cyberbullying and cyberthreats

responding to the challenge of online social aggression, threats, and distress

NANCY E. WILLARD

Research Press | 2612 North Mattis Avenue | Champaign, Illinois 61822

(800) 519-2707

www.researchpress.com

Contents

Acknowledgments

I wish to express special gratitude to everyone who has helped me on the path to greater understanding of these issues. These individuals include Anne Collier of Net Family News (subscribe to her excellent newsletter at http://netfamilynews.org), Larry Rosen, Ph.D., Deborah Finlay, Andy Carvin, Doug Johnson, B. J. Berquist, Scott McCloud, Ron Holmes, Susan Limber, Stan Davis, Art Wolenski, Marion Walsh, and my wonderful online colleagues on WWWEDU (an education technology discussion group). Thanks also to the fine folks at Research Press—Karen Steiner, Russ Pence, Gail Salyards, and Hilary Powers—who distributed the self-published version of this book and helped to bring this new edition to fruition.

Thanks also to my extraordinary children, Jordan, Allegra, and Bakul, who enrich my life and provide me with opportunities to learn new things every day.

Introduction

Cyberbullying and Cyberthreats: Responding to the Challenge of Online Social Aggression, Threats, and Distress provides timely, in-depth insight and practical strategies for school administrators, counselors and psychologists, school resource officers, teachers, and others responsible for helping young people stay safe and healthy in today's interconnected world.

Glimpses of the problem:

> *Brad's blog is filled with racist profanity. Frequently, he targets black and Latino student leaders, as well as minority teachers, in his angry verbal assaults.*

> *Mary, an obese high school student, was changing in the locker room after gym class. Jessica took a covert picture of her with her cell phone camera. Within seconds, the picture was flying around the cell phones at school.*

> *A group of girls at his school had been taunting Alan through instant messaging, teasing him about his small size, daring him to do things he couldn't do, suggesting the world would be a better place if he committed suicide. He discussed this with them. The girls thought it was a big joke. One afternoon, Alan got his grandfather's shotgun, loaded it, and killed himself. He had deleted everything from his computer, except for one message, "The only way to get the respect you deserve is to die."*

These incidents all reflect two disturbing emerging trends related to the use of the Internet and other digital technologies:

- *Cyberbullying:* Sending or posting harmful material or engaging in other forms of social aggression using the Internet or other digital technologies. These online communications can be vicious. Cyberbullying can be happening 24/7. Damaging text and images can be widely disseminated and impossible to fully remove. Teens are reluctant to tell adults—for fear of overreaction, restriction from online activities, and possible retaliation by the cyberbully.

1

- *Cyberthreats:* Sending or posting direct threats or distressing material that raises concerns that the person may be considering committing an act of violence against others or self. It is highly likely that young people who are distressed and contemplating an act of violence are posting clues to this distress and their potential actions online.

The response to cyberbullying and cyberthreats is emerging as one of the more challenging issues facing educators, as young people embrace the Internet and other mobile communication technologies. While much of this activity is occurring off-campus, the impact on the well-being of students and the school climate can be significant. As this book outlines, there are many effective strategies that schools can—and must—employ to address these serious concerns.

Cyberbullying and Cyberthreats contains background information for administrators, counselors and psychologists, school resource officers, teachers, and parent educators. For administrators, counselors and psychologists, and school resource officers, this book will make it possible to analyze cases involving cyberbullying or cyberthreats and intervene in them more effectively, as well as to provide an introductory level of professional development to other educators. For teachers, it will provide the background needed to educate students about this issue. The guide will also prepare all readers to make presentations about this issue to parents. It can also be used for preservice education.

The appendixes in *Cyberbullying and Cyberthreats* contain a variety of documents that will be helpful in implementing the recommendations in this book. If you represent a school or other nonprofit organization that has purchased this book, you may photocopy these documents for noncommercial, educational use and distribute them to members of your community at no charge. These materials are also available on the Center for Safe and Responsible Internet Use Cyberbullying Web site at http://cyberbully.org, where they will be updated as new information becomes available. Other supplementary materials will also be provided on this site.

An Important Caveat

Cyberbullying and cyberthreats are new concerns that have not been fully researched by the academic community. Writing about these issues is challenging because new insight is constantly emerging. Please do not consider this book to be the final word—it is only a step toward increased understanding.

Some Words about Words

Use of the term *cyberbullying* itself presents some concerns. Some socially aggressive online activities may not fit the classic definition of bullying, which includes concepts of repetition and an imbalance in power. But because the term has become popular and identifiable, it is the best choice for further discussion.

Throughout this book, the young person subjected to cyberbullying is generally referred to as the *target,* not the *victim.* This term has been chosen for a very specific reason. The intent of this book and the *Student Guide* (Appendix J) is to empower youth who are being subjected to cyberbullying so they can respond to these activities effectively without becoming victimized or considering themselves victims.

For ease of communication, the term *online* will be used in an expansive sense, referring to dissemination using the Internet or any other form of electronic communication, such as a cell phone or personal digital device (PDA).

The online communications of youth encompass a wide range of formats, including text, photos, drawings, videos, audio messages, and combinations thereof. The terms *communications, material,* and *speech* will be used in this book to refer to this wide range of communication formats, unless there is a need to reference a specific communication format.

When the term *parent* is used, it means any one person serving in this role—mother, father, guardian, grandparent, foster parent, or the like.

A Final Note

All the materials present on Web sites under the URLs in the notes were accessed in August 2006 and were available as of that date. If they are no longer active at those locations, a search engine may take you to their current location.

CHAPTER 1

Overview of Cyberbullying and Cyberthreats

This chapter addresses the various forms of cyberbullying and cyberthreats and the information and communication technologies or activities they involve. The technologies and activities are described more fully in chapter 2.

CYBERBULLYING AND OTHER FORMS OF ONLINE SOCIAL AGGRESSION

The following list of terms and definitions was developed to better delineate different kinds of cyberbullying activities and other forms of online social cruelty. Readers should be aware that if they are reviewing other literature, there could be variations in the terms used to describe different activities. Additionally, some of these activities may overlap or be interrelated.

Flaming

Joe and Alec have gotten into an online argument about an incident that occurred at school. Each message has gotten angrier and more vulgar. Insults have been flying. In the latest exchange, Joe warned Alec to watch his back in school the next day.

Flaming is a heated, short-lived argument that occurs between two or more protagonists. Flaming generally includes offensive, rude, and vulgar language, insults, and sometimes threats. A longer series of such messages is called a "flame war." Note that the example depicts a flame war that has led to a direct threat.

Flaming generally occurs in public communication environments such as discussion boards, chat rooms, or games. Flames erupt between individuals or a small group of protagonists who are arguing and insulting each other, with bystanders occasionally trying to either fan or douse the flames. A series of private angry messages, sent via e-mail or IM, could also be considered flaming. Sometimes a flame war occurs in a public environment at the same time that the protagonists are engaged in background private flaming.

Flaming is a short-lived event between protagonists who are generally well balanced in terms of social power. It is even appropriate to ask whether this activity should be included in a list of activities under the label of *bullying,* which is commonly described as involving repeated acts and interactions between individuals with different levels of social power.

Public communication environments differ in the degree to which they support, encourage, allow, or disallow flaming. In some environments, new users who make innocent mistakes are considered to be fair game for a flame. Sometimes, individuals engage in what is called "baiting"—posting messages with the intention of creating an online argument.

A key point to know about flaming is that flames can be very heated and include veiled or not-so-veiled threats of violence—which may or may not be real threats. A comment transmitted in a flame war, such as "I gonna kill u," may or may not indicate a real and present threat of physical violence. Therein lies a significant source of difficulty for adults responding to the situation. It is important for students to understand that when they get involved in flaming that includes threatening language, this could lead to a significant amount of trouble, including suspension, expulsion, and even arrest. Cyberthreats are discussed later.

Harassment

Joanne saw some girls bullying Jessica at school and reported the bullying to the office. By the time Joanne got home from school, she had 35 angry messages in her e-mail box and even more angry text messages on her cell phone. Most of the messages were anonymous. Some appeared to be from strangers living in other parts of the country. Now, on a daily basis, Joanne gets many e-mail and text messages using vulgar and insulting language.

Harassment is repeated, ongoing sending of offensive messages to an individual target. Harassing messages are generally sent through personal communication channels, including e-mail, instant messaging, and text messaging. Harassment can also occur in public communication environments. Harassment includes the concept of repetition—multiple offensive messages. Harassment is longer-lived than a flame war. The anguish of the targets is that they are constantly receiving hurtful messages whenever they go online or check their cell phone.

The harm inflicted by harassment is mostly one-sided—a cyberbully sending offensive messages to a target. The one-sidedness is a factor that distinguishes harassment from flaming. With harassment, one person is the protagonist, while the other person is simply trying to make the communication stop. The target of harassment may send messages that are angry and contain offensive, rude, and vulgar language, but the intention of such communication is to end the harassment.

Sometimes harassment can occur by proxy. Many teens have established vast networks of communication with online strangers. In a desire to attack and harass a target, a teen may elicit the involvement of online contacts who have no personal connection whatsoever with the target. The target may end up receiving vicious messages from strangers throughout the world.

If the harassment reaches a certain level of harm, or if it is hate or bias-based, it could constitute a crime in some jurisdictions. This situation is discussed in chapter 5.

Denigration

> *Unknown middle school students created a Web site all about Raymond. On this site, they posted Raymond stories, Raymond jokes, and Raymond cartoons. They posed questions about Raymond's sex life. They invited anyone visiting the site to submit their own comments and had an e-mail link for people to send comments directly to Raymond.*

Denigration is speech about a target that is harmful, untrue, or cruel. This harmful speech may be posted online or sent to others. The purpose for sending or posting the material is to interfere with friendships or damage the reputation of the target. This activity includes spreading gossip and rumors. In the case of denigration, the target is not generally the direct recipient of the material. The intended recipients of the material are others. However, a cyberbully may denigrate a target in a message sent to a discussion group in which the target participates. A specific subcategory of denigration is the public posting or sending of digital images that have been digitally altered to present a false image, such as placing the face of a target on a sexually explicit image of a body obtained elsewhere.

Denigration is the form of cyberbullying most frequently used by students against school employees. A student or group of students who are angry with a particular teacher or administrator may create a Web site ridiculing the teacher or administrator. Or a student may post unflattering and untrue comments about a teacher or administrator in a discussion group or blog.

Denigration includes speech that under civil law may constitute defamation or invasion of privacy. Denigration also specifically raises issues related to free-speech protection. When evaluating online speech that appears to denigrate another, it is necessary to consider where the line between legitimate critical speech and defamatory speech is crossed.

Impersonation

Sara watched closely as Emma logged on to her school Internet account and was able to determine Emma's password. Later, Sara logged on to Emma's account and sent a scathing message to Emma's boyfriend, Alex.

Impersonation occurs when the cyberbully gains the ability to impersonate the target and post material that reflects badly on the target or interferes with the target's friendships. This may occur in the target's personal Web page, profile, blog, or through any form of communication. Frequently, the exchange of passwords is considered evidence of true "friendship" among youth, especially among teen girls. The exchange of passwords allows a cyberbully to gain access to the target's account on a system and pose as the target.

Once the cyberbully gains the ability to impersonate the target, the speech could take the form of any of the other kinds of cyberbullying, or it could include making a cyberthreat. That is, a student cyberbully could access a target's account and send a threatening message to a teacher, thus setting the stage for the target to be falsely accused.

Outing and Trickery

Sitting around the computer with her friends at a Friday night sleepover, Judy asked, "Who don't we like? Who can we mess with?" They chose Sara, who was always trying to fit into the group. Sure enough, Sara was online. So Judy started IM-ing her—with all of the other girls providing suggestions. "Ask her who she likes best, Jack or Nathan," they urged. The next Monday, the girls were passing around Sara's IM at school.

Outing is publicly posting, sending, or forwarding personal communications or images, especially communications or images that contain intimate personal information or are potentially embarrassing. A common form of outing is when a cyberbully receives an e-mail message from a target that contains intimate personal information and then forwards the message to others.

Outing of a sexually suggestive or explicit image may occur in the context of a failed relationship. When one party in a relationship seeks to disengage from that relationship, the other party may respond by distributing private communications or images acquired while the relationship was mutual. As noted earlier, threats to engage in outing can occur in the context of cyberstalking: "If you won't hook up [have sex] with me, I will send that picture you sent me to a newsgroup and tell everyone else you are willing to hook up with them."

Trickery can also occur as part of outing. An innocent target can be tricked into thinking that a communication or sending of images is private, when the cyberbully intends to trick the target into communicating or disclosing something embarrassing that will then be disseminated to others or used as a threat. For example, a teen boy may engage a teen girl in sexually oriented communications through instant messaging, with a group of his friends surrounding his computer. Or a teen girl communicating via instant messaging may encourage another girl to disclose her personal interest in a student under the promise that the information will remain "a secret" and then forward this communication to others.

Exclusion

After he beat another boy in an online game, several of the boy's friends threatened Michael. Now, when Michael tries to play on the site, a group of other players gang up on him and restrict his activities so that he cannot participate.

Millie tries hard to fit in with a group of girls at school. She recently got on the outs with a leader in this group. Now Millie has been excluded from IM buddy lists of all of the girls.

Exclusion cyberbullying is related to the designation of who is a member of the in-group and who is an outcast. As anyone who has been associated with teens knows, the boundaries of who is a member of the in-group and who is designated an outcast can change with mercurial speed. The emotional impact of exclusion can be intense. Recall that in many tribal societies, exclusion of a member is considered an extremely harsh punishment. Likewise, excommunication from a religious community is considered the ultimate punishment.

Exclusion may occur in an online gaming environment, group blogging environment, or any other password-protected communication environment. Exclusion may also occur in the context of instant messaging by pointedly excluding someone from the buddy list of a group of students. For teens, exclusion from a buddy list constitutes ultimate rejection.

Cyberstalking

When Annie broke up with her boyfriend, Sam, he sent her many angry, threatening, pleading messages. When Annie blocked his e-mail account, Sam continued to send messages either by anonymous e-mail or text message. Sam also sent messages to people he knew were Annie's friends, describing her in offensive language. Sam also posed as Annie in a sex-oriented discussion group and posted a sexually suggestive picture Annie had given him, along with her e-mail address and cell phone number.

Cyberstalking is repeated sending of harmful messages that include threats of harm, are highly intimidating or extremely offensive, or involve extortion. Cyberstalkers may also try to denigrate their targets and destroy their friendships or reputations. The line of demarcation between harassment and cyberstalking is not clear. A possible indicator is that when a target begins to fear for his or her own safety and well-being, this line has been crossed.

Direct cyberstalking almost always occurs in personal communication environments. Sometimes, the cyberstalker will use anonymous vehicles for communication in an attempt to hide his or her identity. The cyberstalker may also enlist the involvement of other online contacts, including those who do not know the target. Indirect cyberstalking includes communications sent to others for the purpose of denigrating the target or placing the target in an unsafe situation. This behavior overlaps with denigration and impersonation, as defined earlier.

Cyberstalking is frequently linked to the termination of, or problems within, an in-person or online sexual relationship. In such a situation, the cyberbully may have access to intimate personal material to use or threaten to use in a highly embarrassing manner. For example, if earlier in the relationship the target provided sexually explicit pictures—something that occurs frequently in such relationships—the cyberstalker could send or threaten to send these pictures to others in a way that falsely advertises the interest of the target in meeting others to engage in sexual activities.

It is important to note that cyberpredators do not generally engage in activities that would be considered cyberstalking, especially during the early stages of a "grooming relationship." Cyberpredators seek to seduce and win the hearts of young victims. They do not harass or stalk. However, if a young person who has been involved with a cyberpredator finally recognizes the danger and is trying to get out of the relationship, the attempt to escape could lead to cyberstalking. Or, in the later stages of a predatory relationship, if the victim is hesitant to do something that the predator wants, the predator may alternate between intimidation and seduction.

A key point that must be made in the context of this discussion is that a young person who has done something unsafe—such as providing a sexually suggestive or explicit picture to an individual who is now cyberstalking—could be very hesitant to report cyberstalking because of shame or fear of punishment for this prior unsafe act.

Stalking constitutes a crime in most jurisdictions, but the statute may or may not specifically reference online behavior. Disseminating sexually explicit pictures of youth, even if done by the young person, is also criminal behavior—the dissemination of child pornography.

Cyberthreats

Cyberthreats can be roughly classified as follows:

- *Direct threats* are statements of intent to hurt someone or commit suicide. Direct threats generally contain information about an actual planned event.

- *Distressing material* is online material that provides clues that the person is emotionally upset and may be considering hurting someone, self-harm, or suicide.

Sometimes, the lines of distinction between these two types of cyberthreats are vague. The cyberbullying example of flaming also describes what would be considered a direct threat. Here are some examples of what should most likely be considered distressing material:

> *Philosophy So that's the only way to solve arguments with all you fuckheads out there. I just kill you! God I cant wait till I can kill you people. Ill just go down to some downtown area in some big ass city and blow up and shoot everything I can. Feel no remorse. No shame. Ich sage FICKT DU! I will rig up explosives all over a town and detonate each one of them at will after I mow down a whole fucking area full of you snotty ass rich mother fucking high strung godlike attitude having worthless pieces of shit whores. I don't care if I live or die in the shootout, all I want to do is to kill and injure as many of you pricks as I can, especially a few people. Like brooks brown.*[1]

This is material that was posted online by Eric Harris, one of the Columbine shooters. The mother of Brooks Brown reported this Web page to the local police. This statement came from an affidavit that sought a search warrant. But for unknown reasons, the search warrant was never executed. School officials were reportedly not informed about the presence of this material online.

> *- bring a gun to school, ur on the front of every newspaper*
>
> *- didnt choose this life, but i damn well chose to exit it*
>
> *- i cant imagine going through life without killing a few people*
>
> *- nothing wrong with killion*
>
> *- all god's creatures do it in one form or another*
>
> *- yep people can be kissing my shotgun straight out of doom*
>
> *- i tell it how it is*
>
> *- if u dont like it u die*
>
> *- if i dont like what u stand for, you die*
>
> *- if i dont like the way u look at me, u die*
>
> *- i choose who lives and who dies*[2]

The preceding material was reportedy posted by Andrew Osantowski, then a high school student in Michigan when engaged in a private chat with Celia, a college student in Idaho. Fortunately, Celia recognized the danger, saved the transcript, and reported it to her father, who was, equally fortunately, a college security officer. Her father reported the chat session to the police in Andrew's community. Upon investigation, it was found that Andrew was participating in a hate group and had many weapons, including an AK-47. He has been convicted and is now in prison.

> *I'm a retarded [expletive] for ever believing that things would change. I'm starting to regret sticking around, I should've taken the razor blade express last time around. Well, whatever, man. Maybe they've got another shuttle comin' around sometime soon.*
>
> *I think it takes alot of courage to accept death, if you think that you go to Hell or whatever God-forsaken pit after this life for ending your own personal suffering then you're just. . . . Nevermind.*
>
> *I think most people who say this type of thing have never dealt with people who HAVE faced the kind of pain that makes you physically sick at times, makes you so depressed you can't function, makes you so sad and overwhelmed with grief that eating a bullet or sticking your head in a noose seem's welcoming.*
>
> *If you think you're better than those who take their own lives; you're not. If you think you're stronger than those who have taken their own lives; your not.*
>
> *It takes courage to turn the gun on your ownself, takes courage to face death. Knowing you're going to die and actually following through takes heart, I don't care who you are.*

This text (which was posted in a blog) and screen shots from a Flash animation are material reportedly posted on different sites by Jeff Weise, the school shooter from Red Lake, Minnesota, who killed nine people, wounded others, and then killed himself.[3] It has been reported that Jeff was communicating with another student via e-mail and instant messaging about the attack.[4] It was also reported that other students knew about the attack, but it was not reported how this information had been exchanged. Given the level of communication about the planned attacks disclosed to one other student and knowing the degree to which young people are communicating online, it is possible, or even probable, that some of this information was communicated electronically. It is unknown whether the students were communicating about the planned attack through the school's Internet system. The FBI did gather these school computer records for evidence, but there has been no public report of the agency's findings.

All of these examples would probably fall into the category of distressing material because they lack detail about a specific intended action. However, the communications between Jeff Weise and the other student, which are not currently publicly available, might well constitute direct threats.

Is It Real?

Children and teens make threats all of the time. An analysis of the circumstances under which the threats are made can help adults determine their legitimacy. Just because a threat is disseminated online does not make it more real than one shouted in the midst of a child's tantrum. Here are some stories about threats that were not real threats—but the young person making the threat faced real trouble.

> *A high school student sent an anonymous IM to a friend threatening to harm her and her friends the following day at school. The girl showed the IM to her parents. The parents called the school. The school went into lock-down the following day. The student was arrested and charged with a felony of making a written threat to kill.*[5]

> *A high school student created an animated counter on his profile on a social networking site. Beneath the counter, which counts down days, hours, and minutes, were the words, "Until I kill Mr. [name of his math teacher]." When arrested, the student said that he thought of the teacher as a friend and posting the material was "just something to do." The student was arrested.*[6]

It is exceptionally important for school officials to recognize that what initially appears to be an online threat can be any of the following:

- A joke, parody, or game.

- A rumor that got started and has grown and spread.

- Material posted by a young person who is trying out a fictitious threatening online character.

- The final salvos of a flame war that has gotten out of hand but is unlikely to result in any real violence.

- Material posted by someone impersonating someone else for the purpose of getting that person into trouble.

- Distressing material posted by a depressed or angry young person that could foretell a violent or suicidal intention, but that does not represent an imminent threat.

- A legitimate imminent threat.

The problem is that when school officials or law enforcement are first apprised of an online threat, it may be difficult to tell which of these possibilities might be involved. Obviously, the highest priority is doing what is necessary to protect against a possible legitimate threat. But processes also must be in place to rapidly determine the legitimacy of the threat. Reviewing reports of potentially threatening online material is addressed in chapter 8.

TALKING WITH STUDENTS ABOUT CYBERTHREATS

There are two important messages to communicate to youth about cyberthreats:

- It is important to report online threats or distressing material to a responsible adult. Since the rash of school shootings in the United States in the late 1990s, increased efforts have been made to encourage youth to report threats of violence. Youth reports of threats have made it possible for adults to intervene effectively in potentially dangerous situations.

- It is extremely dangerous to post material online that another person, especially an adult, might perceive as a serious threat. Increasing student awareness of the potential consequences of sending or posting threatening material—suspension, expulsion, and even arrest—is essential.

CHAPTER 2

Cybertechnologies and Activities

This chapter provides an outline of the various Internet and digital technologies and online activities that are implicated in cyberbullying and cyberthreats.

In the recent past, technologies on the Internet were roughly classified as Web technologies and communication technologies. Web sites were more static in nature and did not allow any interactivity, whereas communication activities were interactive and rapidly changing. A significant merger of these technologies has now occurred, making this kind of classification more difficult. However, this distinction is made in the following materials. In terms of hardware, the technologies include computers and various personal digital devices, including cell phones, MP3s, and personal digital assistants (PDAs), such as Palms and Blackberrys.

What is the future of these technologies? Equipment will be increasingly smaller, faster, more interactive, and more ubiquitous, and it will have greater multimedia capabilities.

TERMS OF USE AGREEMENTS

Internet service providers, cell phone companies, Web sites, online communities, and providers of the different communications technologies do seek to place some controls on the material and communications posted on their sites. The sites have a document referred to as "Terms and Conditions," "Terms of Use," or simply "Terms" that outlines the agreement between the site and its users. Generally, the terms of use agreement prohibits harmful speech. These agreements are discussed in chapter 6 as one of the limits on free speech.

ONLINE SOCIAL NETWORKING COMMUNITIES

On the Internet, youth like to hang out in online communities. In these online communities, youth engage in social networking—sharing information, engaging in discussions, exchanging pictures, making connections with others with whom they share interests, and talking about issues of the day, which for teens includes discussing such subjects as school, media stars, sex, relationships, sports, and the like.

Online communities offer a variety of basic information and communication services and activities, such as profiles, personal Web pages, blogs, chat rooms, discussion boards, and gaming. The nature of these services may vary from community to community online. (These individual services or activities are described more fully later in this chapter.) Youth from a particular geographic region or within a specific social institution, such as a school, can form their own online groups within the larger online community, focusing on discussions that relate to their school or region. (Check out www.myspace.com, www.livejournal.com, www.xanga.com, www.facebook.com, and www.bebo.com for examples of these online communities.)

Many online community sites are designed for, and very attractive to, youth ranging from the ages of 13 to 23. Parents and other adults should have some concerns about younger and more vulnerable teens who are actively involved with college-age or older individuals, in an environment where generally no responsible adults are present.

WEB SITE PROVISIONS

Age Limits

In the United States, where many of these online community sites are located, the Children's Online Privacy Protection Act (COPPA) places severe restrictions on the kinds of personal contact information that commercial Web sites can collect from children under the age of 13. COPPA also requires parental approval for registration. More information on COPPA can be found at www.ftc.gov/bcp/conline/edcams/kidzprivacy. Most online community sites require that individuals be over the age of 13 to register.

The problem is that there is no accurate way to verify the age of any young Internet user who wants to claim another age.[1] Most youth over about the age of 10 know that it is possible to lie about their age to register on a site that has an age restriction. Social-networking sites are highly attractive to students in middle school, many of whom are under the age of 13. Many underage students register on these sites, often with the permission of their parents.

Some policymakers have argued that these sites should use age verification. Age verification processes can generally limit access to adult sites because adults have various forms of government or business-issued identifications, such as driver's licenses and credit cards. There are no similar forms of identification for minors.

Registrations and Profiles

To use certain technologies, such as instant messaging, or to fully participate in any online community, it is necessary to register. Individuals who do not register may often read what has been posted but are unable to participate actively. To register, the user must provide a certain amount of personal information. On many sites, an option is offered during the registration process to create a *profile*. Users are encouraged to post information in these profiles about their age, location, interests, and activities, as well as online contact information, including e-mail and IM addresses, Web sites, and the like. There is no mechanism for the site to verify this information. Users can also post a picture on their profile, and many do. Other registered users or visitors can search these registrations or profiles by any of the categories. Registrations and profiles are a vehicle by which users make contact with others who have similar interests.

In the course of registration, users create the *username* by which they will be identified on the site. Many teens have more than one account on these systems, each with its own username and associated persona. This allows them to experiment with different personalities. The usernames a teen creates can often provide a strong clue about the image the teen wishes to convey within the community. Sometimes teens will create usernames that are sexually suggestive.

A review of the online profiles on popular communities leads to the conclusion that youth are posting a significant amount of personal contact information, personal interest information, and images, sometimes with sexual overtones. This is an issue all parents and adults working with youth should be attentive to.

Personal Web Sites

Many teens are creating personal Web sites. A survey in 2005 by the Pew Internet and American Life Project revealed that 22 percent of youth ages 12 to 17 report keeping a personal Web site.[2]

Young people who establish personal Web sites may disclose personal contact information and intimate personal information or may post harmful material on that site. Sometimes, several young people will collaborate in the creation of a site that denigrates another youth. If the creator of the site has established a guestbook or provides the vehicle for people to submit comments, others may post or send harmful material to the creator of the site.

Personal Web sites also provide a location where a young person may post material that constitutes a cyberthreat, generally in the form of distressing material. This may include personal Web sites created by youth with suicidal poetry and other anguished statements or graphics about their troubled lives.

As noted, the Web hosts that allow individuals to create their own personal Web sites always have a terms of use agreement that governs the kinds of material that can be posted. But these Web hosts do not have the facility to review each and every posting, and they must therefore rely on a complaint process to notify them if harmful material has been posted.

COMMUNICATION ACTIVITIES AND TECHNOLOGIES

Electronic communications can be roughly classified in two ways:

- Synchronous (real time) or asynchronous (delayed).
- Public or private.

Synchronous communications are those where the participants are communicating with each other at the same time. With asynchronous communications, the communication is delayed until a user receives or accesses it. Frequently, when communications are synchronous, the user must take specific steps to preserve the communications. Asynchronous communications are generally preserved or archived in some format by the Web site or provider, or by either or both of the users in an e-mail in box or cell phone memory.

The notion that electronic communications are private is actually incorrect. Most communication technologies can be used in a manner that is ostensibly private or initially between a limited number of known individuals. But once a message has been transmitted in electronic form, absolutely no technology will prevent the recipient of that communication from sharing it with anyone, anywhere.

Electronic communication technologies can be used to transmit text and images, including drawings, digital photos, and videos. Using a mobile communications device that fits easily into a pocket and can be used with ease at school, today's teens can instantly access and send e-mail, engage in text messaging, access Web sites, and take and send digital photos.

The providers of the various communication services, including Internet service providers and cell phone companies, also have terms of use agreements that include restrictions on the misuse of communication technology through the dissemination of harmful speech. Some misuse of communication technologies is considered illegal under state or federal laws.

The following are common types of electronic communication activities.

E-mail

E-mail is asynchronous communication that can be sent to one or many recipients. E-mail messages are received in a private e-mail account. E-mail is provided by the user's Internet Service Provider or through a Web-based e-mail service, such as Hotmail. E-mail is accessed through a computer or a PDA.

Instant Messaging

Instant messaging (IM) is synchronous communication. Instant messaging software allows users to communicate with a specific person, create a custom chat room for a specific group of people, and share files. IM can occur only between individuals who have included each other's IM address in their IM *contact* or *buddy list*.

During the IM registration process, the user creates a profile, which involves the same sort of concerns discussed earlier. Any other registered user can search through profiles to find and make contacts. When IM addresses have been shared, it is possible for either user to identify when the other user is online and seek to initiate communication.

Many teens have a large number of IM addresses in their contact list, including many individuals they know only online—not face-to-face. The number of IM contacts has become a new measure of one's social worth. In fact, one IM company recently introduced a new game that allows its members to engage in a challenge to quickly determine which of two users has more IM contacts, a measure of popularity.[3] The company also increased the capacity for individual contact addresses to 450. The reason that IM companies are taking steps to encourage youth to increase their IM contacts list is to support the use of IM for market research and advertising.

It is possible with the IM technology to block communications from another user. But it appears that many teens do not take advantage of this capability to escape a cyberbullying relationship. When your social worth is measured by your number of IM contacts, blocking an IM contact is inconsistent with maintaining a high social worth. In addition, although it is possible to save an IM session, specific steps must be taken to do this.

Chat

Chat is a synchronous communication that is public but also has the capability of shifting to a private environment similar to IM. Chat room services are offered by most of the online community sites. Chat groups are generally established to address a specific area of interest. As with IM, it is necessary for the user to take specific steps to preserve the communications, although the Web site may have some archiving capabilities for public chats.

Discussion Boards and E-Mail Mailing Lists

Discussion boards and e-mail mailing lists are asynchronous public communication vehicles. These groups are organized around specific topics of interest. Discussion boards that are present on youth online community sites tend to be the asynchronous public communication environment of choice for teens. These boards are located on third-party community sites and operate under the terms of use agreement of the site that houses them.

E-mail mailing lists are distribution lists that an individual can subscribe to. The messages are then sent to the individual's e-mail box. E-mail mailing lists tend to be used more by adults. A more dated version of group communication is the Internet newsgroup, which also does not appear to be attractive to most teens.

Discussion boards and e-mail mailing lists are archived and publicly accessible. This means that harmful material posted in one of these communication vehicles can be accessed by anyone for many years into the future.

Blogs and Vblogs

Blogs are a merger between Web sites and discussion boards. The term *blog* is short for *Web log,* which refers to an interactive online personal diary or journal. The owner of a personal blog regularly posts commentary and solicits feedback on that commentary. It is possible to create "blogging rings" that link separate blogs together. Many blogging communities that are attractive to youth bear close resemblance to discussion boards, where everyone tosses in relatively brief and frequently inane comments on a particular subject. However, with a blog, as compared to a discussion board, the creator has more control.

Vblogs (video blogs) are blogs that feature the dissemination of video images. *Moblogs* (mobile blogs) can be updated using a cell phone. The Pew Internet and American Life study revealed that 19 percent of online teens keep a blog, and 38 percent of online teens read blogs.[4]

Concerns about blogging include disclosure of intimate personal information or personal contact information and posting of material that is harmful to others. Sometimes, teens will post scathing exposés or thoughts about their fellow classmates, teachers, and parents in their personal blogs. Other times, the reader of a blog may post offensive or harassing material using the response option in a blog.

Blogs can be sophisticated communication vehicles. Creative teachers are using blogging technology to facilitate classroom discussions and exchange of information and insight. These instructional activities provide a vehicle to teach the principles of responsible blogging.

Text Messaging

Text messaging is the communication of brief messages, generally via cell phones or PDAs. Although the term implies text only, it is possible to text message images. It is also possible to send anonymous text messages through Internet sites or to forward other electronic communications to a cell phone, which will then appear as text messages.

There are a variety of other technologies and activities educators must know about.

Online Games

Many different types of gaming environments appear online. Some games are played against the machine. Other games involve users from different locations who are mutually engaged in a gaming activity, either against each other or cooperatively, against the machine. Many gaming environments also have a chat feature that allows players to communicate with each other as they are playing the games. Boys tend to be more attracted to the gaming environment than girls are.

Many interactions in simulation gaming environments resemble the interactions on the most objectionable reality-TV shows—cruel and mean. Frequently, the games involve inflicting violence on others, including sexual violence or violence against others based on race, culture, class, or other differences.

Multi-player role-playing games, where users take on specific personas to engage in gaming against others, are popular environments for young people. The establishment of these personas involves no requirement of truthfulness. Many youth will experiment with different personalities. The creation of multiple identities allows youth to disassociate themselves from the reality of the impact of their online activities: "It wasn't really me who hurt him, it was my online persona." For more discussion of this phenomenon, see chapter 5.

Frequent involvement in gaming can create a mind-set that online activity is not real and everyone online is just a player in a game. This disassociation can provide a rationalization for engagement in harmful online behavior. It is also possible that this disassociation from reality provides some protection for youth who are the targets of online violence. They might rationalize that people are attacking only their online personas and not them personally. This issue needs to be researched in more depth. These concerns are also discussed in chapter 5.

Another phenomenon associated with these gaming environments must also be considered with respect to a possible relationship to groups of students planning a violent attack, perhaps an attack at school. Within these gaming environments, the players form "guilds"—groups of players who work with each other to execute a series of coordinated violent actions. A group of outcast students who participate in these gaming environments could, foreseeably, shift their online planning activities from the gaming environment to the real-world environment. For some members of such a group, there could be a disconnect between fantasy and reality.

Peer-to-Peer Networking

Peer-to-peer networking software is installed on an individual computer to make some or all of the files stored on each computer available to other individuals throughout the world. Sometimes embarrassing materials, especially sexual images, are transmitted through peer-to-peer networking in the context of cyberbullying. Some of the communication activities just described are also facilitated through peer-to-peer networking.

There are many reasons to discourage the use of this technology on a family computer. Peer-to-peer networking software is provided without charge—but in exchange, the software installs spyware, which allows tracking of Internet activity and delivery of pop-up advertising. A significant amount of computer crime is conducted through computers that have been compromised through the downloading of worms and trojans—software that allows others to use the computer to send unwanted advertisements or conduct other inappropriate activity. The primary purpose of using peer-to-peer networking is to facilitate the illegal downloading of copyrighted material, including music, videos, and software. A significant amount of adult pornography, child pornography, and gross images is also disseminated via peer-to-peer networking, many times deceptively labeled.

Online Matchmaking

Many online communities provide links to matchmaking services. Online matchmaking services allow users to find potential relationship matches by typing in certain parameters, including gender, age, location, and interests. The online matchmaking services are often highly sexualized.

Matchmaking services generally limit registration to those over the age of 18. But as discussed earlier, most youth over the age of 10 have figured out that they can lie about their age to enter sites intended for older users.

It is important to note, in the context of this discussion of technologies, that students can often use the school district's Internet service to access online communities or electronic communication services where they can engage in cyberbullying. It is a mistake to believe that filtering technology will or even can prevent this. The district filtering software may be set to block access to popular online communities. But a moderately intelligent middle school student can easily set up a home computer system that will provide the capability to circumvent the school computer to get to these sites or simply access a proxy site that will facilitate bypass of a filtering system. Conduct a search on the words *bypass Internet filter* to see how easy it is for students to find instructions on how to defeat any blocks established by a school district using filtering technology.

Most students are not foolish enough to try to access pornography through a computer in a school computer lab because the appearance of such material would be rapidly detected and lead to punishment. But cyberbullying, even on restricted sites, looks just like writing. Writing is an activity that is to be expected and is unlikely to lead to suspicion or detection.

Students may also engage in cyberbullying using cell phones or PDAs while at school. Students can now easily access their online social networking profile using their cell phone.

Most school districts have policies that prohibit students from using cell phones during class. But in many schools, there are active programs teaching students to use PDAs for educational activities. The prices of these devices are dropping rapidly. The major emerging concern is how schools will manage student use of technology when many students have wireless personal digital devices that they want to use in the classroom for legitimate educational activities—but that function outside of the school's filtering environment and that also could be used to engage in online social aggression. This issue is addressed more fully in chapters 7 and 11.

CHAPTER 3

Insight and Implications

This chapter presents research into traditional bullying and threats of violence or suicide and discusses the insights this research provides when addressing incidents of cyberbullying or cyberthreats.

SOURCES OF INSIGHT INTO CYBERBULLYING AND CYBERTHREATS

Academic research about cyberbullying and cyberthreats has yet to be done with much depth or quality, so it is important for readers to understand the process by which the material presented in this chapter has been developed. The primary source of insight into aspects of cyberbullying and cyberthreats has been an informal qualitative analysis of news reports and privately reported incidents, visits to online communities, and consultations with other professionals who focus on Internet use concerns.[1]

Greater insight was sought through other resources: academic research addressing traditional bullying, input from school counselors and psychologists, and limited research on cyberbullying and Internet use. Of course, this approach does not meet the standards of academic research. Given the state of understanding of these issues, all information presented in this chapter should be considered tentative, subject to further study and clarification. But with a new phenomenon—one that is causing emotional harm to youth—it is necessary to start somewhere.

DEFINITION OF BULLYING

This definition of bullying is often cited:

Bullying is a specific type of aggression in which (1) the behavior is intended to harm or disturb, (2) the behavior occurs repeatedly over time, and (3) there is an imbalance of power, with a more powerful person or group attacking a less powerful one. This asymmetry of power may be physical or psychological.[2]

Reports of cyberbullying reveal an aspect that is at odds with the generally accepted definition of bullying—that bullying occurs when a more powerful person attacks a less powerful person. It appears that sometimes less powerful young people are using the Internet to attack more powerful people or groups of people. Sometimes, the target of harmful online material posted by a student is a teacher.

Researchers investigating computer-mediated group communications have found that the reduction of social cues related to social status in online communication environments appears to lead to greater participation by those who are at a lower level in a social hierarchy. In an office setting, when engaged in face-to-face group communications, the secretary rarely contributes to the conversation when the boss is present. By contrast, in computer-mediated communications, it has been found that the secretary appears to be much more inclined to offer opinions on matters under discussion.[3]

If this is the case, it stands to reason that students who are at a lower status within the social hierarchy at school, including students who are being bullied by those at a higher social status, may be disinclined to speak up when physically present but may feel more comfortable communicating online. These communications may be retaliation or simply an effort to raise their social status to a sufficient level to stop the bullying.

Some preliminary data appear to support this analysis. Kowalski and Limber studied cyberbullying among students in middle school.[4] Based on the results assessing involvement in traditional bullying, the researchers divided the students into four categories: victims (11.5 percent of the overall student population), bullies (4.7 percent of the overall student population), bully/victims (1.9 percent of the overall student population), and none of these categories (81.8 percent of the overall student population). The researchers then examined the percentage of individuals within these groups who had engaged in cyberbullying and who had been cyberbullied.

- Of the victims who had been bullied at school (but who had not bullied back), 3.1 percent had engaged in cyberbullying. Meanwhile, 12 percent of the bullies at school had also engaged in cyberbullying. Close to 19.7 percent of students who reported that they had bullied and were victims at school had also engaged in cyberbullying. And 1 percent of students who reported no involvement in bullying at school, as either a bully or a victim, had engaged in cyberbullying. Since this last group constituted 81.8 percent of the student population, the small segment of this group who had engaged in cyberbullying obviously constituted a significant portion of those who reported engagement in cyberbullying.

- Of the victims who had been bullied at school, 17.7 percent had also been cyberbullied. Of the students who reported they had bullied at school, 11.9 percent had been the victims of cyberbullying. Of students who reported that they had both bullied and been victims, 22.2 percent had been cyberbullied. Of the large group of students who had reported no involvement in bullying at school, as bully or victim, 3.5 percent had been cyberbullied.

The Kowalski and Limber data demonstrate two phenomena:

- Students who are not currently involved in bullying at school, either as bully or as victim, are becoming involved in cyberbullying, both as cyberbullies and as victims.

- There appears to be some role switching. Some students who were victims at school but had not engaged in bullying at school reported engaging in cyberbullying. Some students who had bullied, but had not been victimized at school, reported being victims of cyberbullying.

BULLYING ACTS

Many researchers have noted that bullying aggression is of three different types:

- Physical—hitting, kicking, spitting, pushing, taking personal belongings.

- Verbal—taunting, name-calling, teasing, or threats.

- Emotional and psychological—spreading rumors, manipulating social relationships, social exclusion, and extortion. (Also called *indirect relational aggression.*)

Applying the framework outlined in chapter 1, cyberbullying has no physical equivalent, but it does have equivalents for the other two types of bullying:

- Direct verbal bullying—flaming, harassment, and cyberstalking.

- Indirect relational aggression—denigration, outing and trickery, exclusion, impersonation, and cyberstalking.

INCIDENT RATES

A nationwide survey on bullying in the United States, funded by the National Institute of Child Health and Human Development (NICHHD), involved 15,686 students in grades 6 through 10.[5] This survey found that 10.6 percent of the students reported they engaged in bullying "sometimes," and 8.8 percent admitted to bullying once a week or more. Students reported being victimized at similar rates, with 8.5 percent reporting being bullied sometimes and 8.4 percent reporting being bullied once a week or more. A significant number of students reported that they were both bullied and bullied others. The survey found that bullying occurred with greater frequency at the middle school level than at the high school level and that males reported bullying or being bullied at higher rates than females.

The NICHHD study asked about five types of bullying: belittled about religion or race; belittled about looks or speech; hit, slapped, or pushed; subject of rumors or lies; and subject of sexual comments or gestures. For males, physical and verbal bullying was more common. For females, verbal bullying and spreading of rumors were more common.

A survey of middle school students conducted by Bosworth revealed significantly higher rates of bullying.[6] The researchers in this study asked students if they had engaged in certain behaviors without telling them those behaviors were defined as bullying. In addition to reporting significantly higher rates of bullying than the NICHHD study, the researchers found that adolescents did not fall neatly into categories of either bullies or nonbullies. Many students who engaged in bullying had also been bullied.

The rates of sexually related bullying in the NICHHD study were significantly lower than the rates of sexual harassment reported in a survey conducted by the American Association of University Women (AAUW).[7] The AAUW used this definition of sexual harassment: "unwanted and unwelcome sexual behavior that interferes with your life." The AAUW survey revealed that 59 percent of 8th through 10th graders reported they had been sexually harassed often or occasionally, with 27 percent reporting that such harassment was frequent. Thus, a total of 86 percent of the students were subjected to sexual harassment.

Several reservations about the accuracy of survey data on bullying have been identified: Lack of clarity among youth responding to the survey about what actually constitutes bullying behavior or the meaning of the terms used by the researchers, risks that youth may not be reporting accurately for fear of being identified, and a desire by survey respondents to manage their image.[8]

Recognizing the limitations of all survey research related to bullying, and of definitions, the following are reported results of surveys that provide some insight into the incident rates of cyberbullying:

- Fight Crime: Invest in Kids reported in 2006 the results of a survey of 1,000 U.S. youth.[9] Key findings: One-third of all teens (12–17) and one-sixth of all children (6–11) had mean, threatening, or embarrassing things said about them online. Ten percent of the teens and 4 percent of the children were threatened online with physical harm. About half of the children told their parents, but only 30 percent of teens told their parents. Forty-five percent of the children and 30 percent of the teens indicated that the cyberbullying occurred at school.

- The Crimes Against Children Research Center released its second Youth Internet Safety Survey in 2006.[10] (An earlier study had been released in 2000.) This survey of youth between the ages of 10 and 17 revealed that 9 percent of youth reported they had been harassed online. Fifty-eight percent of the targets were girls. Sixty-eight percent of the girls received "distressing harassment." Seventy-two percent of the harassment happened to teenagers. Half of the harassers were known to be male; 21 percent were known to be female. Forty-four percent of the harassers were off-line friends or acquaintances. Three percent of the incidents occurred at school.

- The Kowalski and Limber study asked about both traditional bullying and cyberbullying incidents in the preceding two months.[11] Twenty-five percent of girls and 11 percent of boys reported being electronically bullied at least once within that period, while 13 percent of girls and 8.6 percent of boys electronically bullied someone at least once. In comparison, only 12.3 percent of girls and 14.1 percent of boys reported having been bullied at school at least two or three times a month in the last couple of months. Just over 5 percent of girls and 8 percent of boys admitted to having bullied others at school at least two or three times a month in that period. This study provides a helpful side-by-side analysis that allows for a comparison of the two forms of bullying.

- Media Awareness Canada conducted a 2005 study titled "Young Canadians in a Wired World, Part II."[12] Among the findings were that 34 percent of students in grades 7 to 11 reported being bullied, while 12 percent reported having been sexually harassed. Among those who reported being bullied, 74 percent were bullied at school, and 27 percent were bullied over the Internet. For those reporting sexual harassment, the situation is reversed: 47 percent said they were harassed at school, while 70 percent were harassed over the Internet. Of those young people who reported being sexually harassed over the Internet, over half (52 percent) said it was someone they knew in the real world.[13]

- A 2004 survey of youth and their parents in the United Kingdom, conducted by UK Children Go Online, revealed that 31 percent of youth between the ages of 9 and 19 had received unwanted sexual comments and that 33 percent had received nasty comments sent via e-mail, chat, instant message, or text message.[14] This study also revealed that parents underestimate the potential concerns. Only 7 percent of parents thought their child had received sexual comments, and only 4 percent thought their child had been bullied online.

The limited research on cyberbullying appears to present the same difficulties as research on traditional bullying and harassment—different studies resulting in different incident rates. It is probable that some of the different results are related to the differences in labeling for specific acts. A question phrased "Has anyone bullied you online?" may receive a different response from "Has anyone spread hurtful rumors or gossip about you online?" Additionally, there are concerns related to assessing the intensity or impact of the reported incidents. Simply asking about incidents will not effectively distinguish between a student who received one or two harmful messages and a student who was the subject of a "We hate [name of student]" Web site upon which many other students posted hurtful comments. Research in the future, including needs assessment activities by a school district, will provide more accurate insight if young people are asked about specific activities and impacts, rather than using labels such as "bullying" and "harassment."

Despite the difficulties in determining incident rates and impacts, however, it clearly appears that cyberbullying is as great a concern as traditional bullying, if not greater.

BULLY AND VICTIM PROFILES

The following is common profile information conveyed about the characteristics of children as bullies, passive victims, and provocative victims. These descriptions, quoted from an article published in *American Family Physician,* were based on numerous research studies.[15]

Bully Characteristics

- Impulsive, hot-headed, dominant personalities; many are physically strong, with good or inflated self-esteem, and feel little or no responsibility for their actions.

- Easily frustrated; have difficulty conforming to rules.

- Expect others to pick on them; see threats where none exist.

- Antisocial; defiant toward adults.

- Unable to understand the emotional experiences of others.

- Have a positive attitude toward violence.

- May have a psychiatric disorder contributing to aggressive behavior (for example, antisocial personality disorder, attention-deficit/hyperactivity disorder).

- May experience peer rejection and social isolation, contributing to an increased risk of depression, suicide, and antisocial personality disorder.

- May experience or witness violence and abuse at home (for example, by parents or other caretakers).

- May experience lack of parental involvement, supervision, and nurturing during childhood.

- At increased risk for school failure and dropout and for future problems with violence, delinquency, and substance abuse; in boys, increased risk for multiple criminal convictions in adulthood.

Passive/Submissive Victim Characteristics

- Quiet, cautious, sensitive, insecure; may have difficulty asserting themselves; appear to do nothing to provoke attacks and are unlikely to retaliate if attacked or insulted.

- May be perceived as being different or weak.

- May be isolated socially and report feeling sad or lonely.

- May experience psychosomatic symptoms (for example, sleep disturbances, enuresis, unexplained abdominal discomfort, or headaches).

- If bullied chronically, may have problems with social and emotional development and academic performance.

- May become cynical if they think authority figures let the bullying persist.

- May accept that they deserve to be taunted, teased, and harassed (similar to victims of domestic violence and other forms of abuse).

- In rare cases, may harm themselves or others or even consider suicide rather than endure continual harassment and humiliation.

- At risk for depression and poor self-esteem later in life.

Bully/Victim (Provocative Victim) Characteristics

- Are targets of bullying and also bully younger or weaker children.

- May be difficult to identify at first because they seem to be victims of other bullies; a reactive victim may provoke a bully into action, fight back, then claim self-defense.

- Hyperactive, quick-tempered, and emotionally reactive; prone to irritating and teasing others to create tension; attempt to fight back when insulted or attacked.

- At particular risk for persistent social and behavior problems, including social isolation, failure in school, smoking, and drinking.

This bully/victim group has been called by various names in research literature, including bully-victims, provocative victims, ineffectual aggressors, and aggressive victims.

ANALYSIS OF THE STATED CHARACTERISTICS: SOCIAL CLIMBER BULLIES AND RESILIENT TARGETS

While the descriptions just outlined clearly characterize some of the players involved in bullying and other acts of social aggression, it appears that two key groups of youth have not been adequately recognized or noted in research and informational literature: social climber bullies and resilient targets. The reason it is critical to look closely at social climber bullies is that these kinds of youth appear to be very actively involved in cyberbullying. Further, increasing the resilience of targets, especially when dealing with online aggression, will be very important.

Social Climber Bullies

Social climber bullies are students who do not bear much similarity to the *Family Physician*'s description of a bully. They are the in-crowd, the jocks, preps, and the like. The bullying activities are generally occurring within the context of the interrelationships between the in-crowd, the wannabes (those who want to be part of the in-crowd), and the losers (as defined by the in-crowd).

In the school environment, bullying by social climber bullies can be very sophisticated and subtle. Sometimes, the socially aggressive behavior demonstrated by social climber bullies may not be recognized as bullying by school staff—despite the emotional harm it inflicts on the targets. Members of the in-crowd tend to be school leaders and athletes who are admired by the school staff. Wannabes will rarely report aggressive behavior to school staff because tattling would totally undermine their ability to gain admission to the in-crowd. Losers may also not be inclined to report aggressive behavior because of the degree to which the in-crowd is admired by school staff, the subtle nature of the bullying, and fear that any report will lead to retaliation.

Reflect on the incidents surrounding the bullying that had been inflicted on students involved in school shootings. Eric Harris and Dylan Klebold were not, reportedly, being bullied by aggressive bullies. They were being bullied by the school's jocks. Many adults in the school community apparently refused to acknowledge the possibility that students perceived to be school leaders and acclaimed athletes were inflicting cruelty upon the shooters.[16] The same pattern of social aggression by the in-crowd against students who engaged in school shootings was outlined in Newman's book *Rampage: The Social Roots of School Shootings*.[17]

Some attention has been devoted to the issues of bullying within the dominance structure of the school. Pellegrini and Long describe bullying as deliberate aggression to achieve high or powerful status in the peer group.[18] Their studies document the significant increase in bullying behavior that occurs when students move from elementary to middle school and the decrease in bullying behavior that appears to occur as more stable social status patterns solidify within middle school.

Adler and Adler address peer culture issues and note that the popular group of students makes up approximately 30 percent of all students in any given grade level.[19] This group drives the school climate and is motivated to protect its members' power. There may be a select group of leaders within the popular circle that determine the ever-changing status of the followers. The next group, the wannabes, makes up about 10 percent of students in a grade level. These are students who have their own small group of friends but would prefer to be in the popular group. The third group includes about 50 percent of the students of a class. These students mostly operate on their own and are generally accepting of others, but they do not wish to be a part of the popular clique. They are also critical of the wannabes. The remaining 10 percent of the class is made up of isolated children, the outcasts. These children lack support and even tend to reject one another.

The children with the most social power have tremendous influence on the behavior of the rest and determine the status of others in their group. They use their popularity to control the group and manipulate the hierarchy. They establish their power by manipulating the feelings and status of other children and may also manipulate clique members into bullying others and then withdraw themselves so that others take the blame.

Unfortunately, neither the work of Pellegrini and Long nor of Adler and Adler appears to have resulted in any reassessment of the information that is commonly disseminated about aggressive bully characteristics.

Resilient Targets

The descriptions of victims also appear to leave out one whole class: resilient targets. These are students who may not fit the mold of acceptability as established by the in-crowd, for which they have been subjected to denigration. Or they may have been the recipients of bullying from the aggressive bullies or bully/victims because they are perceived as different and therefore fair game.

But not all targets of bullying are passive, provocative, or retaliatory victims. Many resilient targets are youth who are simply determined to walk their own path and recognize that it is okay to be different despite the challenges this causes them. Sometimes they figure out how to obtain a sufficient level of power to get most of the bullying to stop. That which remains, they may be able to dismiss as irrelevant. Or they find ways to simply avoid the bullies and ignore the bullying. They are probably still emotionally harmed by these experiences, but they appear to have sufficient internal resilience to grow through this harm and to find ways to deal with the situations they face. Many creative and visionary leaders in our society report that they were bullied in their youth. These leaders do not fit the description of passive, provocative, or retaliatory victims. We need to figure out how to help more students become resilient targets, rather than thinking that the targets of bullying are, and will always be, passive, provocative, or retaliatory victims who will not be able to handle bullying situations without the assistance of adults.

Application to Cyberbullying

This discussion is necessary because it appears that a significant amount of cyberbullying is occurring most frequently in the context of social climber relationships. It takes a certain amount of sophistication and frequent access to technology to engage in cyberbullying. The students who are most likely to be engaged in this kind of behavior are the ones who have such sophistication and access. A counselor colleague who has paid close attention to the phenomenon of cyberbullying describes the youth involved as follows: "Cyberbullies are typically from upper class . . . nice families . . . top kids in the school . . . ones 'we' rely on for honor societies, athletes, etc."[20]

The targets of cyberbullying appear most often to be from the wannabe crowd. The wannabes are the ones who are most likely to be intentionally involving themselves in electronic communication with in-crowd students—because they want to be part of this community. Other students are generally less likely to be involved in communications with this group, so they are probably less frequently the targets. Some reports appear to indicate a pattern of behavior where a member of the in-crowd will encourage a wannabe to anonymously attack another wannabe, a competing member or group within the in-crowd, or an outcast as the price of admission to the group. This could be considered to be cyberbullying by proxy.

Are the aggressive bullies and bully/victims involved? This may depend on the degree to which these youth are seeking to be part of the social-climbing environment within a school and are participating in the online environments with other students. It is probable that youth who match the description of aggressive bullies and bully/victims are actively involved in online violent gaming activities. They are also the youth most likely to be at risk for recruitment by or involvement in online hate groups. Or they may form their own troublesome youth group with other similarly minded youth in the school. These youth are less likely to engage in direct cyberbullying of others at school through interactive communications and are more likely to create personal Web pages or blogs that target others or simply express hateful or hurtful perceptions.

Cautions

These descriptions are interpretations of cyberbullying situations that have been reported in the news or directly to this author. They have been supported in communications with several school counselors and psychologists who have begun to focus on these concerns. It also appears that the findings of Kowalski and Limber indicate that we may be dealing with different populations. Their data suggest that cyberbullying may represent a qualitatively different phenomenon from school bullying. They note that future research is needed investigating the physical and psychological characteristics of cyberbullies.

There has been insufficient academic research attention paid to the activities of social climber bullies at school, including a certain amount of denial by school officials and researchers that the good students and top athletes could be involved in bullying. The new phenomenon of cyberbullying may force a reassessment of all bullying behavior and increase the recognition that there is more than one kind of bully. The underlying caution to all readers is to remain very open-minded when seeking to address the concerns of cyberbullying with respect to the characteristics of the students who may be involved.

GIRLS OR BOYS?

It is commonly reported that boys bully at higher rates than girls.[21] Both boys and girls report being bullied by boys more frequently than by girls.

In more recent years, greater insight has emerged into the damaging ways in which girls indirectly engage in bullying through relational aggression.[22] Male bullies tend to engage in direct physical or verbal aggression. Male bullies have positive reactions to the use of violence to solve problems. They tend to be impulsive, have a need to dominate, display little empathy, and demonstrate aggressive emotional reactions if teased or taunted. Female bullies tend to engage more in indirect bullying, often called relational aggression. Female bullies tend to assume the role of leader in a core group of peers. They are socially cruel and manipulative. They attempt to ostracize targets through backbiting, spreading rumors, trashing reputations, and rewarding others for refusing to interact pleasantly with the target.

As noted, the primary forms of cyberbullying are direct verbal and indirect relational aggression. Thus the type of bullying that boys engage in more frequently—physical bullying—is not as relevant. Survey research on youth online activity reveals that the most popular online activity of boys is gaming and that the most popular online activity of girls is communication.[23] Cyberbullying is primarily occurring in the online communication environments. Therefore, it stands to reason that there is a high probability of greater involvement of girls in cyberbullying, as compared to boys.

The Kowalski and Limber study revealed that 13 percent of girls and 8.6 percent of boys electronically bullied someone, whereas 5 percent of girls and 8 percent of boys admitted engaging in in-school bullying. None of the other studies has reported cyberbullying incident rates by gender. Anecdotal reports from educators, counselors, and psychologists also indicate that girls are more actively engaged in cyberbullying.[24] However, it appears from these reports that boys may be more likely to engage in threats of violence and significant denigration activities, which may be more likely to come to the attention of adults.

RETALIATION

The U.S. Secret Service study of school shooters determined that more than two-thirds of the shooters had been the victims of bullying, some of which reportedly reached the level of severe tormenting.[25] Clearly, armed attack on schoolmates is the ultimate retaliation. Unfortunately, the issue of retaliation does not appear to have been the focus of academic research. Many studies note that there is a class of young people who are both bullied and engage in bullying, but it is unclear whether the young people within this class are engaging in bullying of others who hold an even lower social status or whether this includes retaliatory aggression against bullies with higher social status. It is likely that both activities are occurring.

The disinhibited environment of the Internet and other technologies appears to allow the targets of bullying more freedom to retaliate against their aggressors. A target of bullying at school who is physically smaller than the bully may feel more comfortable engaging in online retaliation, especially anonymous retaliation, than in-person retaliation. Also, in an online environment, the target does not have to face a group of supporting friends who might be surrounding the bully at school. Given greater perceived freedom to retaliate online, the rate of retaliation online may be higher than the face-to-face retaliation rate. That is, targets in face-to-face settings who are more passive may be more inclined to retaliate online because it appears to be a safer environment to do so.

This phenomenon is also likely to be at work in the reported cases where a student has created a Web site or sent e-mail that targets a teacher. Teachers clearly have higher social status. It is highly probable that the student would not have delivered such messages to the teacher in person.

As the Kowalski and Limber data indicate, 1 in 10 students who reported having bullied others at school also reported that they had been the targets of cyberbullying. Of the victims who had been bullied at school (but who had not bullied back), 3.1 percent reported that they had engaged in cyberbullying. The report does not state whether these incidents involved retaliation.

For teachers, it is important to educate students about the dangers of engaging in online retaliation. Unfortunately, students who retaliate against bullies online can be mistakenly perceived as the source of the problem. This can be especially true under circumstances where the original victimization left no tangible evidence, but the cyberbullying did. It is essential to educate students about the significant risks of engaging in online retaliation and to suggest other ways to address the fact that they are being victimized.

It is also important for counselors, psychologists, and administrators responding to a report of cyberbullying to recognize that the student who is engaging in cyberbullying may be seeking to retaliate against a bully or use the Internet as a vehicle to gain sufficient social power over an in-school bully to get the face-to-face bullying to stop.

Counselors and psychologists or administrators who receive reports of cyberbullying are likely to receive at least two different kinds of material:

- "Put-down" material created by a higher social status bully (power bully), either an aggressive bully or a social climber bully, who is targeting a lower social status target.

- "Get-back-at" material created by a lower social status target (a retaliator) attempting to turn the tables on a higher social status bully.

So how can a counselor, psychologist, or administrator tell which is which?

- Obtain information about the overall relationships between the involved students. Determine which student tends to have a higher social status or level of power.

- Closely evaluate the substance of the online material. The power bully material is likely to reflect communications from a person in a position of dominance, power, or control against a person who is perceived or characterized as inferior. It is likely to reflect strength and power. The retaliator material is likely to reflect the emotional anguish of a person who has been demeaned by others—responding to harm that has been inflicted on the person who has posted the material. Get-back-at material is likely to be far more emotional and may cross over into what would be considered to be distressing material or even threats.

An additional issue with respect to retaliation must be kept in mind. Reports are emerging of youth who have been targets of cyberbullying or other online altercations engaging in physical retaliation at school. A 2004 news report from Japan addressed claims that an 11-year-old girl had slashed the throat of a 12-year-old girl at school because she was angry at what the girl had posted about her online.[26] There have been other anecdotal reports of cyberbullying leading to in-school violence.

SEXUAL HARASSMENT AND RELATIONSHIP ISSUES

Sexual harassment, as well as other forms of harassment (based on race or religion), is behavior that is in violation of civil rights laws. Frequently, the term is used in a more general sense to describe a range of socially harmful behavior that involves sexual issues. There is also some amount of confusion with respect to labeling social aggression based on perceived gender orientation differences. Many times, such behavior falls under the description of sexual harassment. But such behavior is also referred to as hate- or bias-based behavior, which is discussed later in this chapter.

The NICHHD study included questions about bullying behavior that involved "sexual comments or gestures."[27] Of those who reported being bullied, 52 percent reported having been sexually bullied, with 18.9 percent reporting this as frequent. But as discussed earlier, the rates of bullying reported by NICHHD were significantly lower than the rates of sexual harassment reported in the AAUW survey.[28] Harassment and bullying of students who are lesbian, gay, bisexual, or transsexual (LGBT) is, unfortunately, extremely commonplace. In a 2003 study reported by the Gay, Lesbian, Straight Educational Network, 84 percent of LGBT students report being verbally harassed because of their sexual orientation. Of even more concern is the finding that 82.9 percent of students reported that faculty never or rarely intervene in such incidents when present.[29]

Most research analysis of these issues does not address socially aggressive behavior that is related to social or sexual relationship issues. Arguments over "who is going with whom" or "who can be seen talking to whom" are frequent among middle and high school students and can provide the basis for bullying.

A variety of sex-related types of situations seem to be involved in cyberbullying incidents:

- Offensive sexual propositioning or harassment.

- Harassment or cyberstalking that is related to failed relationships or the response of a student who has been spurned by another. Some of this activity may be related to risky online sexual behavior engaged in by the target, creating the perception that the target was engaging in false advertising.

- Sexually bias–based harassment of youth who are perceived to be lesbian, gay, bisexual, or transsexual. The most frequent targets of this behavior appear to be boys who do not fit the masculine standard. Of significant concern is that many of the reports of youth suicide related to cyberbullying appear to involve younger adolescent boys (middle school) who are being targeted in a manner that appears to be related to their failure to fit the masculine standard or to dissemination of rumors or harassment based on the perception that the boy is gay.

- The dissemination of rumors about sexual activities and proclivities.

- Tricking a student into revealing sexual interest in another student and then making this information public in an embarrassing manner. This seems to be especially prominent among young girls.

- The establishment of Web sites or Web-based rating systems that focus on sexual attractiveness or activities.

- Relationship-based fights, including arguments about who can go out with whom. This also seems prominent among teen girls.

- Disseminating sexually explicit images that were provided privately. In one reported incident, a teen girl sent a digital video of herself masturbating to a fellow student—who promptly sent the video to all of his friends, showed it at school, and posted it via peer-to-peer networking.[30]

- Creating defamatory sexually explicit images by incorporating the face of a student into a pornographic image obtained on the Internet.

It must be recognized that teens who have placed themselves in vulnerable positions by engaging in risky online sexual behavior are likely to be very hesitant to report to an adult if they are being exploited or harmed because of their concern about the possible consequences to them of revealing their own inappropriate behavior. Imagine the difficulty of reporting to your mother that the sexually explicit video you sent to a boy is now being widely disseminated online. Online risky sexual behavior is discussed further in chapter 4.

Cyberbullying actions that are related to sexual behavior may be in violation of a variety of criminal laws, including production and dissemination of child pornography, sexual abuse, sexual harassment, and stalking.

CYBERBULLYING MOTIVATED BY HATE AND BIAS

The NICHHD study noted that of those who reported being bullied, 25.8 percent reported that they had been bullied on the basis of religion or race, and 8.08 percent reported this type of bullying as frequent (once a week or several times a week).[31]

It appears that some cyberbullying is motivated by hate and bias. As discussed earlier, frequently this is connected to bias related to sexual orientation. It is also probable that some young people engaged in cyberbullying are also involved in online hate groups and online hate activity, a topic discussed in chapter 4.

Hate-motivated behavior is a crime in many jurisdictions. When criminal acts are motivated by hate, they are classified as hate crimes.

THE ROLE OF BYSTANDERS

Observations of behavior provide the greatest insight into the various roles that young people play within the bullying dynamic. Researchers engaged in behavioral observation research have noted a variety of roles that bystanders may take.[32] Some bystanders take the role of assistant to the bully and join in the activities against the target. Others may support and reinforce the bully by laughing at the target or cheering the bully. Others may simply stand by quietly. A small group of bystanders might try to help or defend the target. Pellegrini and Long used behavioral observations to assess bullying in 5th and 6th grades.[33] The observations revealed connection between the need for dominance in one's peer group and bullying behaviors. That is, it appeared that the reinforcing attention provided by the bystanders played a significant role in encouraging the bullying behavior.

Influencing bystanders to intervene in face-to-face bullying by expressing disapproval, providing public or private support to the target, or reporting such bullying to responsible adults is recognized as a critically important prevention strategy.[34]

It appears that a significant amount of cyberbullying is occurring either as a group function or within group online communication environments. However, the bystanders may or may not be as evidently present. The role of group bullying, active participants, and passive bystanders within the online environment needs to be more fully explored.

Influencing bystanders to respond appropriately to denounce cyberbullying, provide support for online targets of cyberbullying, or report concerns to adults takes on even greater importance when it is recognized that most cyberbullying is occurring in online environments where no responsible adults are present.

FAMILY DYNAMICS

Family dynamics, the manner in which family members treat one another, teach children lasting lessons. A family that uses bullying as a relationship tool teaches the child that bullying is an appropriate way to relate to others. Domestic violence teaches that the world is hostile and that the way to survive is to strike first.

Children who engage in aggressive bullying often come from families that are described as having characteristics such as these:[35]

- Lack of warmth and involvement on the part of parents.

- Overly permissive parenting (including a lack of limits on children's behavior).

- Lack of supervision by parents.

- Harsh physical discipline.

- Serving as a role model for bullying behavior.

While this list is likely to describe the family conditions of aggressive bullies and bully/victims, it may not describe the situation of the social climber bullies.

Studies on youth use of the Internet demonstrate a significant disconnect between what teens say about their parents' involvement in their online activities and what parents say. The Pew Internet and American Life Project recently reported that 62 percent of parents said they check on teens' Internet activity after they have been online, but only 33 percent of teens said that they believe their parents monitor their activity.[36] There was much higher agreement on another question: Sixty-five percent of parents and 64 percent of teens agreed that teens do things online that they would not want their parents to know about.

It is highly likely that the parents of youth engaged in cyberbullying are failing to provide supervision and set limits for their child's use of the Internet and that this failure to pay attention has resulted in harmful and aggressive online behavior. The degree to which the online behavior of the youth who are engaged in cyberbullying emulates the values or aggression common in the home, or whether such online behavior is not in accord with such values, is unknown and probably varies.

MEDIA INFLUENCES

The influence of media on violence, bullying, and other harmful behavior has clearly been demonstrated through research. In a joint statement presented to the U.S. Congressional Public Health Summit on July 26, 2000, six major health organizations stated:[37]

> At this time, well over 1,000 studies—including reports from the Surgeon General's office, the National Institute of Mental Health, and numerous studies conducted by leading figures within our medical and public health organizations. . . . point overwhelmingly to a causal connection between media violence and aggressive behavior in some children. The conclusion of the public health community, based on over 30 years of research, is that viewing entertainment violence can lead to increases in aggressive attitudes, values and behavior, particularly in children.

Advertising may also play a role in encouraging bullying. Advertisers seeking to capture the teen market promote products and services based on what is considered cool.[38] Advertising standards generally emphasize the importance of looks and possessions. This emphasis can contribute to bullying and harassment of students who do not meet these advertising norms. Those who fail to meet norms for physical attributes are frequent targets of bullying.

Community and blogging sites are offered as free services for teens. The revenue generated by such sites comes from companies engaged in market research and advertising directed at the teen market. Companies creating such online environments receive income by allowing market research companies to profile and analyze teen online activity, to better create and market products and services to teens. Such companies also receive income based on teen exposure to online ads or other promotional activities that are present on these sites. A recent news report on the online community MySpace demonstrates this:[39]

> MySpace has 41 million registered users and ranks 19th on the list of most-visited Internet sites. . . . That makes MySpace the prime gateway to marketing's dream demographic: 14- to 30-year-olds. . . . MySpace says it already

carries more than 10 percent of all advertising viewed online. The ads range from cola and cell phones to dating services ("eSpin-the-Bottle: Search for Hotties near you"). . . . News Corp. reportedly plans to mine MySpace's vast repository of personal information on young people (demographic profiles, personal interests, spending habits) in an effort to become the dominant seller of Internet display advertising.

Funding schemes like this lead teen sites to encourage a significant amount of personal exposure of information (very helpful for market research firms), to heavily promote concepts of what is to be considered cool (which helps to establish social norms for teens), and to encourage exposure of personal stories and outrageous behavior (because this builds audience). The end result is that for teens, the Internet has become an environment like reality-TV for self-disclosure of personal and intimate information and attacks against others in order to draw traffic to a blog or Web page. Attention is the objective.

Cyberbullying appears to have become an entertainment activity for some youth. A group of friends may gather at one student's house for Friday night fun. Parents may think that all is well because they are safely gathered in the family room engaging in some activity online. What may be occurring is that the group of friends are involved in cruel cyberbullying as a party game. Adult readers likely recall similar telephone gag games they played as youth.

IMPACTS OF BULLYING

It is necessary to consider the impacts of bullying and online social aggression on both targets and the aggressors.

Impacts on Targets

The NICHHD study noted that youth who reported being bullied also reported poorer social and emotional adjustment, greater difficulty making friends, poorer relations with classmates, and greater loneliness.[40]

Children and youth who are the target of bullying can become tense, anxious, and afraid.[41] Bullying can affect their concentration and school performance, and it can lead to school avoidance. If bullying continues for some time, it can begin to affect the targets' self-esteem and feelings of self-worth. It also can increase their social isolation, leading them to become withdrawn and depressed, anxious and insecure. Bullying can have long-term consequences. Researchers have found that years later, long after the bullying has stopped, adults who were bullied as youth have higher levels of depression and poorer self-esteem than other adults.

It is possible that the situation of cyberbullying is more emotionally damaging to the targets than traditional bullying. A number of reasons can be cited for this:

- Online communications can be extremely vicious and cruel.

- A target of in-school bullying has the ability to escape such bullying when at home. The same is not true with cyberbullying. Cyberbullying can be occurring 24/7, whenever a teen uses a technological device—or even if the teen does not use any device (as in the case where students create a Web site defaming another student).

- Degrading incidents that may occur to a target at school are witnessed by a limited number of other students. Degrading images and text can be transmitted worldwide and can be very difficult, if not impossible, to retrieve.

- Sometimes cyberbullies are anonymous, so the target does not know whom to trust. When a young person is the target of cyberbullying by proxy, it can seem like everyone has turned into an enemy.

- Because social norms in some teen communities support a certain amount of cyberbullying, there may be the expectation that the targets should consider such harm to be "no big deal."

Impact on Aggressive Bullies

The NICHHD study reported that youth who bullied others were more likely to report being involved in other problem behaviors, such as drinking, use of alcohol, and smoking.[42] Bullies also showed poorer school adjustment. However, they were not socially isolated. They reported ease in making friends. Unfortunately, this probably means that youth who bully have the ability to make friends with a group of peers who promote or support bullying and engage in other antisocial behaviors.

The Internet provides an excellent vehicle for youth to associate with others who hold common norms. Bullies who are also involved in other antisocial behaviors will have ample opportunity to expand their circle of friends to include other online youth who engage in antisocial behavior. The expanded opportunity for mutual reinforcement of such behavior is cause for significant concern.

REPORTING BULLYING

Youth who are targets of bullying frequently do not report such bullying.[43] It appears that many factors contribute to this phenomenon. Both children and adults often communicate the position that tattling is not acceptable behavior. Some anti-bullying programs seek to help children distinguish between tattling and telling, but this is likely a distinction without a difference within the social norms of youth. Some youth may feel that bullying is deserved because of their personal faults. Some youth do not tell because they perceive that adults, teachers, or parents will not understand or know how to deal with the situation effectively. Youth who do tell risk the possibility that adult actions will make the situation worse, either through diminished social status in the eyes of other students or through generating retaliation by the bully when no adult is present.

Similar pressures against reporting are highly likely in cases of cyberbullying. It is possible that teen targets of cyberbullying may feel even less inclined to report the situation than they would if the bullying was taking place in person and therefore feel even more alone in facing the harm that is being inflicted. Bystanders may also be less inclined to report cyberbullying.

Concerns such as these militate against reports of cyberbullying:

- Many teens think that adults do not understand the Internet and their new online world and will not understand or know how to respond to cyberbullying. Unfortunately, they are probably right.

- Teens fear that their parents will overreact to reports of incidents involving the Internet and respond by limiting Internet access—which would be the social kiss of death—for most teens Two strong online social norms work against the reporting of cyberbullying:

  "What happens online should stay online." This norm promotes the idea that online activities are, or should be considered, separate and distinct from real-world activities. Since adults are generally not present in online environments, reporting online activities would violate this norm.

"On the Internet, you have a free-speech right to say whatever you want without regard for the harm it might cause to another." This is an extremely strong social norm that leads to the assumption that cyberbullying is a free-speech right.

- Teens know that if they anger, challenge, or report a cyberbully, that bully or his or her friends have great potential to cause even more harm through anonymous online retribution and cyberbullying by proxy.

- Some teen targets have engaged in risky online behavior, especially risky sexual behavior, that has placed them in a position of exploitation, and they fear punishment for this prior unsafe act.

To increase the potential of reporting, it is necessary to educate adults about these issues so that they can respond effectively and provide greater education to students about the limits against harmful speech (discussed in chapter 6) and the full range of response options (discussed in chapter 9). Knowing of possible response options that can be implemented without requiring limited access may provide comfort to the targets who fear that reporting will lead to online restrictions.

It is essential that schools establish an anonymous and confidential reporting mechanism. One of the advantages of Internet communications is how easily they are accessed and can be disseminated. This factor, combined with an anonymous and confidential reporting mechanism, provides some distinct advantages to encourage reporting. The student cyberbully may not be able to find out who has reported and therefore would not know whom to retaliate against. This provides a measure of safety for the target or a bystander to report incidents of cyberbullying.

An additional advantage of Internet communications is that the evidence of the behavior is (or at least can be) retained in permanent form. As compared to a "he said, she said" argument about an event, a counselor, psychologist, or administrator has solid evidence of the activities. Unfortunately, there is also the possibility of impersonation.

TEACHERS WHO BULLY STUDENTS

Alan McEvoy has initiated research in an area where there has been little or no focus: teachers who bully students.[44] McEvoy defines bullying by teachers as "a pattern of conduct, rooted in a power differential, that threatens, harms, humiliates, induces fear, or causes students substantial emotional distress." He describes this phenomenon as follows:

> Bullying by teachers shares some similarities to peer-on-peer bullying. Like peer-on-peer bullying, it is an abuse of power that tends to be chronic and often is expressed in a public manner. It is a form of humiliation that generates attention while it degrades a student in front of others. In effect, the bullying can be a public degradation ceremony in which the victim's capabilities are debased and his or her identity is ridiculed.

> Similarly, it is deliberate, it is likely to distress the target, and it tends to be repeated. Equally significant, the teacher who bullies usually receives no retribution or other negative consequences. This too parallels peer-on-peer bullying. The classroom is the most common place for such bullying to occur, although it may occur in any setting where students are under adult supervision.

> The process of targeting students and the consequences of being bullied by a teacher may also be similar to peer-on-peer bullying. Victims may be chosen on the basis of apparent vulnerability (e.g., someone who can't or won't fight back), or because the target is seen as someone others will not defend (e.g., gay or lesbian), or because of some devalued personal attribute. Once targeted, the victim is treated in a manner that sets him or her apart from peers. There may be frequent references to how this student differs from others who presumably are more capable or valued. As a consequence, the student may also become a scapegoat among peers.

> Teachers who bully feel their abusive conduct is justified and will claim provocation by their targets. They often will disguise their behavior as "motivation" or as an appropriate part of the instruction. They also disguise abuse as an appropriate disciplinary response to unacceptable behavior by the target. The target, however, is subjected to deliberate humiliation that can never serve a legitimate educational purpose.

> Students who are bullied by teachers typically experience confusion, anger, fear, self-doubt, and profound concerns about their academic and social competencies. Not knowing why he or she has been targeted, or what one must do to end

the bullying, may well be among the most personally distressing aspects of being singled out and treated unfairly. Over time, especially if no one in authority intervenes, the target may come to blame him- or herself for the abuse and thus feel a pervasive sense of helplessness and worthlessness.

McEvoy conducted focus group discussions with students and teachers. His findings included these points:

In many schools—perhaps most schools—at least one or more teachers can be identified as abusive toward students. Students will be in substantial agreement about which teachers are high rate offenders. The same degree of agreement may hold true for the colleagues of these offenders. They too appear to know which colleagues are abusive. The public nature of bullying patterns increases the likelihood of consensus on those who are most extreme in their behaviors. Simply stated, the faculty and students within the institution often are in private agreement about who the few culprits are, and express deep frustration at feeling powerless to stop the problematic behavior.

It is known that sometimes students create Web sites that target teachers or other school staff. Sometimes, these Web sites may be put-down sites. But there is a very real possibility that when a student or group of students has created a Web site or posted material in some other manner that reflects anger and frustration about a school staff member, such online material is in response to the "pervasive sense of helplessness and worthlessness" that is the result of teacher bullying. Administrators seeking to address an issue related to harmful material posted about a teacher must remain very mindful of the possibility that the harmful online material has been posted by a student who is suffering as the result of the harmful activities of a teacher or other staff member.

DIRECT THREATS

In a report titled *The School Shooter: A Threat Assessment Perspective,* the Federal Bureau of Investigation (FBI) states:[45]

Specific, plausible details are a critical factor in evaluating a threat. Details can include the identity of the victim or victims; the reason for making the threat; the means, weapon, and method by which it is to be carried out; the date, time, and place where the threatened act will occur; and concrete details about plans or preparations that have already been made.

It is necessary to remember that in face-to-face interactions, young people often make verbal threats that are not real statements of willingness to do harm. As noted earlier, if two young children are involved in a schoolyard fight, one might shout at the other, "I'm gonna kill you." This is apt to be an expression of anger, not a direct threat of imminent violence leading to death. A young person's tone of voice and posture, and an assessment of the overall interaction, allow others to determine whether or not something is a real threat.

Material communicated online that appears to be threatening could be real—or not. Just because what appears to be a threat is written and communicated electronically, it is not necessarily more real than a schoolyard shout. As noted in chapter 1, it is critically important for school officials and others to recognize the possibility that online material that appears threatening is not a real threat.

The cyberbully and cyberthreat situation review process, outlined in chapter 8, sets forth a procedure designed to help avoid making an inappropriate response in either direction.

DISTRESSING MATERIAL

Distressing material raises concerns that a young person is suffering emotionally and is possibly on the verge of taking a drastic and harmful step. This kind of online material bears close resemblance what the FBI refers to in *The School Shooter* as "leakage."[46] Here is the FBI discussion of this phenomenon:

> "Leakage" occurs when a student intentionally or unintentionally reveals clues to feelings, thoughts, fantasies, attitudes, or intentions that may signal an impending violent act. These clues may take the form of subtle threats, boasts, innuendos, predictions, or ultimatums. They may be spoken or conveyed in stories, diary entries, essays, poems, letters, songs, drawings, doodles, tattoos, or videos. . . . Leakage can be a cry for help, a sign of inner conflict, or boasts that may look empty but actually express a serious threat. Leakage is considered to be one of the most important clues that may precede an adolescent's violent act.

An example of leakage could be a student who shows a recurring preoccupation with themes of violence, hopelessness, despair, hatred, isolation, loneliness, nihilism, or an "end-of-the-world" philosophy. . . . Another example of leakage could be recurring themes of destruction or violence appearing in a student's writing or artwork. The themes may involve hatred, prejudice, death, dismemberment, mutilation of self or others, bleeding, use of excessively destructive weapons, homicide, or suicide. Many adolescents are fascinated with violence and the macabre, and writings and drawings on these themes can be a reflection of a harmless but rich and creative fantasy life. Some adolescents, however, seem so obsessed with these themes that they emerge no matter what the subject matter, the conversation, the assignment, or the joke.

Suicide prevention guidance focuses on very similar clues. The following list, provided by Substance Abuse and Mental Health Services Administration (SAMHSA), gives indicators that an individual may be contemplating suicide.[47] Note that many of the clues or signs of possible suicidal intention could easily be expressed in material posted online. The main points are material from SAMHSA. The subpoints set forth in italics are additional information on how these signs might be reflected in online activity.

- Threatening to hurt or kill oneself or talking about wanting to hurt or kill oneself.

  Posting this kind of material online on a personal Web site or in a blog, or including these thoughts in electronic messages.

- Looking for ways to kill oneself by seeking access to firearms, pills, or other means.

  Searching for information on methods to commit suicide on Web sites or requesting information in online discussion groups.

- Talking or writing about death, dying, or suicide when these actions are out of the ordinary for the person.

  Posting this kind of material online on a personal Web site, in a blog, or including these thoughts in electronic messages.

- Feeling hopeless.

  Feeling rage or uncontrolled anger or seeking revenge.

- Acting recklessly or engaging in risky activities—seemingly without thinking.

- Feeling trapped—like there's no way out.

  The preceding four feelings or activities could be reflected in online postings or communications.

- Increasing alcohol or drug use.

- Withdrawing from friends, family, and society.

  Signs of Internet addiction, as discussed in chapter 4, could be implicated in possible suicidal behavior.

- Feeling anxious, agitated, or unable to sleep—or sleeping all the time.

- Experiencing dramatic mood changes.

- Seeing no reason for living or having no sense of purpose in life.

  The preceding three feelings could also be reflected in online postings or communications.

Following are different ways in which there may be an interrelationship between online activity and suicidal behavior. The person who is thinking about self-mutilation or suicide may do the following:

- Express these thoughts and intentions online.

- Search for information on suicide methods online.

- Communicate with others in an online forum who are also contemplating harmful or suicidal behavior and thus receive reinforcement for the idea that suicide is an appropriate answer, information on suicide methods, and encouragement. Communication with others may also result in arrangements for joint participation in suicide.

- Communicate in an online forum with others who are contemplating violent actions against others, followed by suicide.

- Form a relationship with a very sick, dangerous stranger who takes perverse pleasure in convincing people that suicide is the answer and providing assistance and encouragement for such action.

- Respond to intense cyberbullying by resorting to suicide or be encouraged to commit suicide by other teens in the context of cyberbullying.[48]

- Consider that suicide is the answer to some other online situation that has led to feelings of helplessness and hopelessness, including involvement with an online sexual predator or online gambling.

Technology facilitates open disclosure of personal thoughts. Educators and other adults who work with youth must assume that emotionally distraught youth with Internet access will be posting material that provides significant insight into their distressed mental state. It is critically important to learn how to find, analyze, and respond effectively to distressing online material. Finding this material will require the education and involvement of youth—because they are the ones who are likely to see the material without making a specific effort to search for it.

CHAPTER 4

Related Youth High-Risk Online Behavior

This chapter provides an overview of additional concerns related to youth risk online. All the behaviors discussed here are significant concerns in and of themselves, but the discussion will focus on their relationship to cyberbullying and cyberthreats.

WHO IS AT RISK?

The first question that must be asked concerns what kinds of youth are most likely to engage in risky online behavior. The answer to this question is quite predictable: Youth who are at risk in general are also the ones who are most at risk of engaging in online activity that is not safe or healthy.

The researchers at the Crimes Against Children Research Center (CACRC) evaluated data from a national sample of Internet users, ages 10 to 17, to explore the characteristics of youth who had formed close relationships with people they met on the Internet.[1] Researchers found that girls who had high levels of conflict with parents or were highly troubled were more likely than other girls to have close online relationships. Boys who had low levels of communication with parents or were highly troubled were more likely than other boys to form such relationships. The researchers were unable to ascertain the quality of the online relationships, but clearly these youth are more vulnerable and at risk for exploitation.

In other words, youth who are "looking for love in all the wrong places" are likely to be looking for attention and connections with others online. These youth are vulnerable to predators. They may also align themselves with other hurt, angry, or disconnected youth and adults to form dangerous online communities and are vulnerable to the contagion that can occur within such groups. They may also be much more likely to follow through with harmful real-world activity when encouraged to do so by their online community.

It is very difficult to get these at-risk youth to disengage from dangerous online communities because it is within these communities that these young people have—perhaps for the first time—actually found what they perceive to be caring and acceptance.

PRIVACY EXPECTATIONS AND CONCERNS

Online communities are public places. Unfortunately, many youth simply do not seem to understand the public nature of these environments or the permanency of the material they are posting. Teachers and parents have reported instances where they have discovered that youth have been posting intimate personal details about their lives or harmful comments about others in an online community Web site. When questioned about these postings, the startled young people usually retort with a question of their own: "Why have you invaded my privacy?" Clearly, educating youth about the lack of privacy, the ease with which their postings can be communicated to others, and the permanency of their online communications is extremely important.

Too often, basic Internet safety guidance teaches a simplistic and ineffective rule: "Do not provide personal information online." It is not possible to register on a new site or make new friends without violating this rule. Better guidance is essential. Young people must learn to distinguish between personal contact information, personal interest information, intimate personal information, and reputation-damaging material. They must also learn how and where different types of information can be reasonably safely shared online.

Personal Contact Information

Personal contact information is any information that will allow someone to find a person in real life: full name, last name, address, phone number, permanent e-mail address, and school or workplace name. Young people should rarely disclose any of this information online without the permission of their parent. Most Internet-savvy adults also avoid providing personal contact information unless it is absolutely necessary, such as for professional contacts or making a purchase.

Personal Interest Information

Personal interest information is more general information about the things and activities the young person is interested in. In most online locations, it is generally safe to share this kind of information. This is the kind of information young people can share with online strangers who might have the same interests, post on Web pages or in blogs, and the like.

Intimate Personal Information

Intimate personal information is private and personal information that should generally remain confidential or be shared only with very trustworthy people. Sometimes, this is information about problems youth are having with others or struggles they might be having in life. It is incredibly important for youth to understand that if they share this kind of information online, especially in public places or with people they do not know personally, they make themselves extremely vulnerable. Others can use this information to exploit them.

It is also important to recognize that there may be circumstances under which disclosure of intimate personal information may be perfectly appropriate. For example, a young person who is being abused or is trying to sort out conflicting sexual issues may be able to find effective professional support services online. Disclosure of intimate personal information is necessary to obtain such support. Young people must be advised of the importance of checking out the qualifications of a support site and not disclosing personal contact information unless absolutely necessary to receive assistance.

It is also likely that young people will ignore guidance categorically warning them against discussing intimate personal information online. It is both essential and far more effective to help them determine the best strategy for discussing such issues. This is actually an important life lesson—knowing how and with whom we ought to share and discuss the intimate details of our lives. Some of the key principles for safe sharing include using more private forms of electronic communication, sharing only with very trusted friends who are known personally or sharing in an environment where no personal contact information whatsoever has been disclosed. It is also important for them to avoid sharing so many details that the information could lead to identification and to understand the risks of relying on any input that comes from such sharing—including the risk that their "trusted friend" might not turn out to be trustworthy after all and may forward intimate personal information to others.

It should be noted that distressing online material involves the disclosure of intimate personal information. While it may be helpful, from an investigator's perspective, to discover the concerns of youth through online writings, the preferable situation is that the young people are not posting information about such concerns for all to see.

Reputation-Damaging Material

Young people are also, unfortunately, posting information and images that could clearly harm their reputation, damage future education or career plans, or provide the fuel for online social aggression. One story reported to this author involved a middle school boy living in a conservative community who engaged in some preliminary sexual "explorations" with an older male—and then described the activities on his public blog.

INTERNET ADDICTION

Internet addiction can be defined as an excessive amount of time spent using the Internet, resulting in lack of healthy engagement in other areas of life.[2]

Internet addiction is itself a concern, as well as an indicator of other concerns. Excessive amounts of time spent on the Internet may become a slippery slope leading teens into the darker side of Internet activity, including cyberbullying and the other risky behavior outlined in this chapter.

Internet addiction is a behavioral addiction. Individuals who appear to be most at risk of Internet addiction are those who are under stress or suffer low self-esteem. Behavioral addictions have common themes:

- Addictive behavior becomes a way to avoid other stressful issues.

- Addicted individuals require increased involvement with the addictive activity to maintain their feelings of wellness.

- Addicted individuals cover up or lie about their activities.

- Addicted individuals become preoccupied with the addiction activity. When not engaged in the activity, they are thinking about the last time they were involved or planning for the next time.

- Efforts to cut back on addictive activity are unsuccessful. Attempts by others to restrict activity lead to anger.

- Addicted individuals are generally the last to recognize the addictive behavior or the harm it has caused.

The Internet offers a time-warped place where youth can get away from their real-world concerns—they can be free, independent, and uninhibited, and they can find acceptance. The Internet is available 24/7. The game is always going on. Friends are always available. Life online constantly beckons.

One large part of the problem is that commercial Web sites have designed *stickiness* into their operations—activities that are designed for the specific purpose of enticing young people to spend as much time as possible on their site and to return frequently. The sites foster addiction because it is good for their bottom line. The more young people use these sites, the more information they disclose and the more advertisements they are exposed to, which translates to more money for the site operators. Young people may not recognize how these sticky features are being used to manipulate them.

These, then, are the main indicators of Internet addiction:

- Excessive amounts of time spent on the Internet.

- Excessive fatigue—the result of extensive nighttime Internet use.

- Preoccupation with Internet activities.

- Decline in grades—the result of fatigue and preoccupation with Internet activities.

- Decline in interest and involvement in other life activities.

- Withdrawal from friends and family.

- Use of deceit and lies to cover up time spent online.

- Intense anger in response to any attempt to limit Internet access, along with efforts to get around any restrictions.

When youth are caught up in Internet addiction, they go into withdrawal when they are not engaged in online activities. They are also preoccupied by their online activities to an extent that limits their involvement in other necessary activity, including spending time with friends or doing homework.

Preventing Internet addiction among young people requires focusing on the quality of their individual relationships with family and friends and helping them practice effective stress management and learn to keep life in balance—spending an appropriate amount of time engaged in important life activities: school and homework, chores and work activities, time with family and friends, organized activities and personal interest time, physical activities, and sleep, as well as time online.

Internet addiction can be implicated in cyberbullying because a young person who is addicted to the Internet can find it very hard to leave the online environment, even when being abused there. For some youth, being disconnected from their online community may be even more painful emotionally (or so it may seem) than the victimization. Internet addiction is also highly related to school failure.

SUICIDE AND SELF-HARM ENCOURAGEMENT COMMUNITIES

It appears that many distressed teens are forming online social communities that support and encourage self-destructive behavior— including self-injury, anorexia and bulimia, drug use, and suicide. Most of these communities express a "pro-choice" approach to self-destructive behaviors. In this context, pro-choice means that whatever a person decides—to commit suicide or not, to cut or not—is perfectly justified and appropriate.

These communities frequently involve teens and young adults and can provide strong emotional support for their participants. But this support is provided through a community of like-minded distressed teens and adults who have adopted attitudes and behaviors that are destructive or injurious as the means by which they are seeking to deal with their social and emotional difficulties.

The most attractive feature of these dangerous communities is online discussion, groups where individuals support each other, exchange stories about events in their personal lives, and swap tips and techniques to engage in injurious behavior and hide the evidence of such engagement from others. One of the reasons that young people are inclined to share in such an environment is the disinhibition that occurs when they believe they are anonymous. This could be considered a positive aspect of disinhibition—that young people are willing to open up and share their hurts and pains. The problem is that such sharing is occurring in an environment with other distressed teens who are unlikely to provide effective guidance.

A teen's need to belong and to feel accepted, combined with group norms for injurious behavior, presents an extremely troubling situation. Teens without strong real-world social connections readily attach themselves to online communities that provide them with feelings of acceptance and belonging. But to be a participant in such communities leads to adoption or continuation of unhealthy thoughts and engagement in injurious behavior. Self-destructive behaviors are socially contagious. Exposure to information that others are engaging or have engaged in certain self-injurious activities can lead more individuals to engage in these behaviors or increase already existing behavior.

It is estimated that more than 500 Internet discussion groups bring together individuals who engage in self-injury—defined as inflicting harm to one's body without the obvious intent of committing suicide. A recent study of such sites and groups revealed that much of the dialogue was supportive in nature, but a significant portion of the dialogue reinforced the self-injurious behaviors by providing information on techniques for cutting and concealment.[3] While this study focused on self-injury, it is likely that the same activities are occurring in groups focused on other self-destructive behaviors.

Such environments also appear to attract predatory individuals who pose as participants or supporters for reasons of their own. They may attract individuals who gain some psychological (or even financial) benefit by promoting harmful or injurious behaviors. Self-injury discussion groups have connections with Web sites that sell self-injury products such as bracelets and clothing. Communities that promote drug use are most certainly attracting or have been organized by drug dealers. Sometimes individuals within the communities appear to distinguish themselves as mentors, making themselves available to assist others in following through on certain harmful actions. Some of the communities appear to have been created by young adults who began engaging in self-injury as teens and who now apparently see their role as supporting other teens and young adults along the same path.

Use of the Internet to form actual suicide pacts is a trend that is also of concern. In the past, suicide pacts tended to involve older individuals, people who had a long-standing relationship, such as older married couples who were facing declining health. The emergence of Internet Web sites and discussion groups that promote choice for those contemplating suicide is also leading to the creation of online suicide pacts. The people who become involved in these activities tend to be teens and young adults who did not know each other prior to their involvement in these communities. The majority of suicide pacts have been reported in Japan. However, the trend appears to be expanding to other countries.

The use of digital imagery, including cameras and webcams, in conjunction with participation in self-injurious behavior, is also increasing. Participants in discussion groups post images of themselves vomiting or graphic displays of cutting. Young people are no longer committing suicide alone. Some are broadcasting the images of their suicide via webcam to their online "support" group.

HATE GROUPS, GANGS, AND OTHER TROUBLESOME GROUPS

Hate groups, gangs, and other troublesome groups are another form of dangerous online community providing support for violence and hatred for others. Hate groups and gangs have common characteristics that are not shared with other troublesome groups. Hate groups and gangs generally have a well-formed leadership structure and include both youth and adult members. They also have a tendency to employ mechanisms such as a formal group name and symbols to identify members of the group and distinguish members of the group from others. Adult members of the hate group or gang may engage in recruiting behavior. Other troublesome groups are less formal and generally include only teens.

Hate Groups

Hate groups are groups that "advocate violence against, separation from, defamation of, deception about, or hostility towards others based on race, religion, ethnicity, gender, or sexual orientation."[4] Hate group members are generally from the dominant race, religion, or ethnicity in their social community and direct their hostility at members of one or more minority groups. Hate groups do not refer to themselves in those terms; on the contrary, they perceive that their beliefs of superiority and their justifications for the denigration of others are perfectly acceptable.

Hate group propaganda present on Web sites generally places heavy reliance on conspiracy theories that describe ways in which other people or groups are intending to restrict or interfere with the rights of the majority group. Frequently, there is reliance on scripture or pseudoscientific language to justify their belief in their own superiority. The sites will often present revised versions of history to justify their disapproval of certain groups. Some may present their material in the context of patriotism or nationalism.

Teens are prime targets for hate groups in search of members, and the Internet has become a significant recruitment ground. Lonely and angry teens of the appropriate cultural group who do not have strong affiliations with their families and friends are the most frequent targets for recruitment. Some hate Web sites are relatively up-front about their intentions and philosophy. Others may initially be more disguised. The first impression is that they are presenting historically accurate information. Some sites may masquerade as fun sites for children—complete with activities like crossword puzzles, stories, and cartoon characters that communicate prejudicial thoughts.

Hate Web sites often offer free downloads of "white power" music—with highly racist and violent lyrics. Many also offer the ability to download hate-based games that allow the player to engage in violence to kill and maim members of minority groups, who are depicted as subhuman. The most popular features of such sites are the discussion boards or chat rooms. These discussion groups allow socially alienated and angry teens to vent and form strong, cohesive support environments based on a mutual agreement to hate others.

Chat rooms and discussion boards are also locations for recruiters to identify and form relationships with likely recruits. Most community sites have strict policies against the posting of hate or gang-related material and regularly remove such material if they find it or if users report it. But it is more difficult for such sites to identify and remove recruiters who are simply communicating within the discussion groups. Teens who present themselves in these environments as lonely, angry, and searching for support are probable targets. Although not studied, recruitment techniques are likely to be very similar to the techniques used by online sexual predators—with the additional value (as perceived by the victim) of an emotionally supportive online group to welcome the new recruit.

Gangs

Gangs tend to be formed by members of minority groups within a society. It is not illegal to be a member of a gang. Unfortunately, many gangs are involved in criminal activities, especially drug trafficking, money laundering, and human trafficking. Gangs are now moving into Internet piracy, computer security crime, and online identity theft.

Gangs are using the Internet and other technologies to communicate with each other, coordinate criminal activity, and avoid detection by legal authorities.[5] They can also use the Internet to track, identify, and target victims. Gangs are creating their own Web sites to facilitate recruitment and communication among members, brag about their accomplishments, or issue challenges to other gangs. They are also using chat rooms and discussion boards for recruiting, in a manner similar to that of hate groups. Social networking sites and other teen sites generally have terms of use that prohibit display of gang symbols.

Teens who are having difficulties fitting into a healthy group of friends may seek involvement with a gang. Sometimes teens are gang "wannabes" and establish sites or engage in discussions that make it appear that they are gang members.

Other Troublesome Groups

Sometimes teens form more informal troublesome groups. For example, a group of students who are being bullied and excluded at school may form an online group where they support each other in expressing anger at other students. They may create their own Web sites where they denigrate the students who are bullying them and engage in continual online dialogue expressing their anger. Activities such as this can become very dangerous.

It is also highly probable that the members of these troublesome groups also actively engage in online violent gaming. In the online role-playing simulation environments, groups of online participants engage in planning and executing violent online strategies within the context of the gaming environment. The use of the Internet to plan violent attacks on their schools or communities may seem to some members of a student outcast group to be a continuation of this common violence planning behavior.

In the spring of 2006, a number of groups of five or six male students were arrested for reportedly planning or threatening an attack at school.[6] The plans were discovered because the students were communicating about them online. In the past, most school shootings have involved one or two shooters. The trend toward larger groups of students planning school violence is of significant concern. It was reported that the students involved were the recipients of bullying, were considered outcasts within the school community, and were involved in online gaming.

RISKY ONLINE SEXUAL BEHAVIOR

Youth are engaged in a range of risky online sexual activities. The teen community Web sites frequently promote sexuality and the use of the Internet for matchmaking activities. The fact that these communities attract youth from the age of around 13 (or younger if they lie about their age) to young adulthood, in addition to attracting older men who troll these communities for potential victims, creates a dangerous environment for younger teens who are exploring their emerging sexuality.

Online Activity Leading to Sexual Encounter

The CACRC has released two studies that addressed sexual solicitation of youth.[7] The first study, in 2000, revealed that 19 percent of youth had received sexual solicitations online. However, the second study (released in 2006) showed a decline in sexual solicitations to 13 percent. This is quite an interesting finding, considering the incredible increase in the amount of time young people are spending online in 2006 as compared to 2000. This indicates that young people appear to be gaining greater skills in avoiding the online places where such contacts are being made.

However, the CACRC definition of "sexual solicitation" was quite expansive. Basically, any unwanted communication that was sexual in nature was considered a sexual solicitation. And 43 percent of the sexual solicitations were from other youth. It appears that this survey was actually picking up on activities that could also be characterized as sexual harassment—a frequent phenomenon in secondary schools.

Youth who are at risk emotionally are clearly most at risk of being manipulated by older youth or adults who are using the Internet to make connections that will lead to sexual involvement. When participating online, they may receive contacts from others who are trolling for relationships. Teens who are uninterested in such relationships appear to be quite capable of ignoring or blocking the author of such a proposal or telling the person to leave them alone. In the CACRC study, only 4 percent of the incidents were considered by the youth to be distressing. One teen out of the 1,500 young people surveyed did meet with an older man who sexually solicited her online.

Teens may make contact with other teens for the purpose of "hooking up," which is the current term applied to sexual encounters that are in the context of a relationship that has no commitments. An excellent *New York Times Magazine* article titled "Friends, Friends with Benefits and the Benefits of the Local Mall" explored these youth sexual encounters.[8]

Other times, youth enter into relationships with older men who are appropriately called "online sexual predators." Frequently, material presented to youth about online sexual predators presents the picture of an innocent victim who is entrapped by a scheming predator. This is indeed the situation involved in many cases, but in other incidents the behavior of the teen has materially contributed to the level of risk. Yahoo just made a decision, under legal pressure, to close chat rooms. Here is more information:[9]

> Among the illicit chat rooms removed were those with labels such as "girls 13 & up for much older men," "8–12 yo girls for older men," and "teen girls for older fat men." Many of these were located within the "Schools and Education" and "Teen" chat categories.

> An undercover investigator, posing as a 14-year-old while visiting one of those chat rooms, received 35 personal messages of a sexual nature over a single 25-minute period, the attorneys general said.

How many chat rooms?

> In June, while still in discussions with the attorneys general, Yahoo removed or barred the posting of about 70,000 user-created chat rooms whose names suggested they facilitated illegal conduct, including promoting sex between adults and minors.

With the names cited and others like them, it should not have taken all that much intelligence and insight on the part of teens to know what kind of conversations were likely to be occurring in such chat rooms. Yahoo is just one of many sites that allow users to create chat rooms. Educators and parents cannot understand or address concerns related to risky sexual behavior if they fail to understand the context in which such interactions occur. This requires addressing the reality of the situation—which is that in many of these cases, young people who are emotionally at risk to begin with are engaging in sexually provocative behavior online with knowledge of what they are doing.

Another study by the CACRC involved interviews with law enforcement officials who had pursued cases of sexual offenses against minors that originated on the Internet.[10] In these cases, it was found that victims were between 13 and 15 years old. Seventy-five percent were girls, and 25 percent were boys (presumably boys who were exploring gender orientation questions). The majority of offenders were over 25. The victims met the offenders in Internet chat rooms. The offenders had apparently conducted research about the victims through the victims' profiles. The offenders frankly stated that they were adults interested in sexual relationships, and the victims met with them knowing that they were going to be engaging in a sexual encounter. Most victims met and had sex with the offender on more than one occasion. Half of the victims were described as thinking they were in love with, or had positive emotional feelings toward, the offender. (While not addressed specifically by the study, this presumably means that the rest of the victims knowingly met with an online stranger to engage in sexual activities without having positive emotional feelings toward this person.)

While risky online sexual behavior and sexual predation are significant concerns in and of themselves, it is important to note the two potential connections between this issue and the cyberbullying and cyberthreats that are the focus of this book:

- Whether the relationship is with an adult predator or another youth for the purpose of engaging in sexual encounters, there is the always-present possibility that the victim may at some point seek to disengage from the relationship. A predator or other youth seeking to retain the relationship could then engage in exploitive behavior that could be classified as harassment or cyberstalking.

- A youth who is engaging in these kinds of online sexual activities (and who is likely to be at risk to begin with) will be engaging in encounters with exploitive individuals. These experiences are likely to exacerbate the existing emotional difficulties. Whenever an educator, counselor, or psychologist is reviewing distressing materials related to suicidal intentions, the possibility that the young person is engaging in these kinds of risky online sexual activities should be explored.

Sexually Explicit Images

Some teen girls and boys are posting sexually suggestive images in their profiles or Web pages. Some are providing suggestive or explicit images or videos via e-mail, webcam, digital messaging, and the like. Sometimes these images are shared more privately in the context of seeking to establish a personal relationship with someone met online. Youth who are providing these images do not seem to understand that images that are shared in private can easily become public. Some teens are even setting up online businesses where they are providing sexual images of themselves or performing for webcams in exchange for gifts that online admirers can purchase for them. Youth may be groomed for such activity. A teen who posts a sexually suggestive image in a profile may receive contact from a child pornographer offering money or a gift in exchange for a slightly more revealing image. If a teen is willing to take this first step, the pornographer is likely to provide successive offers of gifts or money in exchange for increasingly more revealing images.

In relationship to the focus of this book, these images can be used in a number of unfortunate contexts:

- Harassment or cyberstalking—threatening to disclose such images.

- Outing—posting or disseminating the images.

- Impersonation—pretending to be the person who created the image and posting or disseminating it publicly, frequently with the suggestion that the person is interested in sexual contact.

It is highly probable that a young person who has shared a sexually explicit image, and is then victimized or extorted in the context of this image, will be very reluctant to disclose the situation to a parent or teacher. The inability to obtain adult assistance in addressing such a situation can exacerbate the emotional distress experienced by the youth.

VIOLENT GAMING WITH SEXUAL OR BIAS-BASED VICTIMS

Gaming sites are very popular among youth, especially boys. Many of these sites offer role-playing games, where the user will take on a specific persona and participate in an extensive 24/7 "simulated society" game. These games can be extremely violent—including sexual violence and violence based on hatred toward certain others.

The research evidence on youth involvement in violent media demonstrates that such involvement can lead to violent behavior.[11] Attitudes developed in the context of violent gaming can be transferred to other communication forums and the real world.

Simulation gaming activities themselves can also involve cyberbullying. One or more personas in a game may be involved in attacking another persona. Although it is "just a game," the emotional damage to the target can be real. Many gaming sites also have chat features that allow discussions between players, and cyberbullying can occur in these chat rooms.

For some young people, frequent participation in online gaming may lead them to assume the perspective that all online activity is "just a game"—an attitude that supports the continuation of violent attacks in other online environments.

CHAPTER 5

You Can't See Me—
I Can't See You

This chapter explores how young people learn to engage in responsible behavior in the real world, then considers how information and communication technologies may affect their decision making regarding the appropriateness of certain choices. Based on this knowledge, strategies to promote more responsible online behavior can be developed.

EXTERNAL FORCES THAT PROMOTE RESPONSIBLE BEHAVIOR

As young people grow, four external forces play a significant role in helping them learn to engage in safe and responsible behavior: moral values and social expectations, tangible feedback leading to an empathic recognition that an action has caused harm, social disapproval, and negative consequences imposed by a person in authority.

Moral Values and Social Expectations

Moral values and social expectations establish the standards by which behavior is to be measured.[1] Parents are the primary source for the transmission of moral values and social expectations to their children, especially to younger children. For many families, religious beliefs provide a valuable source of values and expectations for behavior. As children become teens, peer norms become an important part of the picture. Child care facilities and schools are other major sources of such values and expectations, operating especially through the establishment and enforcement of rules or policies for students.

Given the potential for differences in moral values and social expectations from these different sources, the level of global agreement on many core values and expectations is amazing.[2] Moral values, especially, are grounded in a near-universal recognition of the need to promote behavior that is necessary to support the health and well-being of people and our planet. It should be noted that every religious tradition in the world has some version of the Golden Rule—a maxim that seeks to encourage responsible behavior toward others. Demonstrating kindness to others appears to be a universal value.

Unfortunately, many advertising and media messages, especially those targeted at young people, promote values that do not encourage behavior that supports the health and well-being of others or the value of kindness.[3] The substance of many advertising messages is that personal value is directly related to physical appearance and acquisitions—thus contributing to an attitude that supports rejection and ridicule of those who do not meet these standards.

There are ample concerns that entertainment media foster disrespectful attitudes and violence directed toward others, especially "different others." The very popular violent video game Grand Theft Auto, which allows users to gain points by killing hobos and Haitians, is an example of such promotion of disrespect and violence. Entertainment media in various forms of reality-TV shows also promote the value of public disclosure of personal concerns and denigration of others. Ample evidence from extensive research reveals that these kinds of media strongly influence the values, attitudes, and behavior of young people.[4]

As young people grow, the values and expectations transmitted by others become internalized. Children's understanding of moral values and social expectations is tied to their cognitive development, especially their ability to take the perspective of others.[5] A major task of adolescence is the development of personal identity.[6] This personal identity incorporates a moral code—an internalized set of values and expectations that will guide decisions relating to ethical and responsible behavior. One of the key ways in which young people internalize values during the teen years is through experimentation with different identities to find what values fit or do not fit.

Recognition That an Action Has Caused Harm

When a young person engages in action that harms another and receives tangible feedback that the action has caused harm, this generally will result in empathic recognition—feeling bad inside as a result of harming another.[7] This bad feeling, combined with the value and expectation of kindness, can lead to feelings of remorse.

Empathic recognition that an action has caused harm to another is viewed as a significant vehicle by which external values and expectations become internalized.

Empathy has both an *affective* (feeling) component and a *cognitive* (thinking) component. Affectively, people appear to differ in the degree to which they are sensitive to the emotional states of others. Differences appear to relate, in part, to biologically based personality traits. People appear to vary in the degree to which they are sensitive to others and to situations unfolding around them. Differences also appear to relate to life experiences. A child whose own feelings are not recognized or properly responded to will frequently have difficulty being emotionally sensitive to the feelings of another person.

Empathy is also connected with cognitive development. As young people grow, they gain greater cognitive ability to recognize and understand the perspectives of others—to put themselves in someone else's shoes. This ability to take the perspective of others influences how a person responds to the perceived distress of others. The early teen years are a time when a major cognitive development shift leads to a significantly greater ability to understand the perspectives of others.

When a younger child perceives that another child is hurt, this generally stimulates a direct empathic response—feeling hurt inside when seeing that someone else is feeling hurt. Younger children are not as likely to have an empathic response if they are not directly in the presence of the child who is hurt. Simply being told that another child has been harmed or is feeling hurt will generally not stimulate significant internal empathic feelings in a younger child. The emerging ability to take the perspectives of another person increases the probability that a growing child or young teen will have an empathic response upon learning that an unseen other person has been harmed or is feeling hurt. This process of internalization leads to what is sometimes called "predictive empathy."

Empathy-induced remorse is a bad feeling about oneself when one is aware of having taken actions that have harmed another. Empathy-induced remorse may lead to efforts to remedy the situation. Alternatively, the person who becomes aware of actions that have harmed another may seek to prevent feelings of remorse by rationalizing those actions. Rationalizations will be discussed later in this chapter.

Educational interventions can enhance the potential that a young person will have an empathic response to another person who has been harmed or is feeling hurt. Programs used in schools today to counteract violence and bullying contain components that seek to enhance empathy, perspective taking, and recognition of the feelings of others. Increasing the potential that a young person will have an empathic response to the hurt of another and feel remorse for taking actions that caused this hurt is a critically important foundation for the prevention of violence and bullying.

Social Disapproval

When a young person engages in irresponsible or harmful behavior and recognizes that others are aware and disapprove of this behavior, this recognition can lead to feelings of shame and loss of face. Parents, teachers, and peers are key providers of social approval or disapproval.[8]

Because their survival depends on it, younger children are clearly influenced by the approval or disapproval of their behavior by their parents or care providers. Active parental involvement, including supervision and appropriate responsiveness to behavior that is not in accord with values and expectations, is the key to raising responsible young people.

Parental involvement also plays an important role with respect to peer influence. Active parents play a strong role in a young person's selection of friends and in moderating the impact of peer pressure. When parents are permissive or uninvolved, peer groups can assume what should be the role of parents in approving or disapproving behavior.

Negative Consequences

When a young person engages in irresponsible or harmful behavior that is detected by a person with authority over the young person, this will generally lead to a negative consequence. Parents and school officials are the most common authority figures to impose negative consequences on young people. Law enforcement officials impose even more significant negative consequences.

The nature of the negative consequence that is imposed in response to irresponsible or harmful behavior is of critical importance.[9] A disciplinary response that forces the young person to recognize the harm that was caused can enhance an internal empathic response and feelings of remorse. Further, a response that focuses on how the young person's actions were not in accord with established values and expectations can enhance feelings of shame. Additionally, a very effective disciplinary response is one that requires the child or teen to take a positive action to cure any harm that was caused.

An ineffective negative consequence is that of punishment—a consequence that merely demonstrates the power of the person in authority to impose a penalty on the young person and is unrelated to the action that was irresponsible or caused harm. A punitive response will frequently shift young people's focus away from the harm that their actions have caused to anger at the person in authority. While feelings of remorse or shame can influence future behavior, feelings of anger at an authority figure generally will not influence future behavior, other than promoting behavior to ensure future detection.

Unfortunately, a common negative consequence used in schools—suspension for a period of days—can be applied in a manner that makes it an ineffective response. Suspension, in and of itself, does nothing to force a young person to confront the harm caused to another. Suspension also fails to provide a vehicle for the young person to take an action that will cure the harm and might even be viewed by some youth as a reward. In cases of egregious behavior, suspension may be an appropriate disciplinary response, but it will be effective only if combined with other consequences that force recognition of harm caused by failure to abide by established values and expectations and if it allows for a cure of that harm.

RATIONALIZATIONS

When youth (or adults) perceive that they have acted in a way that is not in accord with established values, social expectations, or their own internal moral code, they will generally feel guilty—unless they can rationalize their actions in some manner.[10] It appears that everyone is willing, under certain circumstances, to act in ways that are not in accord with established social expectations or their internal moral code. Individuals appear to have an internalized limit about how far they are willing to depart from the ideal set forth in their personal moral code. This limit may vary from person to person. The internalized limit protects against unlimited inappropriate activity.

A number of factors appear to influence the degree to which individuals will waver from their own personal moral code.[11] People are more likely to waver when they can tell themselves:

- "I won't get caught." The chance of detection and punishment is low to nonexistent.

- "It didn't really hurt." The inappropriate action will not cause any perceptible harm.

- "Look at what I got." The harm may be perceptible but is small in comparison with the personal benefit gained as a result.

- "It is not a real person." The harm is to a large entity such as a corporation, and no specific or known person will suffer any loss.

- "Everyone does it." Many people engage in such behavior, even though it may be illegal or unethical.

- "They deserve it" or "They made me do it." The entity or individual that is or could be harmed by the action has engaged in unfair or unjust actions, thus justifying a damaging response.

IMPACT OF INFORMATION AND COMMUNICATION TECHNOLOGIES

When people use the Internet, they are often quite willing to do or say things that they would be much less likely to do or say in the real world. This phenomenon has been termed *disinhibition,* as in the following description:

> With regard to individual's behavior on the Internet [disinhibition] could be summarized as behavior that is less inhibited than comparative behavior in real life. Thus disinhibition on the Internet . . . is seen as any behavior that is characterized by an apparent reduction in concerns for self-presentation and the judgment of others.[12]

Disinhibition on the Internet is a neutral aspect of online behavior. It may lead to either negative or positive results. Disinhibition in Internet communication may lead to hostile exchanges, or it may allow individuals who feel disenfranchised or disempowered in the real world to express their thoughts more effectively in an online environment. Disinhibition with respect to searching for information on the Web may allow a person to more comfortably look either for pornography or for help with a sensitive health issue.

Information and communication technologies can have a profound impact on the external forces that influence behavior. Because the use of the Internet and other technology-facilitated communications is fairly new, researchers are still exploring various aspects of human behavior when using such technologies. However, it appears that information technologies allow users to more easily create rationalizations for irresponsible online behavior. Disinhibition, therefore, appears to be grounded in the process by which people rationalize behavior that varies from legal or social standards or their own personal norms. The perception of invisibility or anonymity and the reduction of tangible feedback about the consequences of online actions appear to be at the heart of this state of disinhibition.

"You Can't See Me"—The Perception of Invisibility and Anonymity

When using information and communication technologies, people perceive themselves to be anonymous, or they can take specific steps to establish the condition of anonymity. The perception (or illusion) of invisibility can influence behavioral choices. Invisibility undermines the impact of the potential for a negative consequence administered by an authority or through social disapproval. Invisibility also makes it easier to rationalize an irresponsible or harmful action due to the lack of potential for detection leading to social disapproval or punishment. If a transgression cannot be detected and a person is unlikely to be punished, threats of punishment are not likely to have any impact on behavior. Thus strategies that seek to influence responsible behavior by threatening legal action or some other punishment are not likely to be influential unless they include clear information regarding how those engaged in irresponsible or harmful behavior can be identified.

In fact, people are not totally invisible or anonymous when they use information and communication technologies. In most cases, they leave "cyberfootprints" wherever they go. Every computer that uses the Internet can generally be identified by its IP address. Despite this reality, the illusion of invisibility persists. Some actions using technology are rather invisible, such as borrowing a friend's software and installing it on your own computer. It is also possible to increase the level of invisibility with the use of anonymizer tools. Establishing an account with an anonymous username enhances invisibility. The fact that many people may be engaged in a similar activity also leads to a perception of invisibility because individual actions are such a drop in the pond that they are unlikely to be detected.

The issue of the impact of invisibility on human behavior is not new. Plato raised this very same issue in his story about the Ring of Gyges. In this story, a shepherd found a magical ring. When the stone was turned toward the inside of his hand, the shepherd became invisible. Thus the question was raised: How will you choose to behave if you are invisible?

Complicating this issue is the recognition of very good reasons for the creation of anonymity on the Internet. Certainly, steps taken to remain anonymous from potential spammers, such as creating an anonymous e-mail account that is used for registrations and other activities that are likely to lead to harvesting of that account for spammers, are beneficial. The ability to search for sensitive information without revealing your identity—for example, to seek information related to questions regarding sexual orientation—is also of great value. From a global perspective, individuals living in countries with repressive regimes that restrict access to information or seek to detect communications that are contrary to the interests of the regime have a strong interest in the use of tools that can create anonymity.

All young people should be taught to create an anonymous username to employ in any public Internet environment, including profiles, blogs, and any communication activities. The use of anonymous usernames is an essential strategy to protect young people from anyone who might misuse their personal contact information, including predators, cult recruiters, cyberstalkers, and marketers.

Unfortunately, from a developmental perspective, young people tend to rely heavily on external forces that influence responsible behavior; they have not fully developed an internal behavior control mechanism. Therefore, we are presented with a direct conflict: Actions that are deemed necessary to protect a young person's personal safety can lead directly to the perception of anonymity and thus undermine the inclination to engage in responsible behavior.

"I Can't See You"—The Reduction of Tangible Feedback

When people use technology, they lose the tangible feedback of face-to-face interaction that provides clues about the impact of their actions on others.[13] People are distanced from a perception of the harm that their behavior has caused. This lack of tangible feedback undermines the empathic response and thus undermines feelings of remorse. The lack of tangible feedback also makes it easier to rationalize an irresponsible or harmful action as not having caused harm to anyone.

Developmentally, it is important to recognize that the cognitive ability to take the perspective of another emerges in the teen years.[14] This cognitive perception taking is an essential foundation for a predictive empathic response to harm suffered by an unseen other. Therefore, children and younger teens are communicating with others online prior to and during the time when they are developing the cognitive perception abilities that enable them to detect or predict how another might feel in response to their communication.

In addition to eliminating an empathic response, the reduction of social and contextual cues can influence behavior by reducing the impact of social disapproval. The reduction in social cues that influence social norms may result in behavior that is not in accord with such norms. A negative aspect of such deregulated behavior may appear as hostile communication. Virtually everyone who has used Internet e-mail has had the experience of sending or receiving electronic communication that expressed thoughts rather more forcefully than would have occurred in the context of in-person communication.

As discussed in chapter 3, a positive aspect of the reduction of the impact of social cues related to social status is that it appears to result in greater online participation by those who are at a lower level in a social hierarchy. A student who is of relatively low status in the social hierarchy of a school may be disinclined to speak up in the classroom. But the impact of the reduction of social cues online may allow that lower status student to feel more comfortable in speaking up online. If this student is the target of bullying by someone of a higher social status, this student may be better able to communicate online in a manner that would demonstrate enough strength to get the cyberbullying to stop. The obvious negative aspect of this situation is that the student who is the target of bullying at school may simply use the Internet as a vehicle for retaliation.

As discussed, the ability to take the perspectives of others is developmental in nature. Therefore, young people may be potentially even less sensitive to the perspectives or needs of others online than they are in real life and therefore may fail to be adequately sensitive to the actual or potential consequences of their online speech. They are at a stage when they need all the clues they can get, so communicating or acting in an environment with reduced social cues can lead them into misbehavior.

"Everybody Does It"—The Impact of Online Social Norms

The social norms of online communities or groups may vary widely. Within some communities or groups, the norms support respectful online communication and responsible online behavior, whereas other environments support more volatile communication or other irresponsible or harmful behaviors. Therefore, while the influence of in-person social cues might be diminished, it appears that most online groups establish a mechanism for transmitting social cues regarding their expectations.[15]

Unfortunately, several online social norms common in youth online communities and groups support cyberbullying and cyberthreats, as well as other risky or irresponsible behavior. These social norms can be viewed as new Internet-based rationalizations for unsafe, irresponsible, or harmful behavior. Some of the more troubling norms include the following.

"Life online is just a game."

This norm allows the individual to ignore the harmful real-world consequences of online actions. It also creates the expectation that young people will simply ignore or "blow off" any online action by another that has caused harm.

"Look at me—I'm a star."

This norm supports excessive personal disclosure of intimate information, generally done for the purpose of attracting attention. In social networking communities, an individual's social status is measured by the number of contacts or connections the person has. Many young people appear to be emulating forms of modern entertainment media (especially reality-TV) to attract attention to their postings. This includes disclosure of titillating information and outrageous attacks on others. Such disclosure is promoted by the Web sites because it allows for market research and creates an audience.

"It's not me. It's my online persona."

On the Internet, it is possible to maintain multiple identities—called *personas*—within different communities.[16] Each persona may have different motives and operating parameters. During adolescence, young people are inclined to play out a range of roles and identities anyway, because this facilitates their development of a core sense of their own personal identity.[17] Internet technologies significantly enhance the ability to experiment with multiple identities. The ability and inclination of teens to maintain multiple identities on the Internet allows them to deny responsibility for actions taken by one of their online personas.

"What happens online stays online."

This norm supports the idea that one should not bring issues related to what has happened online into the real world. It specifically wards against any disclosure of online activity to adults.

"On the Internet, I have a free-speech right to post anything I want, regardless of the harm I might cause to another."

This norm supports cruelty and aggression as a free-speech right. As discussed in chapter 6, this norm is strongly promoted by advocates for civil liberties on the Internet.[18] As important as the rights of free speech are, there are limits on speech that causes harm to others.

STRATEGIES TO ADDRESS NEGATIVE INFLUENCES OF TECHNOLOGY ON BEHAVIOR

It is important to recognize that the following strategies are dependent on certain levels of cognitive development. Younger children simply do not have the cognitive ability to understand the various perspectives of others. Therefore, their online activities must be limited to *safe places*—environments that have been previewed by a responsible adult and determined to be safe and appropriate—and under close supervision. Teens will be more independent in their use of the Internet. The following strategies are addressed toward the teen audience.

Be Kind Online

Emphasize the importance of kindness and the avoidance of harm to others. Moral values and social expectations are frequently transmitted to children in the form of rules—for instance, "Do not call other children bad names." Unfortunately, this approach to the transmission of values fails to include the reason for the rule, which is grounded in the value of kindness and not causing harm to another. This information must be conveyed to children in the context of discussions of the rules: "Why is it important not to call other children bad names?"

If rules are enforced using a punitive approach rather than a disciplinary approach, the child's focus is shifted from recognition of the harm caused to another to anger at the adult authority who is enforcing the rule. If you ask a child, "Why should you not hit another child?" and that child responds, "Because it is against the rules" or "Because I will get into trouble," the child's response indicates a failure to connect the rule with the underlying value of not harming another.

A child who learns to base behavioral choices on the chances of getting into trouble is a child who will be more likely to misbehave when in an online environment that allows for invisibility. Grounding rules, values, and expectations in the concept of the importance of kindness and avoiding harm to others is a strategy to enhance responsible behavior under conditions when one perceives oneself to be invisible.

They Are Real People

Help young people recognize harm caused to unseen others. Since the feeling aspect of empathy is absent in online communications, young people should be guided to learn to rely on the thinking aspect of empathy. They should be encouraged to think about and consider the perspective of others whom they cannot see. Social skills and violence and bullying prevention curricula that emphasize the importance of empathic awareness, especially predictive empathy or "thinking empathy," provide an essential foundation for efforts to address cyberbullying.

Providing young people with real-life examples where others have been severely emotionally harmed by cyberbullying will help to combat the misperception that actions taken online have no impact on others.

What You Do Reflects on You

Help young people learn to do what is right in accord with their own personal values and enhance their reliance on their own internalized personal moral code, while recognizing that young people are in the process of developing this kind of code. Shifting the focus away from rules and threats of punishments to a focus on the harmful consequences of behavior that is not in accord with established values is an important strategy to accomplish this goal. Threats of punishment are ineffective when the likelihood of detection and punishment is perceived to be remote.

The key to such preparation is education and appropriate discipline. We must focus the attention of young people on the reasons for the rules rather than the potential for detection and punishment. By focusing on the reasons for the rules, we can help young people develop a more understanding and caring moral code, as well as increase their reliance on this internal code rather than on external enforcement measures.

Another important factor is enhancing the role of a young person's emerging personal identity and moral code as the primary focus of their attention in making behavioral choices. A consistent reminder that "the choices you make reveal the kind of person you are" is a message that should be regularly imparted to children as they grow.

Think First

Help young people learn to use effective decision-making strategies. The decision-making strategies listed here can enhance action in accord with maintaining personal values and avoiding harm to others. Help youth learn to ask themselves questions like these:

- *Am I being kind and showing respect for others and myself?* This question focuses on the social norm of kindness and the need for self-protection.

- *How would I feel if someone did the same thing to me or to my best friend?* This Golden Rule question suggests an analysis of how one would feel if one were the recipient of a certain action.

- *What would my mom (or dad, guardian, or other adult who is important in my life) think?* Philosophers call this the "moral exemplar." Young people can be encouraged to model the behavior of those whose opinions are important to them. This strategy also brings in the importance of acting in accord with the values that have been established by the family.

- *Is this action in violation of any agreements, rules, or laws?* It is important for young people to recognize the basis upon which rules have been created. Rules are created to protect the rights of people and to serve the common good.

- *Would it be okay if I did this in the real world?* This question also seeks to address the perception that online actions should be judged by real-world social norms.

- *Am I trying to rationalize a wrong act?* Combined with a discussion on rationalizations, this question helps to focus young people's attention on excuses they might be making that are interfering with responsible decisions.

- *How would I feel if everyone could see me?* One way to make good decisions is to act as if the whole world can see what you are doing. Another form of this question is "What would happen if what you just posted showed up on the front page of the newspaper?" This question can help enhance the influence of real-world social norms.

- *How would this action reflect on me?* This question seeks to enhance reliance on youths' personal values. All actions taken on the Internet are a reflection of the values of the individual taking those actions. Ultimately, this is the most important question.

Life Online Is Not Just a Game

Educate youth about real-world consequences of online actions. To combat the misperception that online abuse has no consequences, provide youth with insight into the school standards, terms of use agreements, civil law theories, and criminal law standards that could be applied to harmful online speech. This discussion can also be expanded to address family values and personal values. Private religious schools should certainly also expand the discussion to address religious values. These issues are discussed in depth in chapter 6.

It is critically important to address the legal ramifications of making cyberthreats. Youth must understand that if they post material online that appears to be a threat, they run the risk of ending up suspended, expelled, or under arrest if an adult sees the post—even if what they posted was just a joke! An excellent news story that can be used as the basis for this discussion is the *Washington Post* article "Message Is Clear in N. Va.: IM 'Threats' Can Bring Teens Trouble in an Instant."[19]

You Are Leaving "Cyberfootprints"

Educate youth about the strategies that can be used to detect their identity (and increase adult monitoring and supervision). Although it is preferable that young people learn to make decisions without regard for the potential of detection and punishment, young people should also understand that, in most cases, if they have engaged in inappropriate online behavior, their identity could be traced.

It is necessary to recognize that the development of an internalized personal moral code is a task that is accomplished primarily during the teen years and requires a certain stage of cognitive development. We should thus not be surprised if, in an unsupervised environment, teens fail to act in accord with the values that we would hope are part of their emerging internal personal moral code. Active adult involvement in the form of supervision, monitoring, and appropriate discipline will still be necessary.

Within the school environment, there clearly should be a lack of invisibility provided by effective supervision and monitoring. Unfortunately, effective monitoring is not occurring in many schools. Students should be fully aware that they have limited privacy with respect to their online activities and files, that routine monitoring (including technical monitoring) is occurring, and that individualized investigations may occur if there is a reasonable suspicion that they may have engaged in misuse. The effective monitoring of student Internet use is addressed in chapter 11.

Parents should also be advised about the importance of keeping the computer in a public place in the home and the need for ongoing supervision. Because parents are legally responsible for any injury to others caused by a teen's online behavior, it is important for parents to establish a ground rule giving them access to files on any computer in the home. Parents should regularly check the history file, should know all the public locations where their children are posting information, and should review those public postings regularly. Young people might object that this is an invasion of their privacy, but any material posted in a public online site is just that—*public*.

Some inexpensive keystroke monitoring technologies can be installed on home computers that will allow parents to monitor every online action, including private communications. The use of these technologies raises concerns about trust and the parent-child relationship, so the better approach is a solid relationship and agreed-upon standards. However, the parents of a young person who has acted in an inappropriate manner online are perfectly justified in installing monitoring software.

The recommendation made to parents about the use of this software in the *Parent Guide* (Appendix K) is that they inform their child of the presence of the software and the conditions under which they will review their child's private communication activities. The same standard that is used in school, "Activities that raise a reasonable suspicion of inappropriate behavior may lead to a search," is an excellent guideline for use in the home. Parents should advise their children about the circumstances that could lead to a decision to investigate their private online activity as well as a more in-depth analysis of their public activities. These circumstances might include late-night use, excessive use, declining grades, emotional distress, reports of inappropriate online behavior, clues detected in a review of public postings, and the like.

In the *Student Guide* (Appendix J), students are advised that the best way to address parental concerns about their online activities is to talk and share. They are encouraged to show their parents where they are going online and tell them what they are doing, show them their Web site and blog, introduce their parents to online friends, and avoid spending too much time online or immediately switching computer screens when a parent approaches. Additionally, students are advised to talk with their parents about what is happening online, especially if any problems arise, and to talk with their parents about expectations for online behavior—even better, tell their parents what their personal standards are. And, of course, they are advised not to engage in inappropriate online activities that could justify their parents' paying closer attention to their time online.

KNOWLEDGE AND SKILLS

In addition to these strategies, which all focus on influencing the motivation to do what is right, students should be educated about the risks and responsibilities related to online actions and should receive age-appropriate, realistic, practical guidance on how to respond to troubling situations in a safe and responsible manner.

CHAPTER 6

The Limits: Values, Rules, Agreements, and Laws

This chapter addresses the range of limits on online speech, the legal issues that arise, and the possible legal consequences of engaging in cyberbullying and cyberthreats.

FREE SPEECH

It is necessary to educate students about the limits on their free-speech rights to post or disseminate material online. As noted in chapter 5, a strong social norm for Internet communications is "On the Internet, I have the free speech right to write or post anything I want, regardless of the harm it might cause to another." This is not just a youth norm. Many of the organizations that focus on Internet issues, such as the Electronic Frontier Foundation (EFF), place a high degree of emphasis on free speech rights and anonymity and an unfortunately limited emphasis on the need for responsible speech.

There is no question about the essential value of the protection of free speech as a core value in a democratic society. But freedoms must be exercised with responsibility. People also have the right to be free from harm caused by irresponsible speech.

It will be helpful for purposes of illustration if readers will review EFF's *Blogger's FAQ on Student Blogging* before continuing to read this chapter. (This document is available online at www.eff.org/bloggers/lg/faq-students.php.)

In some parts, this document echoes the guidance found in this chapter. But it lacks reference to personal values and standards with respect to kindness and respect for others. For example:

What If I Want to Advocate Civil Disobedience on My Blog?

If you want to, for example, call for a student walk-out or otherwise advocate for civil disobedience that might be considered a "material disruption" at school, or if you just want to be able to freely criticize teachers and students without fear of getting unjustly punished, you should blog anonymously. [Instructions on how to blog anonymously are also provided.]

The online social norms and free speech guidance being recommended to today's youth provide a useful context for our discussion on limits.

There are, essentially, seven sources of limits—"lines drawn in the sand"—when it comes to the exercise of online free speech: personal values, religious values (which are probably only appropriate for full discussion in private religious schools), family values, school rules, terms of use agreements, civil law standards, and criminal laws. The most important limit is personal values, which one would hope will embody all of the other standards.

BENEFITS OF A DISCUSSION ON LIMITS

Family values, school rules, terms of use agreements, civil law standards, and criminal laws all embody the concepts that people should not act in ways that cause harm to others and that they can be held responsible for such harm should they ignore these standards. It is very important that young people—and their parents—know that these standards and potential consequences are in effect when they use the Internet. Information about these standards and the potential consequences to those engaging in cyberbullying can help in the following ways:

- Targets of cyberbullying will receive some assurance that it is possible to stop the aggression. This knowledge can help them gain the courage to directly challenge the cyberbully to stop. The knowledge will provide assurance that if they report the cyberbullying to an adult, action can be taken to stop the harm.

- Potential cyberbullies will be more aware of the possible consequences of harmful online speech, which could act as a deterrent. Such knowledge may also be helpful in convincing parents of the need to pay closer attention to what their children are doing online.

- Bystanders will have better insight into strategies that they can suggest to targets to stop the cyberbullying, as well as arguments they might make to directly challenge the actions of cyberbullies.

RELIGIOUS VALUES

This book has been written in a secular manner to serve the needs of public schools and nonreligious private schools, and therefore it does not discuss religious values in detail. For many families and private religious schools, religious values will provide an important reference point for a discussion of limits on free speech. Religious values can either be discussed as an additional source of limits or incorporated into a discussion of family and school values. An additional question could be added to the list of responsible decision-making questions discussed in chapter 5: "Is this action in accord with my religious values and the values of my religious community?"

FAMILY VALUES

The *Parent Guide* (Appendix K) encourages parents to address their family values about communications and behavior. Because most parents will reinforce messages about the importance of kindness and personal responsibility, it is possible that schools can also reinforce the importance of students' acting in accord with their family's values.

The *Student Guide* (Appendix J) encourages students to talk with their parents about family values and to use their understanding of such values as their guide for making decisions about online behavior. The decision-making strategy suggested by the question "What would a trusted adult, someone who is important in my life, think?" is also based on the goal of encouraging students to think about the values the important adults in their lives are seeking to transmit.

Both guides recommend that parents review all material that is posted by their child in any public location and review more private communications if there is a reasonable suspicion that their child might be engaged in unsafe or irresponsible behavior. One way that students can be encouraged to ensure that the material they post online—especially in any public location such as a blog, Web page, or discussion group—is in accord with their family values is to think about their parents' reaction to reading such material.

It is presumed that school districts have a student disciplinary code that prohibits bullying and harassment. Districts should also have an Internet use policy that incorporates the standards of the student disciplinary code. Chapter 11 provides an extensive discussion of district policies.

The legal standards related to student speech at school and outside school are fully addressed in chapter 7. It is recommended that schools take action that will raise the level of awareness of students to the provisions of the Internet use policy and disciplinary code that relate to communications through the district Internet system. This may involve a brief statement that appears on the logon screen as well as on signage in the computer lab.

TERMS OF USE AGREEMENTS

Internet Service Providers, Web sites, and cell phone companies place controls on the material and communications transmitted through their technologies or posted on their sites. The sites all have a document that is referred to as "Terms and Conditions," "Terms of Use," or simply "Terms" that outlines the agreement between the site and users. Generally, these terms of use agreements prohibit harmful speech.

On Web sites, terms of use agreements are generally accessible through a link on the home page of the site or through the pages related to registration. There is generally a check-off box as part of the registration process that indicates the user's willingness to abide by the terms of use. Terms of use agreements can be extensive and legalistic. It is highly probable that most youth have not read the fine print of these agreements.

Here is a representative example of such language—taken from the MySpace community, a very popular online community for youth—which addresses the kinds of material that can be posted (material that is not related to harmful speech or protection of personal privacy has been omitted):[1]

a. You understand and agree that MySpace.com may review and delete any content, messages, MySpace.com Messenger messages, photos or profiles (collectively, "Content") that in the sole judgment of MySpace.com violate this Agreement or which may be offensive, illegal or violate the rights, harm, or threaten the safety of any Member.

b. You are solely responsible for the Content that you publish or display (hereinafter, "post") on the Service or any material or information that you transmit to other Members. . . .

d. The following is a partial list of the kind of Content that is illegal or prohibited on the Website. MySpace.com reserves the right to investigate and take appropriate legal action in its sole discretion against anyone who violates this provision, including without limitation, removing the offending communication from the Service and terminating the membership of such violators. Prohibited Content includes Content that: i. is patently offensive and promotes racism, bigotry, hatred or physical harm of any kind against any group or individual; ii. harasses or advocates harassment of another person. . . . iv. promotes information that you know is false or misleading or promotes illegal activities or conduct that is abusive, threatening, obscene, defamatory or libelous. . . . vii. provides material that exploits people under the age of 18 in a sexual or violent manner, or solicits personal information from anyone under 18; viii. provides instructional information about illegal activities such as making or buying illegal weapons, violating someone's privacy, or providing or creating computer viruses. . . .

e. You must use the Service in a manner consistent with any and all applicable laws and regulations.

f. You may not include in your Member profile any telephone numbers, street addresses, last names, URLs or email addresses. . . .

g. Although MySpace.com cannot monitor the conduct of its Members off the Website, it is also a violation of these rules to use any information obtained from the Service in order to harass, abuse, or harm another person. . . .

i. You may not attempt to impersonate another user or person who is not a member of MySpace.com.

It is quite apparent that the terms of use of the MySpace site specifically prohibit much of the activity that is involved in cyberbullying. But just because a Web site has terms of use that prohibit harmful speech, that does not mean that the operator of the site has the ability to review all material posted on its site.

One problem is that some of these sites hide these excellent provisions in an extensive, legalistic document that most users do not read. On some sites, there is no easy way to figure out how to report infractions of the terms of use, although with increased expressions of concern about these sites, this situation appears to be changing. The responsiveness of service representatives from these sites may vary widely.

For the purpose of educating youth, the language in terms of use agreement clearly outlines the standards by which users should behave. These provisions are an important place to begin a discussion with youth about their online conduct. They also provide the basis upon which someone harmed by material posted on the site can seek the removal of such material and the termination of the account of the person posting the speech. Doing so requires filing a complaint. It is very important for youth and adults to know about the existence of these agreements because filing a complaint is an important strategy to stop and remove the harmful speech. This topic is discussed in chapter 9.

CIVIL LAWS

Civil law theories could provide the basis for lawsuits for financial damages or injunctive relief to be filed against offending students and their parents by the targets of cyberbullying. In civil litigation, the injured person, called a *plaintiff,* can request financial damages from the person who has caused harm, called the *defendant.* In cases where the defendant is a minor, the case is filed against the minor's parents or legal guardians. The financial damages can include loss due to pain and suffering, costs of counseling, losses related to lowered school performance or school avoidance, and the like. The target can also request an *injunction,* which is a court order requiring certain behavior or the cessation of certain behavior. The cyberbully could be required to remove all material over which he or she has control and cease and desist from placing any further material.

Intentional Torts

Many reported instances of ongoing cyberbullying that have resulted in significant emotional harm to young targets involve situations that could give rise to successful civil litigation for financial damages. It is possible that it will take a number of well-publicized cases where the parents of cyberbullies are held financially responsible for the harm caused by their children to provide greater incentive for parents to establish standards and supervise their children's Internet use.

The *Student Guide* and *Parent Guide* discuss the legal theories that will provide for claims to be filed against cyberbullies and their parents and also recommend contacting an attorney for assistance as one of the options in response to cyberbullying. The following legal theories are considered *intentional torts:* offenses that are committed by a person who intends to do an act that results in harm—essentially, an intentional wrongdoing.

Defamation (or Libel)

The cause of action of defamation (or libel) is based on the publication of a false and damaging statement. The statement must identify the target, and the statement must harm the target's reputation in the community. It must also be demonstrated that the person committing the defamation intentionally published the statement or failed to prevent its publication when he or she should have acted to prevent such publication. The defense to a claim based on defamation is that the statement is true.

The fact that the target of defamation may be a child should not matter. Children have the right to protect their reputations, and damage to their reputations can have a significant negative impact on their lives.

Invasion of Privacy: Public Disclosure or False Light

An invasion of privacy claim involves the public disclosure of private facts or false light. Public disclosure of private facts occurs when a person publicly discloses a nonpublic detail of another person's private life, when the effect would be highly offensive to a reasonable person. False-light invasion of privacy occurs when information is published about a person that is false or places the person in a false light, is highly offensive to a reasonable person, and is published with knowledge or in reckless disregard for whether the information was false or would place the person in a false light.

Defenses to actions based on invasion of privacy are that the facts are newsworthy or that the target gave consent. Activities of young people are unlikely to be sufficiently newsworthy. Minors are incapable of giving legal consent.

Intentional Infliction of Emotional Distress

The claim of intentional infliction of emotional distress supports a legal action when a person's intentional or reckless actions are outrageous and intolerable and have caused extreme distress. To support this claim, actions must be considered very outrageous and regarded as utterly intolerable in a civilized community.

State Laws Supporting Civil Litigation

Sometimes, state laws will support a civil cause of action based on acts that are in violation of a state criminal law. For example, under Oregon Revised Statutes (ORS) 30.198 (Actions for intimidation) provides the basis for a civil action in cases that meet the requirements of the crime of intimidation (ORS 166.155), which is the state's "hate crime" law. This law prohibits acts that meet this condition: "Intentionally, because of the person's perception of race, color, religion, national origin or sexual orientation of another or of a member of the other's family, subjects such other person to alarm by threatening." ORS 30.198 provides that any person injured by a violation of the hate crime law can file a civil action for damages and injunctive relief. This is in addition to any criminal proceeding and also does not require that any criminal activity even take place. The law specifically provides that parents can be held liable for the actions of their child, in an amount not to exceed $5,000. There is also the potential to recover attorneys' fees. Other states or jurisdictions may have similar legal provisions.

Holding Parents Financially Liable

Two legal approaches outline terms under which parents can be held financially responsible for cyberbullying harm caused by their child: negligent supervision and statutory parental liability.

Negligent Supervision

Under the doctrine of negligent supervision, parents can be held liable for the intentional or negligent actions of their child. Parents have a duty to use reasonable care to control and supervise their children when they know, or should know, of the necessity to exercise control or supervision and if they have the ability and the opportunity to exercise such control or supervision at the time it is needed.[2] Under the claim of negligent supervision, the parents are considered at fault for their failure to supervise. To prove a claim of negligent supervision in a case of cyberbullying, the target will have to show that (a) the parents were aware of or should have been aware of specific instances of cyberbullying and (b) the parents had the opportunity to control the child.

Parents generally would be considered to have the opportunity to control their child's use of a computer located in their house. Whether or not the parents know or should know that their child is engaged in harmful online activities would be a question that would be decided differently, depending on the facts of a case. School district activities to educate parents about the concerns of cyberbullying and the need to monitor their children's online activities could help to establish the fact that parents should have been aware of the potential that their child was engaged in cyberbullying.

If a child is identified as having engaged in cyberbullying, the parents are warned that their child is engaging in such behavior, and the behavior continues, then the parents clearly know there is a concern. Their failure to adequately address the known concern could increase the potential for liability.

The increased potential for financial liability is a very powerful lever that school officials can use to encourage the active involvement of parents in stopping cyberbullying, ensuring that harmful materials are removed to the best degree possible, and preventing retaliation from the student's online friends. The fact that school officials have informed parents that their child is engaging in behavior that is harming another child significantly increases the potential for liability under the theory of parental negligence—because now it is very clear that the parent has knowledge of the harmful behavior. The *Parent Guide* specifically notes the increased potential for liability and the steps that parents should take to address the issue. Providing this material to the parents, with that particular section highlighted, may provide great incentive to the parents to respond appropriately.

Parental Liability Statutes

The vast majority of states have what are most frequently called "parental liability" laws. For example, in Oregon, ORS 30.765 (Liability of parents for tort by child) provides that parents can be held liable for damages caused by any tort intentionally or recklessly committed by the child. In most states, there is an upper limit on the liability of parents. In Oregon, the liability is limited to not more than $7,500.

Under parental liability laws, parents of a target of cyberbullying who has been victimized in a manner that meets the requirements for intentional torts, as outlined here, could file a claim against the parents of the child posting or sending the material.

Under the doctrine of negligent supervision discussed earlier, the focus of attention is on the negligence of the parent in failing to supervise the child. Under parental liability laws, the focus is on the intentional tort committed by the child. If it is demonstrated that the child committed the tort, the parent is liable, regardless of the negligence of the parent—that is, regardless of whether or not the parent knew or should have known that the child was engaged in such activities or had the opportunity to control the child's behavior.

Small Claims Action

In some cases, the financial damages to a child due to cyberbullying may be relatively minor. Unfortunately, lawsuits can be very costly. If the damages are expected to be limited, it may be difficult to find an attorney willing to file a lawsuit (although sometimes a certified letter from an attorney might be enough to get the bullying behavior to stop).

In cases where the amount of financial damage is small, there may be another option (note the word *may*). Parents may be able file a claim in state small claims court. The parent will need to do some additional legal research to prepare for such a claim and may want to consult with an attorney for assistance. Parents should be made aware that most small claims actions involve matters of disputed bills and the like, and the judge may therefore not know exactly how to respond to a small claims action involving cyberbullying. It is also possible for the defendant to file a request for a jury trial. In small claims court, it is possible to request financial damages, but these are limited by state statute to a modest sum, such as $5,000.

Taking action through small claims court should be considered a tentative recommendation because, to this author's knowledge, this kind of action has never been tried.

CRIMINAL LAWS

One difficulty in providing general information addressing criminal law is that different jurisdictions and states have different laws that could be applied to cases involving cyberbullying or might apply to cyberthreats. However, it is useful to provide general guidance to students and parents that posting online material that meets the following standards may constitute a crime in their state or jurisdiction:

- Making threats of violence to people or their property.

- Engaging in extortion or coercion (trying to force someone to do something they don't want to do).

- Making obscene or harassing telephone calls (this also includes text messaging).

- Harassment or stalking.

- Hate or bias-based crimes.

- Creating or disseminating material considered harmful to minors or child pornography.

- Sexual exploitation.

- Taking a photo image of someone in a place where privacy is expected.

Teachers may wish to identify relevant local laws or make this a student assignment. These laws are posted online through government Web sites.

CHAPTER 7

Legal Considerations for Schools

This chapter addresses legal questions schools need to consider when dealing with cyberbullying and cyberthreats. When can and when should an administrator respond? That is:

- When *can* a school administrator monitor or conduct an individualized search of student Internet use records through the district Internet system—or of electronic records on a cell phone or PDA?

- When *can* a school administrator intervene with formal discipline to address cyberbullying?

- When *should* a school administrator seek to prevent and intervene in cases of cyberbullying?

This chapter has been written from the perspective of U.S. law and general common law standards. U.S. constitutional law applies to public schools but not to private schools. For readers in other countries, different country or jurisdictional laws may be applicable.

Important Disclaimer

The following material will discuss areas of law that are unclear, especially related to the question of when an administrator can intervene in cases of off-campus cyberbullying. Thus the material should not be interpreted as providing legal guidance. It is absolutely critical for school officials to consult with the district's legal counsel on these matters.

MONITORING AND SEARCH OF INTERNET USE RECORDS

When can a school administrator monitor or conduct an individualized search of student Internet use records through the district Internet system?

Legal Standards

Monitoring student use of the Internet in schools necessarily raises the issue of legal standards related to student privacy. Most of the case law related to privacy issues has emerged in the context of criminal cases and has involved an interpretation of Fourth Amendment restrictions on search and seizure. This case law has also been interpreted in the context of searches of student personal belongings in school, as well as school lockers and desks.

The initial analysis in such cases relates to the expectation of privacy. The U.S. Supreme Court, in *Katz v. United States,* first enunciated the constitutional standards related to expectations of privacy and established a two-part test.[1] The first part of the test states, "The person must have had an actual or subjective expectation of privacy."[2] The second part requires that this subjective expectation "be one that society is prepared to recognize as 'reasonable'."[3] If these two tests are satisfied, then there is said to be a "reasonable expectation of privacy."

Two additional doctrines that appear to be relevant have emerged in this area. The first is the "plain view doctrine." Under this doctrine, if a public official is in a legitimate place and sees something in plain view, there are no privacy expectations, thus no privacy protections.

The second doctrine is that of "consent." In *United States v. Simons,* a government agency network services administrator found patterns of use that indicated that an employee was accessing Internet pornographic material.[4] Further search was made of the employee's computer, and a significant number of pornographic files were found. The employee objected to the search on Fourth Amendment grounds. The court upheld the search, indicating that the government agency's policy on computer use indicated the potential for audits of Web usage to identify instances of inappropriate activity.

In the case of *New Jersey v. T.L.O.,* the Supreme Court enunciated the standards for school officials in conducting a search and seizure of a student's possessions in the school setting, where there is a legitimate expectation of privacy.[5] These standards are as follows:

- Was the search "justified in its inception?"[6] A search is justified when there are reasonable grounds for suspecting that it would turn up evidence that the student has violated or is violating either the law or rules of the school.[7]

- Was the search "reasonably related in scope to the circumstances which justified the interference in the first place?"[8] A search is reasonable when "the measures adopted are reasonably related to the objectives of the search and not excessively intrusive in light of the age and sex of the student and the nature of the infraction."[9]

Most school districts have search and seizure policies related to student lockers and desks that are in accord with the *T.L.O.* legal standards. The policies establish that students should expect only limited privacy and provide that a general inspection may occur on a regular basis. Specific inspections of individual lockers or desks may be conducted when there is reasonable suspicion to believe that illegal or dangerous items or items that are evidence of a violation of the law or school rules are contained in the spaces in question. These same standards can be applied in the context of analysis of Internet usage records and computer files.

Monitoring and Search of Internet Records

Following is an outline of the manner in which the standard school locker and desk search standards can be applied in the context of Internet usage.

Notice

Provide notice and establish presumption of consent. A recommended statement is "Users have a limited expectation of privacy in the contents of their personal files, communication files, and record of Web research activities on the district's Internet system. Routine maintenance and monitoring, using both technical monitoring systems and staff monitoring, may lead to discovery that a user has violated district policy or the law. An individual search will be conducted if there is reasonable suspicion that a user has violated district policy or the law."

Reinforce the warning on logon screens and in computer labs. A recommended statement is "The district's computer and Internet system is to be used for educational purposes. Users are reminded that the district monitors all Internet use. An individual search of usage and files may occur if there is reasonable suspicion of misuse." One important reason to provide effective notice is the deterrent effect of such notice.

Monitoring Techniques

Routine monitoring can be performed in a number of ways:

Staff monitoring of student use. This is the most obvious method. Most computer labs are set up in a way to facilitate such monitoring. All activities of students are considered to be in "plain view."

Routine review of activities and usage data. One easy way to do this is to require students to print their browser history file at the end of any computer lab session and have staff collect and review these logs.

Use of technical monitoring tools. These tools can operate in real time, allowing an administrator to directly but remotely view what is on the screen of any computer in the computer lab or building.

Use of intelligent content analysis monitoring technologies. These advanced monitoring tools analyze Internet use traffic based on key words, looking for communication patterns that may reveal instances of inappropriate activity. The system then provides reports to administrators of activity that raises a suspicion of inappropriate behavior. Essentially, these systems function in accord with the "locker search" standard.

Monitoring Practices and Expectations

All staff members who routinely involve their students in computer use should receive professional development in the concerns of cyberbullying and the activities to watch for when students are using computers. Regular substitute teachers should also receive this training. One problem with staff monitoring is that from a reasonable distance, a student engaged in cyberbullying will appear to be a student who is working on a writing project. It is very important for staff members to be sensitive to the clues students might exhibit if they are the recipients of hurtful material. Staff members should be exceptionally attentive to any student who appears to be emotionally upset or shocked when using a computer.

It is very important to recognize that no monitoring system will ever be entirely effective. Students also need to know the importance of reporting instances of misuse, especially cyberbullying and cyber-threats. They should not be taught to rely on any monitoring system.

Special inspection of the online activities of a student would occur when there are indicators that raise a reasonable suspicion misuse has been or is occurring. Any of the monitoring methods described here may give rise to this suspicion, as may reports of inappropriate activity occurring on or off campus.

School administrators must understand that it is technically possible for students to get around a school filtering system to post cyberbullying or cyberthreat material on a Web site or send harmful material through various Internet communications methodologies. For example, students can set up a simple-to-install system that on their home computer that will allow circumvention of the district filter.[10] A student engaged in cyberbullying will not raise the suspicions of a lab monitor because the student simply looks like he or she is writing.

As discussed later in this chapter, it is more difficult to formally discipline a student if the harmful activity is occurring off-campus. But if a student is reported to be cyberbullying another student, even if it appears to be an off-campus activity, such cyberbullying could be occurring through the district Internet system. In this event, the district could face some liability. This being the case, the demonstration that a student is cyberbullying another student, even if this activity appears to be off-campus, provides a sufficient reasonable suspicion that the student may be violating district policy, thus justifying an individualized search of that student's Internet use activity through the district Internet system. This search may reveal evidence of inappropriate or harmful use of the district Internet system.

Only authorized staff should approve and conduct an individualized search of student Internet use activities and computer files. Generally, the administrator who is responsible for the student should authorize the search, and the district's technology director should conduct the individualized search or designate someone to do so.

Monitoring and Search of Personal Digital Device Records

Unfortunately, the legal authority of school officials related to search and seizure of records of activity on personal digital devices is far from clear. Students may use cell phones while on the school campus in a manner that is in violation of the disciplinary code. Increasingly, students will be bringing personal digital devices, including laptop computers and PDAs, into the classroom for instructional purposes. These devices will operate outside of the school's filtering system. Therefore, while students are in class and using a personal digital device, presumably for note taking, they could also send a cruel message to a student in another class, download and send a pornographic image, or engage in other inappropriate activities.

A recent court case, *Klump v. Nazareth Area School District*, has addressed the ability of school officials to review records on a personal digital device, in this case a cell phone.[11] Unfortunately, in this case, the school officials quite clearly engaged in unwarranted search activity. The school district had a typical policy indicating that cell phones are not to be visible during the school day. The student's phone fell out of his pocket and was confiscated by a teacher. School officials then searched the cell phone records, called numbers, and engaged in text messaging with the student's brother. None of these activities appeared to be at all justified by the precipitating incident—a cell phone's falling from a pocket.

In the context of a motion to dismiss, which occurs prior to any evidence gathering, the court upheld the legitimacy of the claim of action that the school officials had engaged in an inappropriate search, based on the search and seizure legal standards, given that there was a lack of reasonable suspicion. If this were the only ruling of the court, this would not present concerns—because this ruling would imply that in cases where the standard of reasonable suspicion has been met, school officials would have authority to conduct a search.

But another claim made by the student and his parents alleged that by reviewing the electronic records retained on the cell phone, the school officials had violated the state's wiretapping law. The court also allowed this claim to proceed. We are therefore left with the possible situation that it would be illegal under wiretapping laws for a school official to review the records of any personal digital device—even if used on campus in a manner that raised a reasonable suspicion that the student had violated the disciplinary code.

As discussed in chapter 11, it is likely that the most effective way to address the lack of legal clarity and the potential finding that reviewing records on personal digital devices is illegal will be through contract. Parents of students who desire to use such devices on campus would be required to sign an agreement allowing school officials to review the records retained on the device; otherwise, use of such devices on campus would be forbidden.

FREE-SPEECH STANDARDS

When can a school administrator intervene with formal discipline to prevent cyberbullying?

Many school administrators regard it as essential to be able to respond to instances of cyberbullying with formal discipline. This assumption is incorrect. As outlined in chapter 9, a school official has many ways to address cyberbullying that do not require the ability to impose a formal disciplinary response.

Student Free-Speech Cases

U.S. Federal Courts have recognized that students have rights to free speech and free expression that must be balanced against the schools' interest in maintaining an appropriate learning environment and protecting the rights of other students. A number of Supreme Court cases have addressed students' First Amendment speech rights. Three of these cases provide the greatest guidance for educators in addressing issues of student speech on the Internet: *Tinker v. Des Moines Independent Community School District,*[12] *Bethel School District v. Fraser,*[13] and *Hazelwood School District v. Kuhlmeier.*[14]

In *Tinker,* school officials had disciplined students for wearing black armbands to protest the war in Vietnam. The court noted:

> There is here no evidence whatever of the petitioners' interference, actual or nascent, with the school's work or of *collision with the rights of other students to be secure and left alone.*[15] [Emphasis added.]

The standard established in *Tinker* was as follows:

> In order for the State in the person of school officials to justify prohibition of a particular expression of opinion, it must be able to show that its action was caused by something more than a desire to avoid the discomfort and unpleasantness that always accompany an unpopular viewpoint. Certainly where there is no finding and no showing that engaging in the forbidden conduct would "materially and substantially interfere with the requirements of appropriate discipline in the operation of the school," the prohibition can not be sustained.[16]

In *Fraser,* the Supreme Court found in favor of school officials who disciplined a student whose speech before a school assembly included sexual references. The Court distinguished between the purely political speech in *Tinker* and the student's vulgarity and held that school officials had the authority "to prohibit the use of vulgar and offensive terms in public discourse."[17] Justice Brennan's statement in his concurrence in *Fraser* is particularly relevant to the present discussion. Brennan noted that "if respondent had given the same speech outside of the school environment, he could not have been penalized simply because government officials considered his language to be inappropriate."[18]

The issue involved in *Hazelwood* was a principal's decision to remove several articles from publication in the school newspaper. The Court found that the school newspaper was not a public forum because the school did not intend to open the paper to indiscriminate use by the students. Therefore, the court indicated that it was appropriate for school officials to impose educationally related restrictions on student speech.[19]

Subsequent lower court cases that addressed student underground publications, which are a form of off-campus speech, have applied the *Tinker* standard to such publications. In *Thomas v. Board of Education,* students created a newspaper that contained sexually related articles and parodied several school officials.[20] The newspaper was sold off-campus. The students were punished. The court ruled that such punishment was inappropriate. The court's ruling was based on the "supposition that the arm of authority does not reach beyond the schoolhouse gate."[21] The court indicated that it was not appropriate for school officials to attempt to restrict free speech in the general community, "where freedom accorded expression is at its zenith."[22] But the court did indicate that school officials were entitled to discipline students if the off-campus speech "incites substantial disruption within the school from some remote locale."[23] In *Boucher v. School Board of the School District of Greenfield,* the court held that the imposition of discipline against a student who published instructions on how to hack into the school's computer system was justified because it was reasonable for school officials to believe the article would cause a substantial disruption of school activities.[24] However, the court noted that "school officials' authority over off-campus expression is much more limited than it is over expression on school grounds."

Threats are a distinct form of speech and are not protected by the Constitution.[25] The standard necessary to determine whether or not there is a "true threat" is proof, in light of the circumstances in which the statement was made, that (a) the person intended that the statement be taken as a threat, even if the person had no intention of actually carrying out the threat, and (b) the statement was in fact threatening.[26]

To summarize the relevant standards, under *Hazelwood,* schools may impose restrictions on speech that appears to be school sponsored—that an observer would view as coming from the school—based on any legitimate educational concern. Under *Fraser,* schools can limit lewd, vulgar, or profane language, but not if such speech takes place off campus. A "true threat" is not protected speech. All other speech is subject to the *Tinker* rule: It may be regulated if there is a well-founded reason to believe it would materially and substantially disrupt the school. This includes speech that disrupts the rights of other students to be secure and left alone.

Application to Off-Campus Online Speech

These legal standards have been applied in cases involving off-campus harmful online speech posted by students in a number of cases. Unfortunately, all but one of these cases involved student off-campus speech that targeted staff. In many of the cases, the material was quite outrageous and harmful. The one case involving speech directed at students did not involve truly harmful speech. This distinction is important because of the specific language in *Tinker* related to disruption of the rights of students.

It is useful to compare two of the cases involving material directed at staff: In *Killion v. Franklin Regional School District,* a high school student was suspended for writing e-mail that derided the school's athletic director.[27] The e-mail addressed the teacher's weight and sex life. Another student reformatted the e-mail and distributed it at the school. The court determined that the school district would need to establish that there was a "substantial disruption" before it could take action against someone for off-premises speech. The court noted that the school district could not identify any actual disruption at the school that resulted from the e-mail. There was "no evidence that teachers were incapable of teaching or controlling their classes. . . . [The e-mail] was on school grounds for several days before the administration became aware of its existence, and at least one week passed before [the school] took any action."[28]

In *J.S. v. Bethlehem Area School District,* an 8th grader's Web site included derogatory comments about his math teacher, including: "Why should she die?" and "Take a look at the diagram and the reasons I gave, then give me $20.00 to help pay for the hitman."[29] The student voluntarily removed the Web site a week after the principal learned of it. The school officials contacted the FBI but took no action against the student during the remainder of the school year. During the summer, officials decided to impose a 5-day, then a 10-day, suspension, which was transformed into expulsion proceedings. The student then brought a lawsuit, appealing the expulsion.

The court based its decision on the *Tinker* standard and determined that off-premises behavior could be punished if the school could establish that "the conduct materially and substantially interfere[d] with the educational process."[30] The majority thought this was so, given that the student accessed and showed the Web site to other students at school and that the students discussed the Web site while at school and at school-sponsored activities. The statements on the Web site were also considered by the majority to be a threat. They noted that the teacher who was the subject of the Web site was unable to finish the school year and took a medical leave the following year. (The teacher also filed a lawsuit against the student and his parents based on intentional tort claims, as discussed in chapter 6, and prevailed.)

The application of the standards expressed in these cases to instances of off-campus cyberbullying directed at other students is unknown. Note that the *Tinker* language specifically referred to interference with the school's work or the rights of students to be secure. There was no mention of interference with teachers' rights. It is likely that courts would be much more concerned about off-campus activities that are substantially interfering with a student's security or right to education than they have been about the concerns of the teachers who have been targeted by these sites. Clearly, the courts would pay significant attention to the demonstrated relationship between bullying and school violence, as well as to the well-documented negative impact of bullying on the emotional well-being and school performance of young people. There would likely be a greater perceived interest in protecting more vulnerable students than in protecting teachers, a situation that could result in support for formal school discipline.

Some legal commentaries published subsequent to these cases have argued that the application of the *Tinker* standard to these cases is wrong. These writers argue that if the speech is indeed totally off-campus, despite the fact that the speech is targeting someone who is also on campus, schools do not have any authority to act—even if the standard of substantial disruption is met. Some support for this position is found in the *Boucher* decision, where the court noted a distinction between school officials' authority over off-campus expression as compared to expression on school grounds.

Constitutionality of Anti-Bullying and Anti-Harassment Policies

Approaching the issue of student speech from a different perspective, it is necessary to consider the implications of free-speech standards in the context of school anti-bullying and anti-harassment policies. Under both Title VI of the Civil Rights Act of 1964 and Title IX of the Education Amendments of 1972, schools can face liability if they allow a "hostile environment": an environment that is so severe, pervasive, and objectively offensive that it undermines and detracts from the targets' educational experience, thus effectively denying equal access.[31] As established under *Tinker*, schools are justified in restricting speech that interferes with the rights of other students to receive an education.

In a recent decision, *Saxe v. State College Area School District,* the court struck down an overly broad school anti-harassment policy.[32] The court did affirm the principle that "preventing discrimination . . . is not only a legitimate, but a compelling government interest."[33] The court noted the relationship between bullying and school violence in this regard. Unfortunately, the court also stated, "We need not map the precise boundary between permissible anti-discrimination legislation and impermissible restrictions on First Amendment rights."[34] More clarity would have been very helpful.

The court determined that the *Tinker* standard applied to student speech that was not vulgar *(Fraser)* or school sponsored *(Hazelwood)* and that it therefore applied to a consideration of the anti-harassment policy. Essentially, the court ruled that an anti-harassment policy that was so broad as to apply to a student's statement of personal values and could affect speech that was merely offensive to some listeners was unconstitutional. However, the court also indicated, citing *Tinker*, that the "primary function of a public school is to educate its students; conduct that substantially interferes with the mission is, almost by definition, disruptive to the school environment."[35] Therefore, policies that restrict speech that substantially interferes with a school's mission to educate its students should pass constitutional review.

For the purposes of the present application of school policies to cyberbullying, it is assumed that legal counsel for school districts have reviewed the districts' anti-harassment and bullying policies to ensure they are in accord with the (unfortunately unclear) standards enunciated in *Saxe*. The continued ratification of the application of the *Tinker* standard to student speech that interferes with the rights of other students to receive an education in relation to anti-bullying and anti-harassment policies is helpful.

Probable Application of Legal Standards

Because of the lack of extensive case law in this area, the application of the standards described here in cases involving online speech is not certain. School officials should consult with their school legal counsel on these issues. The following are some examples of possible scenarios, with predicted legal interpretations.

True Threat

> *From a home computer, a student sends a message to other students: "A rampage is gonna happen . . . and deaths will occur."*

Speech that meets the standards of a "true threat" would not be considered constitutionally protected speech. Speech that meets this standard should trigger implementation of the district's threat assessment and school crisis plan and result in formal discipline.

School-Sponsored Online Speech

> *A tech-savvy language arts teacher has established a blog for students to use for activities related to persuasive writing.*

The *Hazelwood* standard governs student postings on school-sponsored Web sites, blogs, forums, or other means that in any manner associate the student with the school, such as an e-mail account with the school domain. The standard would be that school officials could impose educationally based restrictions on all student postings and communications. However, if the school does not maintain a clear position of control and sponsorship over these activities, the standard could revert to the *Tinker* standard.

It is essential that teachers understand that if they create an online vehicle for student postings and communications, such a vehicle must be created under conditions where the teacher is expressing the right to control everything the students post, based on educational reasons. It must also be clear that student disciplinary policies and the Internet use policy also apply to any material posted or sent by students.

Off-Campus Speech Facilitated by District Internet System

A tech-savvy student logs onto the district Internet system and goes through this system to access a third-party online community, upon which the student has established a personal Web page. The student posts material to this Web page and then goes to his Web-based e-mail account or uses his cell phone text messaging capabilities to send a message to another student suggesting that she look at the new material he has posted.

It is probable that a court would not consider the *Hazelwood* standard to be applicable because the speech in this case is not school sponsored—that is, it would not appear to others that the speech is school sponsored. It is probable that student use of the school district Internet system to post material on other Web sites or to send messages that are not easily identifiable as being school sponsored or originating from a school district Internet system would be governed under the *Tinker* standard, as would use of a cell phone or other personal digital device on campus. The *Tinker* standard would also probably apply to student off-campus harmful speech that has been brought onto campus through the district Internet system, including accessing the material, displaying the material to others through a school computer, or sending an e-mail to another student that suggests the student look at what has been posted online. The district's anti-bullying and anti-harassment policies would apply to these postings because these policies address speech that is considered to be a material and substantial disruption of rights of other students to be secure.

The courts would also be likely to consider the substance of the district Internet use policy. This policy should clearly express the fact that all student postings and communications made through the district Internet system will be governed by the student disciplinary code and the Internet use policy and that these two policies are in accord. In addition to the passage establishing school policy recommended earlier, it is further recommended that the logon screen on all district computers include a statement such as this: "All computer users are reminded that XYZ District's Student Disciplinary Code and Internet Use Policy govern all communications and material posted or sent through the district Internet system. This includes district policies against bullying or harassment."

As discussed before, when responding to any report of harmful online material directed against a student or staff member, it is highly recommended that an individualized search be conducted of the district system, aimed at identifying the Internet use activities of any students who are suspected of being involved. The presence of off-campus harmful online material, combined with the possibility that the district Internet system could have been used to post or send such speech, should raise a reasonable suspicion of misuse of the district Internet system that will justify such a search.

Totally Off-Campus Online Speech

It appears that three interrelated factors must be considered relevant when addressing incidents of off-campus online harmful speech where there has been no use of the district Internet system or personal digital device by a student while on campus.

Whether or not the creator of the speech has engaged in any on-campus activities related to the off-campus speech sufficient to establish a "school nexus" or connection. That is, the off-campus speech supports the presumption that the speech is tied to the school. Activities that might be sufficient to establish a school nexus could include on-campus bullying activities (even extremely subtle bullying activities that might otherwise be ignored) involving the same students or actions such as downloading harmful material and providing it to other students in the school building. It is very important to advise the targeted student to report any on-campus interactions with the cyberbully and to advise staff to carefully monitor any on-campus interactions.

Whether or not the speech has resulted in a substantial and material disruption or could reasonably be expected to result in a material and substantial disruption. Actual harmful impact on the target can be documented by statements by the target, reports of a counselor or the target's physician, attendance records, school performance, and involvement in school-based activities. Determining the threat of disruption will likely require an assessment of the overall situation and the degree of harmfulness of the online speech.

Whether the target of the speech is a student or a staff member. A strong argument can be made that school officials should be able to intervene in cases where off-campus online harmful speech is damaging a student's emotional well-being and interfering with that student's education and emotional well-being when at school.

It is possible that courts would perceive an inverse relationship between activities that would establish a school nexus and the degree of emotional harm inflicted upon or reasonably expected to be inflicted upon the targeted student. In other words, if the off-campus speech posted or sent by a student is considered to be highly offensive and the significant emotional harm suffered by the targeted student is evident and well documented, or if it is reasonable to expect that due to the highly offensive nature of the online material the targeted student will suffer significant emotional harm, it is likely that the courts would be inclined to support district intervention, absent any direct school nexus. This would be well in accord with the court's decision in *Boucher*.

It is presumed that if the target of the harmful online material is a teacher, the offensiveness of the material and degree of emotional harm suffered or expected would need to be greater than that which would justify a response on behalf of a student. Courts are likely to presume that school staff members should have thicker skins than students. Further, the specific language of the *Tinker* standard references interference with the school's work or collision with the rights of other students and does not mention any concerns about a harmful impact on teachers.

No School Nexus and No Material and Substantial Disruption

Even if school officials cannot establish sufficient school nexus and material and substantial disruption, they still have ways to intervene informally to address incidents of cyberbullying. The school counselor or psychologist or the school resource officer can provide education and support to targets and their parents in seeking resolution of the situation. The school could also seek to informally engage the parents of cyberbullies in an effort to get the aggression to stop, including warnings about the potential for financial liability. Additional intervention action options are addressed in chapter 9.

If the target of the harmful material is a teacher and it is determined that the material is unlikely to meet the standard of a material and substantial disruption, the harmful online material may still meet the standards necessary to pursue civil litigation. Other intervention action options discussed in chapter 9 could also be available to the staff member.

When should *a school administrator seek to prevent and intervene in cases of cyberbullying?*

Schools have a responsibility to protect the safety of students under their care and ensure that there is no substantial interference with their right to receive an education. This responsibility includes student safety and well-being when students are using the district's Internet system or if the district allows cell phones or other personal digital devices to be used by students on campus.

This potential liability rests on two bases: negligence and statutory.

Negligence

Negligence claims will be grounded in state laws related to the imposition of liability on public officials. Some states have enacted immunity laws that provide some protection for school officials against claims based on negligence. The manner in which negligence claims will be decided will therefore vary from state to state. There may be even wider variation among different countries.

Negligence can be described in a number of ways:

- Failing to do something that a reasonable person would do.

- Doing something that a reasonable person would not do.

- Failing to exercise ordinary care under circumstances that create an unreasonable risk of injury to another.

The injured party in a negligence suit must establish four elements:

- A legal duty.

- A breach of that legal duty—failure to exercise reasonable care in the context of a foreseeable risk.

- Proximate cause—the breach of the duty was a substantial factor in bringing about an injury, damage, loss, or harm.

- Actual injuries, loss, or damage.

Schools have a duty to anticipate foreseeable dangers and to take necessary precautions against those dangers to protect students in their care. A breach of duty occurs when a school official fails to exercise a reasonable standard of care in the context of a foreseeable risk. The issue of proximate cause asks whether the student's injury is something that could have been foreseen and prevented by a school official. Damages sustained as the result of bullying may include emotional harm and the costs of addressing that harm (for example, the costs of counseling) and losses to a student due to the student's avoidance of school (for example, lowered school performance, which will interfere with future educational opportunities). There are emerging reports of students' committing suicide as a consequence of cyberbullying—obviously a profound loss.

Is there a legal duty for school administrators to protect the safety and security of students when they are in school and when they are using the Internet through the district system?
Yes, clearly. There is both a general duty and a statutory expression of this duty for all districts that are receiving technology funds through E-Rate or Technology Literacy grants through the U.S. Department of Education. The Children's Internet Protection Act (CIPA) requirements include the following:

> (I) IN GENERAL. In carrying out its responsibilities under subsection (h), each school . . . shall—

> (A) adopt and implement an Internet safety policy that addresses. . . .

> (ii) the safety and security of minors when using electronic mail, chat rooms, and other forms of direct electronic commerce.[36]

Other duties applicable to this situation include the duty to provide effective supervision of students and the duty to provide safe schools. Frequently, these duties are included in state statutes governing the operation of schools.

School officials clearly have a duty to ensure the safety and security of minors when they are using the Internet at school. If schools have established laptop programs that allow students to take district computers home, or if districts otherwise provide students with the ability to access the district's Internet service from outside school, this duty would carry over to student use of the district's Internet system from home. If schools are allowing students to bring and use cell phones or other personal digital devices while at school, the duty of care to properly manage the use of these devices should also exist. But as these are personal devices and the ability of schools to monitor their use is significantly decreased, the standards to determine liability would likely be different.

Is it foreseeable that students could be using these technologies in ways that could harm other students? Given the emerging information about cyberbullying activities and the harm done by such activities, as well as the potential that students could be posting cyberthreats online, it is clearly foreseeable that they could use the district Internet system and personal digital devices in school for this purpose.

What is a "reasonable standard of care"? This is a difficult question to answer, as there have been no cases specifically related to a standard of care associated with student use of the district's Internet system or cell phones and other personal digital devices at school. In general, the standard is expressed as "what a reasonably prudent person would do in similar circumstances."

The following are actions that, in this author's professional opinion, should be considered necessary to meet this duty of care:

- Needs assessment to determine the extent of concern and aspects related to misuse of Internet in school, plus a regular assessment of the manner in which students are using the district Internet system.

- Policy provisions that prohibit the use of the district Internet system and cell phones or other personal digital devices on campus to bully or harass other students. These policies should link Internet and digital device use to the district's anti-bullying and anti-harassment policies.

- Policies and practices that severely constrict the ability of students to use the district Internet system for noneducational ("Internet recess") purposes.

- Effective education and notice to students and staff about these policies.

- Effective supervision and monitoring, which may need to include intelligent technical monitoring of Internet use.

- A vehicle for students to report cyberbullying and cyberthreats confidentially or anonymously.

- An established procedure to respond to such reports.

Statutory Liability

Title IX of the Education Amendments of 1972 prohibits the sexual harassment of students. To prevail in a complaint under Title IX, sexual harassment must be sufficiently severe, persistent, or pervasive that it adversely affects a student's education or creates a hostile or abusive educational environment. Under Title VI of the Civil Rights Act of 1964, no individual may be excluded from participation in, be denied the benefits of, or otherwise be subjected to discrimination on the grounds of race, color, or national origin under any program or activity that receives federal funds.

A violation of Title IX or Title VI may be found if a school has effectively caused, encouraged, accepted, tolerated, or failed to correct a sexually or racially hostile environment of which it has received actual or constructive notice. Although the school may not be directly responsible for all harassing conduct, the school does have a responsibility to provide a nondiscriminatory educational environment.

A school can receive notice in many different ways. Actual notice would occur if a student has filed notice or informed a school employee of harassing conduct, or if a school employee has witnessed the harassment. In cases where the school has not had actual notice, the school may have had constructive notice. A school is charged with constructive notice of a hostile environment if, upon reasonably diligent inquiry in the exercise of reasonable care, it should have known of the discrimination. In other words, if the school could have found out about the harassment had it made a proper inquiry, and if the school should have made such an inquiry, the school will be assumed to have had constructive notice of the hostile environment.

The necessary question that must be posed for schools with respect to notice is this: Should the school, upon reasonable and diligent inquiry in the exercise of reasonable care, know about incidents of students' harassing other students and thus creating a sexually or racially hostile environment via the district's Internet system? In other words, given the knowledge that students are using the Internet to engage in cyberbullying, should school officials make a reasonably diligent inquiry into whether or not students are using the district Internet system to engage in such activities? Clearly, the answer to this question is yes.

States may also have enacted laws that address essentially the same issues as Title IX and Title VI—harassing conduct of a sexual nature or on the basis of race, color, or national origin. States may also have enacted laws that broaden the protected classes or antibullying laws that apply to bullying, harassment, or intimidation of any students for any reason.

A consideration of the reasonable preventive actions presented here under the discussion of negligence is also relevant to the discussion of whether or not the school has accepted, tolerated, or failed to correct a sexually or racially hostile environment.

CHAPTER 8

Cyberbully and Cyberthreat Situation Review

This chapter discusses a systematic method of reviewing situations related to reports of online activity that could be considered cyberbullying, as well as reports of cyberthreats. While the focus of this book is on students, the situation review will also address harmful online material directed at school staff. A chart that displays the steps of this situation review is included as Appendix A.

THREAT ASSESSMENT AND SUICIDE INTERVENTION PROTOCOLS

The U.S. federal government publishes two helpful resources that address threat assessment in schools: *The School Shooter: A Threat Assessment Perspective*[1] and *Threat Assessment in Schools: A Guide to Managing Threatening Situations and to Creating Safe School Climates.*[2] Both publications (which are available online) were created after a series of school shootings in the United States. While these publications focus on school violence, much of their analysis is also pertinent to suicide. These documents can provide valuable guidance for situation review teams. At least some of the members of this team should already be familiar with these reports, and the district should have developed a process to follow to respond to any reported threats.

Many excellent suicide prevention resources can be found through the Suicide Prevention Resource Center.[3] In addition, a number of states and districts are also actively developing suicide prevention protocols.[4]

Given the degree to which today's youth are using online communications, it is critically important for school personnel to understand the following points:

- When students are potentially violent or suicidal, the probability is high that they are posting material or sending communications online that provide important insight into their mental status and plans.

- If a student has shared any plans or thoughts about inflicting violence on others or committing suicide or other self-harm, the probability is high that other students are discussing this information through online communications.

Important Notice

It is absolutely imperative for school districts to incorporate an assessment of the online communications of students into all threat assessment and suicide intervention protocols.

Working with Law Enforcement

A variety of situations could justify contact, at one point or another, with law enforcement. These situations include threats of violence, cyberbullying that may be in violation of a criminal law, and reports that a student has become involved with an online sexual predator. The degree to which local law enforcement in different regions may be prepared to handle these kinds of situations may vary significantly. The school or district's safe schools committee would do well to meet with representatives of local law enforcement to discuss how, when, and to whom in local law enforcement school staff should report concerns about youth online activity. School officials should remain actively involved during any investigation.

Sexual Predation

The concerns of youth involvement with online sexual predators are not the focus of this book. However, the encouragement to students and parents to report worrisome online material to the school is likely to result in increased reports of youth who are involved in risky sexual activities, including youth who have gotten involved with online predators, so it seems useful to provide a few words of guidance on responding to such reports. It will probably be helpful to establish a specific procedure—developed in partnership with local law enforcement—for handling such reports. Staff probably have a clear understanding of when and how to report suspected child abuse, but they may not know how to respond to these kinds of situations.

All school administrators, counselors, and psychologists should know that if they receive any evidence of student involvement with an online predator, they should immediately contact law enforcement. If the predator lives within the state, they should contact local law enforcement. If the predator is in another state, or if the case involves the transmission of child pornography, they should contact the Federal Bureau of Investigation. If there are any questions about such reporting, the professionals at the National Center for Missing and Exploited Children (www.ncmec.org) can provide helpful guidance. All other staff should know to report any concerns or even suspicions to an administrator, counselor, or psychologist.

Law enforcement officials may require access to the child's computer and may need some time to be able to track a predator down and arrest him (it is almost always a "him"). A child who is involved with a sexual predator and who has not independently reported such involvement should not be made aware that there are suspicions about such activity. This child may be under the psychological control of the predator and could warn or even run off with the predator. Unless school officials are advised differently by local law enforcement, it is recommended that the school contact law enforcement first—and follow law enforcement's guidance in contacting the parent. It is possible, and thoroughly understandable, in such situations that the parent could overreact and that this reaction could complicate the ultimate objective of apprehending a dangerous individual. Make sure you have mental health support immediately available to intervene with both the child and the parents.

Avoiding Failure to Act and Overreaction

When conducting a situation review, especially involving threats of violence or suicide, it is critically important to avoid both failing to act and overreacting. Consider two case studies:

Failure to Act

Eric Harris, one of the Columbine shooters, had created a Web site that contained bomb-making instructions and alarming language. This language was set forth in chapter 1. The mother of a child who was threatened on this Web site contacted the legal authorities. An affidavit was filed seeking a search warrant, but reportedly no search ever occurred.

The online material clearly indicated a child who was on the verge of committing violence. Prompt action should have been taken.

Overreaction

An honor student created a Web site titled the "Unofficial Kentlake High Home Page." This Web site contained a statement disclaiming school sponsorship and noting that it was for entertainment purposes only. The site had two mock obituaries of the student's friends. The news media picked up on the story and reported that the student's site contained a "hit list." The student immediately removed the page in response to the story. The school responded with fast-tracking expulsion and then backtracked to a five-day suspension. The student filed a lawsuit. The court found that the school officials had failed to show that the Web site was "intended to threaten anyone . . . or manifested any violent tendencies whatsoever." The school district later settled with the student.[5]

This was a clear case of overreaction. This student posed no risk to anyone. The district paid a price for its overreaction.

Handling Threat Situations That Prove False

It is very important to address how to handle situations where a reported online threat turns out to be false. Unfortunately, it is much more likely that reports of threats that turn out to be false are going to occur in connection with online communications. If the threat appears to be legitimate, the school must respond appropriately. But if the threat turns out to be a joke or unsubstantiated rumor, the fact that the school did respond could have worrisome ramifications for future reports.

In a case reported in *The Washington Post*, a male freshman student made an anonymous online threat as a joke to another student, who reported the threat to her parents, who in turn reported the incident to the school and police. The school went into lockdown, and the boy was arrested on a felony count of making a threat. Of significant concern is the reported reaction of the students to the arrest. Many were protesting and signing petitions against the arrest. The following comment by one student was reported:

> Laura said that after the incident, her parents had a conversation with her. "They, like, talked to me and said, 'If you ever get a strange message, tell us,'" she said. But in light of what happened at Yorktown, she added, *"I think I would try to figure it out first on my own."* [Emphasis added.] [6]

Obviously, the assessment of potential threats is not something young people should try to figure out first on their own. But if young people come to believe that adults are not going to handle troublesome online situations appropriately, they will not report such situations. They will attempt to deal with them on their own. This reticence could have very unfortunate consequences in cases where the online material does present a legitimate threat. An overly aggressive school and law enforcement response to online threats that ultimately turn out to be false can lead to distrust and decisions by youth not to report potential threats in the future.

Two messages must be communicated effectively, and probably repeatedly, to students, parents, and the community. The first is the critical importance of making a report about an online threat, even if the threat might be false. The individuals who report possible threats, whether identified or not, should be widely praised. Reference can be made to the recent school shooting incident in Red Lake, Minnesota, where, reportedly, more than 39 people knew of the potential shooting, but no one reported the concern.[7] Nine people were killed. The disruption of a school lockdown to prevent possible violence is nothing compared to the disruption of an actual incident.

The second message that needs to be communicated is the importance of not posting material that someone else could interpret as a threat. Youth must understand that it is simply not possible in some cases for adults to assess the legitimacy of threatening material posted online. Further, making a threat, even if the threat is not real, can lead to criminal prosecution.

Communicating effectively with news media in such situations will be critically important. The local media will provide the greatest assistance in conveying the correct messages to youth, parents, and the community. It is essential that the two points be framed effectively and be repeated for emphasis.

Key Factors

Supreme caution must be employed when evaluating online communications or activities because there is the ever-present possibility that online postings may not be what they seem. This section discusses the factors that need to be kept in mind when evaluating troubling online material.

- Not all cyberbullying will reach the level of a threatening situation, but some could. The threat could come from the cyberbully—but in other situations, the target may present more of a risk of engaging in violent behavior. The risk could be to others or self.

- If something's "goin' down"—that is, if negative interactions between students or groups of students are reaching a point of potential serious conflict—it is highly probable that these issues are being discussed online by the students who are involved or by other students. School officials and other concerned adults absolutely need to know where their students are gathering online to communicate. (One obvious problem that will emerge as adults start to pay more attention to online communications and activities of youth is that they may take more of these communications and activities underground—into password-protected environments.)

- School officials may be dealing with a situation in which one student is impersonating another for the purpose of getting that student into trouble. If a student wishes to inflict punishment on another student, breaking into that student's account and posting what appears to be a legitimate threat could be a very effective strategy. A few select keystrokes, combined with a scheme to make sure a report of the communication is made, could well lead to the suspension, expulsion, even arrest of the target of the impersonation. Alternatively, a student who is charged with making threats may falsely claim that another student has engaged in impersonation.

- The fact that a statement is recorded in electronic form may make it appear more serious than it really is. Young people often use language online that is far coarser than they would otherwise use. Just about everyone who communicates electronically has engaged in some degree of *flaming*—sending messages that reflect a high degree of passionate anger. Arguments can flare up and reach a level of anger that could raise legitimate concerns to someone who has not been a party to the entire incident—but the degree of anger expressed electronically could bear little resemblance to the actual degree of threat. This is the disinhibition factor at work.

- It is known that teens use the Internet to experiment with different personalities. A mild-mannered student who has never caused any concern to anyone, and who is highly unlikely ever to do so, may be experimenting—playacting—with a totally different online personality that presents threatening characteristics.

- Technology facilitates open disclosure. Online communications can be very self-revealing, especially in blogs, where the whole purpose of the activity is to be self-revealing. Students may be likely to reveal far more deeply personal feelings and perceptions online than they would ever reveal when talking with a school counselor or psychologist. Therefore, the material posted by students might provide entirely realistic insight into their emotional state.

- The original online material provided in a report made to a school administrator may be the last chapter and not the whole story. This material alone may fail to provide insight into events that led up to the creation of the material or the ongoing relationship between the parties involved. It is exceptionally important to search for additional material.

- The most worrisome threat may not come from the student who has posted harmful online material. The vast majority of school shooters were the victims of bullying and tormenting by others. The target of a cyberbully may be emotionally distressed by the harm and may be the one at greater risk of engaging in violence against self or others.

- It is essential to distinguish between "put-down" speech and "get-back-at" speech and to gain an understanding of the underlying relationship between the parties involved. Is the reported material a continuation of what is apparently an ongoing face-to-face bullying situation or simply in retaliation for such face-to-face bullying? The same considerations need to be made in the context of harmful speech directed at teachers. Sometimes teachers bully students, which can lead to online retaliation.

- Troubling and threatening online material may be posted in retaliation for face-to-face bullying or other cruel treatment by other students or by school staff. The student who has posted such material clearly is at risk or may present a risk. But the need to ensure the safety of all concerned should not result in further victimization of an already victimized student.

SITUATION REVIEW TEAM

It is recommended that the existing threat assessment and suicide intervention team be charged with the responsibility to review reports of cyberbullying or cyberthreats. It appears that in some districts these issues are handled by two different groups—an arrangement that is somewhat illogical, given the degree to which suicide and school violence are intertwined. Threat assessment brings a law enforcement perspective to the table, and suicide intervention brings a mental health perspective. Both perspectives should be actively involved in all situations requiring analysis.

The primary recommended change in team membership from the traditional threat assessment and suicide intervention team is the addition of the technology coordinator and the library media specialist. These are the individuals in the district who have the most insight into students' online activities, including knowing the online communities in which students are participating. The library media specialist is likely to be the staff member most proficient in conducting online searches.

In some cases of more basic cyberbullying, it will not be necessary for the entire team to be involved. Most likely, the disciplinary administrator or the school counselor or psychologist will bear the responsibility of evaluating and responding to the reported incident. For more complicated or potentially significant incidents, a number of investigative tasks may need to be designated to specific staff members.

Following are the recommended members of a situation review team and their areas of responsibility related to an evaluation of troubling online material:

- *Administrator.* The school administrator will be responsible for oversight of the review of the report, approving any investigations of student communications and activities through the district's Internet system, and determining the appropriateness of any school disciplinary response.

- *School counselor or psychologist.* The school counselor or psychologist may well have some understanding of the background of the students involved, which will greatly facilitate an appropriate analysis of the situation. The school counselor or psychologist is also likely to be the most appropriate staff member to respond to reported incidents through communications with parents and students, especially those incidents that do not require or do not meet the standards for any school-imposed disciplinary action.

- *Technology coordinator.* For many incidents, additional information on the communications and activities of the participants will be exceptionally helpful. The school or district technology coordinator will have the ability to conduct a search of the student's use files—with authorization from the school or district administrator. The manner in which the district may authorize such a search of computer files and Internet activities may vary.

- *Library media specialist.* It is probable that the school library media specialist has the most up-to-date insight into the online communities in which students are currently active. Also, the school library media specialist probably has the most sophisticated skills in searching the Internet to find evidence of student communications or postings that may be relevant to the current situation. Alternatively, the school technology coordinator may be the individual charged with these responsibilities.

- *School resource officer.* A school resource officer located on campus might be immediately involved in any review process. If a school resource officer is not always present in the school, it is likely that this individual would be called in only on cases that raise significant, potentially criminal concerns. If the situation looks serious and anonymity is a concern, the school resource officer may be able to provide assistance in obtaining a search warrant to reveal the identity of the person posting the material.

- *Mental health community contact.* The school counselor or psychologist may play this role, but it also may be helpful to have sufficient connections with mental health professionals, should the need arise, to call upon their services rapidly. A direct connection with a local suicide prevention network is highly advisable.

- *Key resource person.* Because these are emerging concerns, it will take some time for individuals in each school to gain the expertise necessary to address them. It will be very helpful if states, regions, or large school districts ensure that one or more key resource people are available to assist the situation review teams in responding to a report—especially a highly worrisome report.

LEGITIMATE, IMMINENT THREAT OF VIOLENCE

As noted earlier and discussed in chapter 1, online material that initially appears to be a legitimate and imminent threat could be any of the following:

- A joke, parody, or game.

- A rumor that got started and has grown and spread.

- Material posted by a child who is trying out a fictitious threatening online character.

- The final messages in a flame war that has gotten out of hand but is unlikely to result in any real violence.

- Material posted by a child impersonating another child for the purpose of getting that child into trouble.

- Distressing material posted by a depressed or angry child that could foretell a violent or suicidal intention but that does not represent an imminent threat.

- A legitimate imminent threat.

The problem is that when school officials or law enforcement personnel are first apprised of an online threat, it may not be possible to tell which of these possibilities might be involved. It is essential that at every step of the way, with the addition of any new information, a reassessment be made of the legitimacy of the threat and the appropriate identification of the individuals involved.

It is also important that school officials who have a good understanding of youth Internet use remain actively involved. There is no assurance that all law enforcement officials fully understand this new area of concern. This lack of understanding could lead to inappropriate or incomplete actions. For example, if a law enforcement official does not understand the very real possibility that one student could be impersonating another to make what appears to be a legitimate threat, the innocent target of a cruel hoax could be unnecessarily traumatized.

A high priority must be placed on conducting an effective investigation of material posted publicly by students in the school, as well as of all records of Internet use on the district system by all students involved. It is probable that law enforcement personnel will take the lead in doing this, as they should have greater capabilities. As noted, the school technology coordinator and library media specialist may also play important roles.

A lower level threat, without any other indicators of immediate concern, may not justify immediate law enforcement involvement, but it still may require a risk analysis following the gathering of additional materials that bear on the potential for violence or self-harm.

If the online material appears to present a legitimate and imminent threat of violence and danger to others, the adults in charge should contact law enforcement and initiate a protective response in accord with the school's crisis plan.

Contacting the authorities is not enough in this type of case; it is critically important to immediately continue with the following evidence-gathering and preservation steps.

EVIDENCE GATHERING AND PRESERVATION

The following recommended process is designed to address more egregious, complicated situations. Many situations may not be as complex, thus justifying a more abbreviated approach.

Step 1. Preserve the Evidence

The first step to take in a review of any reported online incident is to preserve initial evidence, both electronically and on hard copy. If the online incident has occurred at home, instruct parents, students, or staff members on how to preserve all evidence and the importance of doing so. The school's technology coordinator may need to offer technical assistance to the parents to fully preserve all information pertinent to the incident.

Step 2. Seek to Identify the Source

The creator (or creators) of the material may be obvious or anonymous—or even impersonating someone else. In many cases, it may not be immediately possible to determine the identity of the source. Other steps in the review and response process may need to proceed at the same time that identification attempts are occurring.

The district's technical services personnel will probably have the greatest in-house skills for determining the identity of the creator. If harmful material is being sent to a student at home and there appears to be a school nexus of any kind, the school may want to offer technical assistance to parents to identify the creator. The parent's Internet Service Provider (ISP) may be able to provide assistance. There are also relatively inexpensive services available on the Internet that parents can use to help them identify anonymous senders of e-mail and instant messages.

An effective interview with the target of the cyberbullying may provide evidence of unhealthy relationships with other students at school that could reveal clues as to the creator's possible involvement. If the evidence provided is sufficient to establish a reasonable suspicion that one or more students may be involved and may have used the district Internet system, a search of their Internet use records may be justified.

A close evaluation of the harmful material and other associated material, including friendship links, will also be likely to provide helpful clues. While students engaged in cyberbullying may seek to establish anonymity, it is highly probable that they lack the sophistication to remain fully cloaked. "Loose lips sink ships," as the old saying goes. Youth who are engaged in bullying and cyberbullying are very likely to have "virtual loose lips."

If the reported situation appears to be criminal in nature, law enforcement officials have significantly greater abilities to learn the identity of individuals posting material online. Officials can have a subpoena served on the Internet company to obtain identifying information.

Step 3. Search for Additional Material

Following the administrative process established by the district for review of student computer records and files through the district Internet system, a search should be made of the files and records of all students for whom there is a reasonable suspicion of involvement. This search may yield some significant insight into the incident.

At the same time, the librarian or technology coordinator (or both) should conduct a further search of the Internet in relation to the reported incident. This search could include a more detailed investigation of the online environment where material emerged and other online community sites that are known to be popular among students. It is also advisable to use an Internet search engine to look for instances of the names and known usernames of the students possibly involved and the name of the school.

Given the degree to which students are using the Internet to communicate with each other and the high potential that these communications can provide helpful insight for school officials, it is strongly recommended that this search for material occur in the context of any threat assessment process, as well as in situations where there may simply be a hint of some trouble brewing. As noted, if something is building toward a violent incident or something more general at school, it is highly probable that students are talking about it online. The search should include records of Internet use on the district Internet system and in public environments.

School staff members should also be aware of the online communities in which students congregate to discuss school issues and should make sure they are in a position to review the postings in these sites to investigate any online commentary that may be occurring. School librarians and computer lab managers are most likely to become aware of which online communities have engaged the school's students. If a threat has emerged, knowing the names and URLs of these communities and how to gain access rapidly could prove invaluable.

RISK ASSESSMENT

At a prior stage of analysis, the question was presented of whether there was a legitimate, imminent threat of violence or suicide. Risk assessment addresses the potential for violence, suicide, or other self-harm. Does the evidence gathered raise concerns that any of the students involved may pose a risk of harm to others or themselves? It is critically important to recognize that the threat of violence, suicide, or self-harm may come from students who posted the material or from students who were targeted by the material.

Here are some of the possible violence or suicide scenarios:

- The creator of the material may have posted material that constitutes a direct threat.

- The creator of the material may have posted material that is distressing and suggests that violence against others, or suicide or some other self-harm, may be in the works.

- The creator of the material may be encouraging another student to commit an act of violence or suicide.

- The degree of emotional harm being inflicted upon the target by a cyberbully, combined with knowledge of the target's underlying personal situation, may raise concerns that the target could respond to the cyberbullying with an act of violence against the creator or may commit suicide or engage in other self-harm.

- A student could be found to have become affiliated with an online hate group—that is, a group with activities such as angry discussions, experimentation with bomb making, fascination and involvement with weapons, and the like.

- The establishment of what could be called a "troublesome youth group" of local students or more formal gang or gang-like activity is possible, involving use of the Internet to coordinate potentially violent activities.

If this preliminary review raises any concerns about the possibility of violence or suicide, the process should shift to a threat or suicide risk assessment and intervention, in accord with district process.

CYBERBULLYING ASSESSMENT

The following steps should be followed in cases of cyberbullying. These steps may occur in conjunction with the risk assessment and intervention, if justified by the risk assessment.

Step 1. Determining Whether the School Can Respond Directly

As discussed in chapter 7, this type of analysis requires considering whether the degree of harm to the target constitutes a material and substantial threat of disruption and whether or not there is a school nexus.

Material and Substantial Threat of Disruption

The legal standards for this threat are that the speech must materially and substantially interfere with the requirements of appropriate discipline in the operation of the school. This includes collision with the rights of other students to be secure and left alone.

This assessment should address actual impact on the student's emotional well-being, school performance, and involvement in school and extracurricular activities. It should also consider the online material and circumstances. The more outrageous and harmful the material, the greater the threat of harm to the student. The question to ask is "Would it be reasonable to suspect that a student being targeted with this material is being or will be emotionally harmed?"

School Nexus

Following are some guided questions to ask to determine whether there is a school nexus:

- Was the material posted or sent using the district's Internet system? If laptops have been provided to students, was a school laptop used to post or send the material, even if used from home? Did a student use a cell phone or other personal digital device while at school?

- Has the creator taken steps to bring the offending material on campus by accessing the material or showing it to others while using the district Internet system or by bringing downloaded copies of the material to school? Has any student at school accessed the offending material through the district Internet system, and can it be established through interviews with the students accessing the material that the creator encouraged such access while at school? (The technology coordinator can search the Internet use records of all students to identify any access by other students to the site upon which harmful material has been placed.)

- Did any of the posted material originate on campus? For example, were harmful digital images taken on campus that were later posted on the Internet or sent via cell phone?

- Have there been any incidents of in-school bullying that involve the same individuals, and, if so, what is the relationship to the off-campus material?

Step 2A. Evaluating Speech Directed at Students

When addressing student-on-student cyberbullying, assess the relationship between the students at school. Who is the bully and who is the target in the overall situation? Knowledge of the relationship between students is necessary to distinguish between put-down speech and get-back-at speech. The situation of a student who has placed harmful speech online in retaliation for on-campus bullying must be handled differently from the situation of an unprovoked student who is putting other students down.

Put-down cyberbullying is bullying that reflects the creator's opinion of superiority and the target's inferiority. Put-down cyberbullying material can be extremely harmful. The creator of the speech will probably appear to be in total control emotionally—calmly and cruelly denigrating the target. Generally, the put-down cyberbullying material will specifically note or provide clues to the reasons for the perceived inferiority of the target. These reasons are likely grounded in some form of bias against the target because he or she is "different" and perceived to be inferior.

It is probable that the put-down cyberbully is also bullying the target at school, possibly in very subtle ways that have not been noticed by the school staff. If the target is a wannabe, it is possible that he or she has not reported such bullying for fear of being cut out of any possibility of being accepted as a member of a desired social group. The target of put-down cyberbullying is the one who has most likely been emotionally harmed. This emotional harm could lead the target to commit an act of violence against the cyberbully or commit some form of self-harm.

Get-back-at cyberbullying material will likely carry a much higher level of emotional anguish. This type of cyberbullying material could fall into the category of distressing material. The get-back-at cyberbully has lost control and is lashing out at those believed to have been tormenting him or her in other ways.

If a student is posting get-back-at speech, it is very likely that this student has also been the target of on-campus or other cyberbullying by the person who is targeted in the material. In such cases, the target of the cyberbullying is the original bully. It is also quite possible that the target, the original bully, has not been emotionally harmed. The get-back-at cyberbullying material may merely provide evidence that the original bully has been successful in getting the original target of the bullying to lose control. This provides reinforcement for the original bullying and justification for further bullying. If particularly vicious, the original bully may report the cyberbullying or obtain the assistance of a friend to report it, with the goal of further victimizing the original target by arranging for punishment.

If the online material appears to be the work of a student who has been bullied by others in the school environment, it is crucial to remember that the student who has created the material could present the greatest risk of violence. Intervention is imperative—but that intervention must take into account that this student has been victimized and needs help dealing with the on-campus bullying.

Too often, students who are being cruelly tormented by other students at school and who finally reach the point where they respond in an angry way are treated as the cause of the problem—when in actuality they are the victims in the overall situation. If, in fact, the get-back-at cyberbully has been victimized on campus, and that situation has either not been reported or was reported but not handled effectively, then the online actions of this student should be viewed, in large part, as a consequence of the failure of the school's program to prevent bullying. The actions of the student in placing the online material are clearly inappropriate. The material must be removed, and harmful online actions need to stop. But what is most important is that the school ensure that the harm inflicted on this student is also stopped and that this student is assisted in finding more effective ways of addressing the bullying.

Step 2B. Evaluating Speech Directed at Staff or School

While the major focus of this book is on student-student communications, it is presumed that the same team will also review situations involving material directed at school staff. In most cases, these instances will not involve direct communications to a staff member; instead, they will involve indirect posting of material that damages the reputation of school staff. The harmful material could also be directed at the wider school community.

Use of Online Speech as a Teachable Moment for the School

The first level of consideration in the evaluation of such material is to use such speech as an opportunity to look within. Internet postings by students about the school and its staff provide an excellent opportunity for staff to see themselves and assess the quality of the school community through the unvarnished words of the students. Such speech also provides the opportunity to learn more about the emotional status of the students posting the speech.

- What does the speech say about the quality of the school environment and the degree to which all students in the school feel welcome and supported and to which their important needs are met?

- What does this speech say about how this particular student is feeling about school and the degree to which he or she feels welcome and supported and is having important needs met?

If the online material is simply nuisance speech, which may include speech that is foul and vulgar, the best response is probably simply to ignore it. If the speech is a legitimate protest, the best approach for a school is to learn from it and seek to engage students positively in addressing any concerns that have been raised.

School officials must understand that youth have the free-speech right to post rude and vulgar speech, even rude and vulgar speech directed at a school or school officials and speech that protests actions of school officials. It is only when such speech reaches the level of substantial and material disruption in the operations of the school that school officials have the right to intervene formally. However, it is quite possible to file a complaint with the company hosting the speech to have offensive language removed (see chapter 9).

Speech Directed at Specific Staff

If the speech is directed at specific staff members, it is necessary to look closely to determine whether the speech is put-down speech or get-back-at speech.

Staff members who are the targets of put-down speech may have personal qualities that some students may consider give the staff inferior status. For example, a teacher may be obese or perceived to be gay. Just as students with higher social status may bully those with lower social status based on qualities perceived to reflect inferiority, some students may engage in the same activities directed at teachers. As noted, put-down speech tends to be delivered in a calm and cruel manner. (Envision the material that the *Harry Potter* character Malfoy might post targeting Hagrid.)

If the site or materials are more in the nature of get-back-at speech, this realization should trigger an analysis of the emotional well-being of the student and the relationship of the student and the targeted staff member. A student who places angry get-back-at speech directed at school staff has been a victim of some emotional harm, somewhere, which has led the student to use the Internet to lash out. Perhaps the student may be the victim of parental neglect, bullying by other students, failed school response to learning disabilities, or some other form of emotional harm.

Despite the other potential causes, when a student posts emotional get-back-at speech targeting a teacher or other staff member, the possibility that the teacher has victimized the student must be seriously considered. Although this type of bullying is not well-researched, it is clear that some staff members do engage in cruel bullying and denigration of students. It should not be immediately assumed that the student is the one primarily at fault and must be punished. While the harmful online material needs to be removed, the more serious aspects of this situation require determining what is going on in this student's life that would lead to the posting of such material. A review of the teacher's instructional practices in general, and as related to this student specifically, should be a priority.

Step 3. Preliminary Assessment of Potential Criminal Law Violations or Civil Remedies

The online material should be evaluated based on the potential that such material meets the legal standards for criminal prosecution or civil litigation. If the speech has targeted a student, the parents are the ones who would make the decision whether or not to pursue the filing of a criminal complaint or investigate legal remedies with the assistance of an attorney. If the speech has targeted a staff member, the district's legal counsel should be consulted. School officials should not be expected to conduct an in-depth legal analysis. However, a preliminary assessment of the necessity for contacting law enforcement or legal counsel may be helpful.

If the online material appears to involve a violation of criminal laws (other than laws against threats, which would be handled in the context of the threat assessment)—including coercion, obscene or harassing text messages, harassment or stalking, hate or bias crimes, creating or sending sexually explicit pictures, sexual exploitation, or taking pictures of someone in a private place— school officials could refer the incident to law enforcement or recommend that parents take this course of action. If a staff member is involved, consultation with district counsel prior to such referral may be warranted.

If the school or district has a school resource officer, this individual should be involved in the analysis and decision making regarding the most appropriate strategy. The parents of the target are the ones who will ultimately decide whether to pursue criminal prosecution, if the material has met the criminal law standards. In some cases, the mere threat of the potential for a referral for criminal prosecution or a home visit by the school resource officer may be sufficient to stop the cyberbullying activities.

If the online material appears to involve defamation, invasion of privacy, or intentional infliction of emotional distress, school officials may want to suggest to parents that contact with an attorney for a review of the situation may be an appropriate response. School officials will need to be careful in making this recommendation to avoid a situation where the parents of the target expect the school district to pay for such legal services. If the online material is directed at staff and appears to meet the standards for a civil remedy, consultation with district or union counsel may be warranted.

An important reason for school officials to consider the potential legal consequences of the cyberbullying is the leverage this understanding might provide both in getting the cyberbullying to stop and in preventing any retaliation as a consequence of intervention. Parents who are informed about potential financial liability or criminal consequences of their child's harmful online speech may be more highly motivated to take steps to ensure that such activities stop.

CHAPTER 9

Response Actions and Options

This chapter provides guidance on the response actions and options available to the school, as well as to parents and students who are the targets of cyberbullying. The response actions and options are also available to staff members who are targeted. A chart outlining these possible actions and options is included as Appendix B.

SCHOOL ACTION OPTIONS

The situation review described in chapter 8 provides the background to determine possible response actions and options by the school.

Formal Disciplinary Action

If the district can establish a school nexus and substantial and material interference with the target's ability to fully participate in school activities, the school can impose a formal disciplinary response. But, as noted in chapter 7, the ability to impose formal discipline may be relatively insignificant in the overall perspective of resolving the problem. School officials should absolutely not simply impose a formal disciplinary response and consider the matter resolved.

A formal disciplinary response will not fully address all of the concerns encountered by the target. Harmful online materials must be removed. There is a possibility that the cyberbully might seek revenge on the target, including revenge via cyberbullying by proxy. If the incident involved a "get-back-at" cyberbully, as opposed to a "put-down" cyberbully, the school must work to stop the on-campus bullying by other students (or possibly by school staff). Parents of the target may need to take some action on their own, as described later in this chapter. School officials can help the parents or the target figure out the most appropriate response and provide a range of assistance in following through, including technical support. It is also essential to help the target gain new skills to prevent further victimization.

Informal Resolution Options

If it is difficult to establish a school nexus, or if there are other reasons a formal disciplinary response might not be advised, all the following recommended school actions are still fully available. The school does not require the ability to impose formal discipline to work with the parents of the cyberbully and the parents of the target or to provide support to the target. Formal discipline is only one method of getting someone's attention to stop inappropriate behavior. There are many other methods, most of which are likely to be more effective, to stop the cyberbullying.

Working with Parents of the Put-Down Cyberbully

The parents of a put-down cyberbully are probably unaware of their child's online activities, likely to be concerned to find that their child has engaged in this kind of activity, and inclined to take steps to get the cyberbullying to stop. On the other hand, they could be very defensive. The manner in which parents are approached will probably play an important role in achieving cooperation. Here are some assumptions that should be helpful in guiding the decision about how to approach parents:

- Chances are, the parents have absolutely no idea their child is engaging in these activities, and the actions of the student are not in accord with the parents' values and the values they have tried to impart to their child.

- When first made aware of the problem, the parents are likely to find it virtually impossible to believe that their child, raised to have good values, would ever engage in this kind of behavior.

- The next reaction will probably be anger—directed at their child and possibly at the school or the target. This anger is likely to be grounded in the humiliation the parents feel that their child could be involved in activity like this, shame that such activity has been discovered, fear that others will hold them in lower regard because of this, and embarrassment that the child's actions reflect poorly on their values and parenting.

- The parents are likely to be relatively naive about effective strategies to address these concerns and improve their management of their child's Internet use.

The goal for school intervention is to help the parents through these initial reactions and bring them to a state where they can work successfully with the school to resolve the concerns and prevent further harmful activity. It is very important in the initial approach to the parents to provide them with hard evidence of their child's online activities, assurance that school personnel recognize that they probably do not know this is happening and would not be allowing it to happen if they did know, and assurance that the school will provide some assistance on how they can better manage their child's harmful use of the Internet.

Parents need an opportunity to work through their immediate negative reaction privately. A recommended approach is to send the cyberbully's parents a certified letter that includes the downloaded material, provides the assurances described in the preceding paragraph, and requests a meeting the following day to address these concerns. Unless there is some sort of emergency situation, it is *not* advisable to call the parents for a meeting at the school, hand them the documentation of the cyberbullying, and expect them to be able to engage in effective problem solving. The "drop it on the table" approach is likely to lead to anger and defensiveness and thus interfere with ultimate resolution. At the meeting, the school official should seek parental commitment to ensure that all material is removed and that they will ward against retaliation. A plan of action should be developed with the parents to better manage their child's Internet use.

As discussed previously, school officials will also need to be aware that in the course of investigation, it may turn out that the student who initially appears to be the cyberbully may, in fact, have been the target of bullying by another student. In other words, what first appeared to be put-down cyberbullying may, in fact, be get-back-at cyberbullying. A plan must be developed to stop all bullying, on campus and online.

School discipline or intervention could cause the cyberbully to try to retaliate anonymously against the target. The cyberbully could also seek to engage other individuals, including those from outside the school environment, such as IM buddies or friends from an online community, to attack the target. Parents should be warned about the potential for retaliation and the need to prevent it and should discuss this possibility with their child: "Asking someone else to engage in bullying on your behalf is just the same as doing it yourself."

The biggest lever school officials have to encourage parental participation in stopping the cyberbullying, removing harmful material, and warding against retaliation is the threat of civil litigation and potential financial liability. As noted in chapter 6, if parents know that their child is engaging in activity that is harming another and fail to intervene, they can face significant personal liability in the form of a claim for parental negligence. The district's action in informing parents of their child's activities clearly brings the harmful activity to their attention (which is why it is advisable to send the letter via certified mail). Options to bring this potential liability to parental attention may include a specific statement in the letter sent home (which should be cleared first by district legal counsel), mention during the in-person meeting, and provision of the *Parent Guide* (Appendix K). The *Parent Guide* clearly outlines the risks of potential liability and the steps that are considered necessary to avoid such liability.

One step parents could take is to install monitoring software on the home computer and to regularly review the results of this monitoring. This software is relatively inexpensive. It provides parents with the ability to monitor all of their child's online activity—every keystroke. Use of the software with children who have not engaged in inappropriate activity could raise trust and relationship concerns. But for the child who has engaged in cyberbullying, trust has already been lost, and the installation of monitoring software is a highly appropriate, logical consequence. Parents who are totally unfamiliar with computers could take computer classes at the local community college or from some other source. If the parents do not know how to install the software, recommend contacting a computer service company. Some computer service companies will even make house calls.

Parents should also attempt to restrict the child's ability to use another computer for access. Computers are apt to be available at the public library, a community technology center, or a friend's house, and it is desirable to close off as many of these avenues as possible.

Working with Parents of a Child in Distress

In some cases, the school may become aware of cyberbullying or distressing material through some other source and will need to contact the parent of the student who appears to be at some emotional risk. The report could have come from some other individual, or the student could have reported the cyberbullying to the school without first reporting it at home. In these cases, the best strategy for working with parents is just the opposite from that for working with an aggressive cyberbully.

The initial reaction of these parents will likely be significant concern for the safety and well-being of their child. Therefore, prior to contacting parents, it is best to engage in a review of the situation and develop a preliminary plan of action to recommend. If there are any indicators that the child is emotionally at risk, a school- or community-based mental health support structure should be accessed. The parents need to know exactly with whom they need to talk, and they need to have a knowledgeable advocate available to them. Obviously, if the child is at immediate risk, this process must be accomplished rapidly.

When the preliminary review has been accomplished and a preliminary plan of action has been developed, the parents can be asked to come to the school to meet with the school counselor or psychologist and any other necessary school officials without fully informing them of what the problem is. During the meeting, the parents should be informed about the concern and provided with documentation of the cyberbullying. The parents will probably need emotional support, so the school counselor or psychologist absolutely must be present.

In other cases, the parents of the child who is the target will be the ones bringing the complaint to the school. If parents bring a complaint to the school, the situation review and development of a plan of action will need to be accomplished in cooperation with the parents and possibly the target.

If the situation involves a get-back-at cyberbully, a child who is being victimized at school and has posted distressing material, the parents should be assured that the school recognizes that a larger picture is involved and that their child's online actions might be related to on-campus bullying. A commitment must be made to address the on-campus concerns. But the parents also need to know the importance of gaining better management of their child's Internet use. The suggestion of the use of monitoring software is totally applicable here also. A child who is posting get-back-at material is in danger of crossing the line and posting threatening material that could lead to criminal charges, so it is very important to get this situation under control.

The objective in the initial meeting with parents will be to create a workable plan of action for addressing the situation. The strategies described in this chapter and in the *Parent Guide* can be reviewed to determine the most appropriate actions. This may be a preliminary plan that will include additional evidence gathering, such as a review of district Internet use records, and a reevaluation of the situation after such evidence has been gathered. The plan will probably include an agreement by the school to seek a meeting with the parents of the cyberbully to resolve the problem informally. If justified, the plan may also describe formal discipline of the cyberbully. Parents who are concerned about the safety and well-being of their child are unlikely to be very attentive to a lecture on the free-speech limitations on school officials. But if there is a lack of clarity about whether or not the school can impose formal discipline, this situation will have to be explained.

Parents of a target also need to be warned about the possibility that the cyberbully could engage in retaliation or enlist the assistance of online friends for this purpose. Parents should be advised to pay close attention to this possibility and to keep all lines of communication open.

School officials will also need to be aware that in the course of the investigation, it may turn out that the target of the reported cyberbullying may, in fact, have been bullying other students at school. Obviously, any plans will require addressing the overall situation and getting all bullying to stop.

The parents of a target should also be made aware of the possible civil litigation options and the fact that since the parents of the cyberbully now know that their child is involved in these harmful activities, if the cyberbullying does not immediately stop and all harmful material is not removed, that knowledge can provide the basis for a claim of parental negligence. As a backup, if deemed necessary, the parents could talk with an attorney and request that the attorney send a certified letter to the parents of the cyberbully stating the same thing.

The parents of a get-back-at cyberbully also need to be made aware of their possible civil liability if their child's online actions do not stop and if all harmful material is not removed. Get-back-at cyberbullies may post material that crosses the line into a criminal offense—especially any online threats. The parents need to be made fully aware of this possibility.

Working Directly with the Target

The school counselor or psychologist or a community-based counselor should provide ongoing support to any students who have been the target of cyberbullying, whether or not they have engaged in get-back-at cyberbullying of their own. The counseling support should address the emotional harm that has resulted from the bullying or cyberbullying and seek to empower the student with effective skills to prevent and respond to bullying that occurs either in person or online. Such skills should give the student options besides retaliation.

Excellent resource materials are available for counselors to provide assistance to students who are bullied, including those who engage in retaliation. There are also ways that the Internet can be used to empower students who traditionally are targets. However, some peculiarities of the online environment and the youth who participate in it should be kept in mind. Appendix J provides student curriculum materials that can provide the basis for education about strategies to deal with cyberbullying.

Addiction to Harmful Online Communities

One important issue to address will be the degree to which the student is addicted to engagement in online activity, especially in the online environment through which the bullying is taking place. In many cases, the target of the cyberbullying is a wannabe—a student who wants to be an accepted member of a popular student group that actively communicates online. To disassociate from the online community may seem to the target as painful as being subjected to cyberbullying. Essentially, the recommendation to avoid participation in the online community will be akin to recommending a state of total self-exclusion or exile—deliberate acceptance of what is traditionally the most severe of penalties in human groups. Making such a decision to exclude oneself would be difficult for a mature adult, let alone an unhappy child.

Unfortunately, at this stage in our understanding of this issue, stating the problem is easier than figuring out how to address it. Two basic approaches come to mind:

- Help the target to see the futility of seeking to remain in this particular online community and then to find other alternatives.

- Help the target to figure out how to remain in the online community but get the cyberbullying to stop.

A counselor or psychologist may help the target make a realistic evaluation of the quality of the online community and the benefits of remaining in it. If the communication environment is public, visit the environment with the student and discuss the values and kindness reflected in the communications—helping the target assess the quality of the communications and importance of participation. If some of the communications are private, the target may be willing to share the communications and discuss them.

If a decision is made to leave this online community, specific steps will need to be taken to engage the student in another, healthier community of peers at school and online. Essentially, this will require figuring out what the student's interests and strengths are and seeking to engage the student with others who share those interests. This may require getting the student involved in a new student organization or a community youth group. Another strategy may be finding a way for this student to become involved in helping others who will express their gratitude for this service. The student could get involved as an aide for an after-school program for younger students, provide support in a soup kitchen, or join a program that addresses environmental concerns. Seeking to engage an older student in an activity that is linked to a future career option may help the student shift attention from the desirability of being an accepted member of a school social group to that of pursuing future opportunities.

The counselor or psychologist can help the targeted student develop a plan of action and commitments related to use of the Internet that will assist the student in achieving the objective identified.

Online Bully Proofing

If a student wants to stay within the online community, or even try a new community, the counselor or psychologist can share some strategies that can help lead this student to success. It is very important in these circumstances to secure from the student a commitment to report any concerns before they get out of hand. Parents should pay close attention and initiate discussions with their child often.

Online communications have several benefits that counselors and psychologists may be able to use to assist targets in dealing more effectively with bullying behavior. A counselor or psychologist can help targets learn how to respond in an assertive but not aggressive way to any harmful online communications and how to use technological communications systems effectively to gain social power and control without retaliation.

The Internet is actually an excellent environment for targets to engage in communication activities that can raise their social power and eliminate the rewards of power and control sought by bullies. Consider this: Which would be easier, standing up to a bully who is 30 pounds heavier or who is surrounded by an aggressive entourage in a face-to-face setting or doing the same through Internet communications? Which communication would be more powerful, a statement made by a fearful child in a face-to-face setting in the heat of the moment or a carefully constructed statement that is delivered online?

Teens are experimenting with different identities online. So it may be possible to encourage targets to create an online persona of someone who has greater social power than they currently think they have at school. They can use the Internet to practice empowerment. This will require translating assertiveness techniques into the online environment—where three features work to make this change in status entirely possible.

The communications are preserved. This allows for an analysis of their substance after the fact. Sometimes youth who are the targets of bullying or cyberbullying may be communicating or behaving in ways that precipitate this treatment or are responding in ways that reinforce the continuation of the bullying. With copies of the communications in hand, the counselor or psychologist can engage the target in a self-assessment of the behavior that may be contributing to the initiation or continuation of the bullying behavior.

Helping students gain greater expertise in evaluating their own communication patterns and behavior is extremely useful. Has the target been posting material or engaging in other actions that are perceived by the online community to be unacceptable and thus is provoking the cyberbullying? Or has the target been overreacting in response, thus providing reinforcement for the cyberbully and friends? It is extremely important to conduct this analysis in a manner that is very supportive of the student.

The impact on the target is invisible. If the target will keep his or her hands off the keyboard, the online target is invisible: The bully can't tell for sure how the target has reacted. The counselor or psychologist can help the student understand that the primary goal of bullies is to get targets to lose their cool. The natural, normal response of anyone who has been attacked is to get upset. But when targets lose their cool, they essentially hand over power to the bully. Bullies want to demonstrate that they can force the target to lose control. It proves their success, raises their status with their peers, and provides ample justification for more bullying—because the target now "deserves it." When targets lose their cool online, this simply amplifies the success of the bully because the target's response is preserved electronically for many bystanders to see.

The communications can easily be delayed. With online attacks, the most important rule is "Do not respond until you have calmed down and can figure out what to do from a position of strength." After the target has calmed down and can think clearly, a decision can be made regarding how to respond. The target should take advantage of the ability to delay online communications to draft a response to the cyberbully, if a response is warranted. Even if the cyberbullying is occurring in a real-time communication venue such as chat or IM, the target can exit until prepared to communicate effectively. The communication can be shifted to a delayed method, such as e-mail.

If the target decides to respond, he or she should take the time to craft a strong message. It is okay to write an initial response when upset, but this response should not be sent. The student can let the message sit, have a friend read it, or even work with the counselor or psychologist to refine the message prior to sending it. In some cases, it may be best simply to ignore a harmful message sent by a cyberbully. But any response that is made should be strong, assertive, and unemotional.

PARENT, STUDENT, AND STAFF ACTION OPTIONS

Parents, students, or staff all have options, some appropriate in the case of milder forms of cyberbullying and others to be taken in the case of a criminal violation. In some cases, a step-by-step approach may be warranted. In all cases, if harmful material is present on any public site, a complaint should be filed with the site to seek the removal of the material.

As noted in chapter 8, saving the evidence and identifying the cyberbully are important first steps in responding.

Deciding When to Tell an Adult

It is necessary to explain the rationale for some guidance set forth in the *Student Guide* (Appendix J) related to deciding when to tell an adult. The following text is from the *Student Guide:*

Decide if you need to involve an adult. Sometimes you can resolve these situations on your own. Tell an adult if:

- You are really upset and are not sure what to do.

- The cyberbully is also bullying you in "real life."

- You have been threatened with harm.

- The cyberbully is doing things that can really damage your reputation and friendships.

- The cyberbully is also bullying other students.

- You tried some of the other steps to get the cyberbully to stop, and it didn't work.

Conventional guidance to students is always to tell an adult if they are being bullied. This guidance is tied to the perception that victims of bullying are incapable of handling the situation and will always need to ask an adult for assistance. Essentially, this guidance does not see any target as capable of handing any bullying situation. We cannot raise resilient youth if we perceive that they are, and always will be, helpless and in need of adult assistance to handle a bullying situation. We should expect that in many situations youth should be able to respond appropriately on their own.

This being said, adult assistance sometimes is necessary or advisable, just as an adult may need on occasion to seek the assistance of an attorney to handle a contentious matter. The *Student Guide* presents information in a way that respects the anticipated competence of the teen to handle some or many situations. It is hoped that teens will feel more empowered in general and be more inclined to seek adult assistance when it is necessary and appropriate.

The guide also provides information on the full range of options to respond to cyberbullying, including those that will require adult assistance. Many teens are leery about telling an adult about online concerns because they do not think the adult will know what to do—or will make matters worse by doing the wrong thing. By providing a list of possible responses, teens will hopefully be more likely to request assistance when such assistance is really needed.

Challenging the Cyberbully

The target should be instructed to send the cyberbully a very clear, unemotional, strong message demanding that the cyberbullying stop and warning that if it does not stop, other action will be taken. Any messages sent to the cyberbully or received from the cyberbully in response to this message should be saved.

Ignoring the Cyberbully

Several strategies can be used to ignore the cyberbully. The target should be advised to try the following measures:

- Block or filter all further communications from this individual through e-mail, IM, and text messaging.

- Avoid going to the site or group where attacks have occurred.

- Get a new e-mail address, account, username, or phone number.

However, as discussed earlier, it may be very difficult for a student to leave a specific online community, despite harm that may be being inflicted there.

Filing a Complaint

This step should be taken in all cases of cyberbullying, though it may need to be delayed while attempts are taking place to identify an anonymous cyberbully. As discussed in chapter 6, cyberbullying is almost always a violation of the terms of use agreements of the Web sites, ISPs, and cell phone companies where it takes place. The target or the target's parents can file a complaint by providing the harmful messages or a link to the harmful material to the company and asking that the account of the cyberbully be terminated and any harmful material removed.

- If the cyberbully is using e-mail, contact the ISP of the cyberbully (determine the ISP from the e-mail address), contact the company at support@<ISP> or look on the ISP's site for a "Contact Us" e-mail address.

- If the material appears on a third-party Web site (for example, www.webhostname.com/~kid'sname.html) go to the site's home page and file a complaint through the "Contact Us" e-mail address.

- If the material is on a Web site with its own domain name (for example, www.xyzkid.com), go to Whois (www.whois.net), a Web site that will allow you to look up a registered domain name and find information about the registrant and the host company. Go to the host company's Web site and file a complaint through the "Contact Us" e-mail address.

- If the cyberbully is using a cell phone, trace the number and contact the phone company.

One advantage of filing a complaint in this way is that it is not necessary to identify an anonymous cyberbully. If the cyberbullying is occurring through e-mail and the cyberbully is using an alias established as part of a family account, the complaint will result in the termination of the family account—an impact that will bring the issue to the attention of the cyberbully's parents quite rapidly.

Be sure to save all communications with the company. Some companies may be more responsive than others. You might have to work up the chain of command to get a positive response. Complaint procedures are worthwhile, despite the cyberbully's ability to set up a new account. Complaints may need to be repeated until other steps take hold.

Contacting the Cyberbully's Parents

The target's parents can send the cyberbully's parents a letter that includes the downloaded material and requests that the cyberbullying stop and all harmful material be removed. This would be an alternative to a school-initiated information intervention response with these parents.

Contacting an Attorney

An attorney can send a letter to the cyberbully's parents demanding that the cyberbullying stop. An attorney can also help file a lawsuit against the cyberbully's parents that provides for financial damages and requires that the cyberbullying stop.

Contacting the Police

If the cyberbullying appears to be a crime, either the school or the parents can contact the police. Alternatively, the school resource officer could be involved in making contact with the parent for a referral to local law enforcement.

CHAPTER 10

Comprehensive Response to Cyberbullying and Cyberthreats

This chapter discusses ways for districts and schools to address cyberbullying and cyberthreats in a comprehensive manner. The recommendations in this chapter are grounded in insight gained through research into other effective programs for the prevention of bullying, suicide, and violence, threat assessment practices and U.S. federal requirements for safe schools planning. This insight has been expanded to address the issues related to youth online behavior, student use of technology, and legal issues affecting a school response.

SAFE SCHOOLS PLANNING

This chapter is relevant across the board, from a small private school to a large urban district with many schools. Nonetheless, the general guidance it provides will require modification, as appropriate, to address the needs of specific organizations. Districts and schools probably already have structures in place to address both safe schools and management of educational technology, which they can adjust to address online risk concerns. Districts and schools should approach this chapter by asking the question "How can we best build on our current approach to incorporate these recommendations?"

The approach set forth in this chapter is designed to be comprehensive. Some districts or schools may not find it necessary to implement such a comprehensive approach. There are also other concerns related to youth risk online that are not the subject of this book. Issues such as online sexual predators, scams, hacking, and the like are of concern, but are not likely impacting the school community as directly as the concerns addressed in this book. For those districts or schools that desire to address the full range of youth risk online concerns, the comprehensive approach described in this chapter can easily be adapted to achieve this objective.

Principles of Effectiveness

In the United States, safe schools planning must meet the requirements of the Safe and Drug Free Schools and Communities Act (SDFSCA).[1] All activities proposed in an SDFSCA plan must meet standards known as "Principles of Effectiveness."[2] The Principles of Effectiveness standards seek to ensure that districts receiving the federal funds are held accountable for achieving measurable results. Programs have been established to independently review programs addressing safe schools, bullying, and suicide prevention and to provide guidance on programs that are deemed to meet appropriate standards.[3] However, if a district is experiencing unique challenges and has ideas for new approaches that have not been fully tested through scientific research, the district may request a waiver of the Principles of Effectiveness requirement.[4] The district must demonstrate that the proposed program or activity is innovative and has a substantial likelihood of success.

The comprehensive approach recommended in this chapter has not been subjected to a rigorous scientific evaluation because these are new concerns and there has been insufficient time to do so. The recommended approach is grounded in insight gained through research into other effective prevention programs and specifically contains elements designed to ensure ongoing evaluation of effectiveness. Further, the approach incorporates the elements necessary to support a waiver of the Principles of Effectiveness. Any U.S. school that seeks to implement the program outlined in this chapter using SDFSCA funds will be required to seek a waiver. Appendix G provides a template that districts can use to request this waiver.

Essentially, the key components necessary to support a waiver should be included when implementing any new program—needs assessment to ensure that the scope of the concern is well understood, a well-thought-out rationale for the new program, an implementation plan, and performance measures and an evaluation plan.

OLWEUS BULLYING PREVENTION PROGRAM

The most widely researched program to combat bullying in school is the Olweus Bullying Prevention Program, which was first developed in the early 1980s in Norway and Sweden. The Olweus program was adapted to meet the needs of U.S. schools and implemented in South Carolina by Dr. Susan Limber under comprehensive research conditions.[5] Limber's excellent study of the Olweus program provides the essential foundation for an understanding of the necessary components of a successful bullying prevention program. The recommended approach to address cyberbullying and cyberthreats builds on this program.

The Olweus Bullying Prevention Program was originally designed to work with interventions at three levels—schoolwide, classroom, and individual. These are the core components of the Olweus Bullying Prevention Program:

- A coordinating committee

- Needs assessment

- Professional development

- Policies that incorporate appropriate consequences

- Increased supervision of problem areas

- Parent involvement

- Student education that provides the opportunity for students to discuss concerns

- Individual interventions that address the needs of the targeted students, the bullies, and both sets of parents

Limber's review of the implementation of the Olweus program in U.S. schools noted several factors that seem relevant to the challenge of addressing cyberbullying and cyberthreats.

- The original Olweus program did not include community involvement. Many schools also include community members on their safe schools committees and reach out to community institutions to assist in the implementation of bullying prevention activities and the dissemination of bullying prevention information. Limber regards the inclusion of community activities as an essential addition to the Olweus program. To address cyberbullying and cyberthreats effectively will require community collaboration, especially with law enforcement and community mental health organizations, as well as with other community organizations.

- Limber identified resistance on the part of staff and parents as a major challenge. Some staff and parents still hold the belief that bullying is a natural process of growing up and that youth can be expected to resolve these concerns on their own. Strong leadership and local needs assessment data was considered necessary in drawing attention to the issue. Cyberbullying and cyberthreat activities are occurring in the hidden world of youth online activities. A local needs assessment will help raise awareness of these concerns and encourage greater commitment in addressing them.

- The desire for simple answers sometimes leads schools to select short-term, easy-to-implement solutions that do not lead to a systemic change in the school community. As discussed in the next section, when seeking to address concerns related to technology, there is too often an effort to rely on simplistic and ineffective technological solutions.

Avoiding Reliance on the Quick Fix

Historically, technological quick-fix solutions have been promoted as ways to address concerns of youth risk on the Internet. As interest in the Internet grew in the late 1990s, concerns were raised about youth access to pornographic material. The quick-fix response in the United States was to mandate that schools use filtering software. At the same time the U.S. Congress was mandating school use of Internet filtering, the National Academy of Sciences released an extensive report entitled *Youth, Pornography, and the Internet.*[6] In the preface to the report, the chair of the committee that investigated this issue, Dick Thornburgh, noted:

> It is the hope of the committee that this report will be seen as comprehensive and authoritative, but I believe it is bound to disappoint a number of readers. It will disappoint those who expect a technological "quick fix" to the challenge of pornography on the Internet. . . . It will disappoint parents, school officials, and librarians who seek surrogates to fulfill the responsibilities of training and supervision needed to truly protect children from inappropriate sexual materials on the Internet.

Internet industry and government policymakers are most concerned with enhancing the growth of the Internet. Filtering and child-safe portals have been promoted to alleviate parental fears. The result of this promotion has been the misperception that all parents and schools need to do is configure a protection tool correctly and children will magically be safe online.

It can be anticipated that some district employees will maintain that their district has done everything necessary to address issues of cyberbullying and cyberthreats because it is blocking access to social networking sites and does not allow students to use e-mail. But students may be able to bypass the school filter. Students can also use cell phones or other personal digital devices to access the Internet and communicate electronically. Further, off-campus online activities of students are having a negative impact on the school climate and on student well-being and school performance. It is essential that educational leaders recognize and dismiss the perception that simple solutions, especially technology-based quick fixes, will address these concerns.

Additional Anticipated Difficulties

Several additional issues could present challenges:

- In the vast majority of districts, student Internet use comes under the authority of the technology department, whereas a totally separate committee is charged with addressing safe schools issues. Generally, technology department staff have a limited understanding of safe schools issues, and safe schools personnel have a limited understanding of technology use issues. To address cyberbullying and cyberthreats, it is absolutely critical to address this systemic structural issue to ensure the collaborative involvement of individuals with both technical and safe schools expertise.

- It is necessary to address the concerns of off-campus activities that are harming the school climate and well-being of students. As discussed in chapter 7, free-speech limitations restrict the imposition of formal discipline. Some educators may take the position that because the cyberbullying is occurring off campus, it is not a matter for schools to be concerned about. The problem with this attitude is that unresolved issues arising off campus can easily escalate and have the potential for a catastrophically damaging impact on campus. Addressing off-campus concerns will require active involvement of parents and the community, along with flexibility in administrative or disciplinary responses.

- Involvement of responsible student leaders in planning and implementation can bring insight that is unlikely to be available through any other source. However, involving students may pose a challenge because of the social norm among youth that online activities should remain hidden from adults. Some students may view any students who participate in planning and implementation activities as traitors.

Appendix D sets forth a template for a comprehensive plan of action to address cyberbullying and cyberthreats. This template can be downloaded from The Center for Safe and Responsible Internet Use Cyberbullying Web site, at http://cyberbully.org, and modified to meet the needs of specific districts and schools.

Coordinated Planning

Cyberbullying and cyberthreat concerns must be addressed at both the district and school level. Some issues—such as policies relating to the use of personal digital devices on campus and management of student use of the district's Internet system—are district-level responsibilities, but many implementation efforts will be school based.

Because online risk concerns are, at their core, safe schools issues, it is recommended that the safe schools committees at the district level and the school level assume responsibility for oversight. However, it is essential that educational technology staff be included on the safe schools committees. This includes both the technical services staff and the library media staff. To develop the initial plan of action, it may be advisable to establish work groups at the district and school level that include representatives from both the safe schools committees and the educational technology committees.

The technology coordinator will have the greatest level of expertise with respect to Internet use management in the district and will also have excellent insight into issues related to off-campus Internet use by students. The district and school library media staff members will have the greatest insight into how students are using the Internet in more open environments in the schools and how effectively the district's Internet use management approach is working. Both technology and library media staff members will also have significant expertise in finding online material related to any specific incidents.

Ideally, student representatives should serve directly on these committees, especially at the school level. As noted, this could present some problems. Alternatively, a separate student Internet use committee could serve as advisory to the safe schools committee or work group. This committee would include more students, and the committee deliberations would be more open—any interested student could be invited to participate. This would probably reduce the risk to any participating students. Further, it would create a larger group of students who could help establish and enforce responsible Internet use norms among the students. Other options for incorporating student input should also be considered.

Needs Assessments

Needs assessment can serve many purposes beyond the obvious ones of determining what problems exist and providing insight into strategies to address such problems. The assessment will provide baseline data that will allow for effective evaluation of the implementation of the comprehensive plan in the future. The results of the needs assessment can also be helpful in educating staff and parents about the kind and degree of concerns in the district and thus generate greater commitment to programs to address the concerns. Last, if a district is going to apply for SDFSCA funds, the needs assessment is an important component of the request for a waiver of the Principles of Effectiveness.

It is recommended that needs assessment be conducted at two levels.

Staff needs assessment. The staff needs assessment can be conducted in a survey format or as a group discussion. The key staff members to include are the members of the district and safe schools and educational technology committees. The staff needs assessment should solicit insight into the perceptions of the extent of the problem, the adequacy of current school policies and implementation of those policies, Internet use management issues, and reporting and response concerns. Appendix F contains a list of questions that can be posed to staff.

Student needs assessment. The student needs assessment should be conducted via a survey of students at the middle and high school level. Appropriate sampling can be done so that not all students need complete the survey. A more informal needs assessment conducted in discussion format involving 4th- and 5th-grade students might also be helpful. The student needs assessment should seek insight into general Internet use, parental involvement in Internet use, personal experiences and perceptions of other students' experiences with these concerns, bystander behavior, and reporting behavior. A student needs assessment survey is included as Appendix E. This document also provides guidance on how the district can interpret and use the data from the student needs assessment.

When the results of the student needs assessment survey have been determined, it will probably be very helpful for key staff members to hold discussions with groups of students. These student focus groups are likely to significantly increase the depth of understanding of the local issues and concerns.

It is anticipated that these needs assessment surveys will be modified as greater insight into these concerns is revealed. The most current versions of the needs assessment documents will be available on the Center for Safe and Responsible Internet Use Cyberbullying Web site (http://cyberbully.org).

Policy and Practice Review

A district level review of Internet policies and practices, as well as policies and practices for the management of cell phones and other personal digital devices, will be necessary. Additionally, the policies and practices around bullying and harassment, threat assessment, and suicide prevention must be reassessed.

Internet and Personal Digital Device Policies and Practices

A thorough review of Internet use management and personal digital device policies and practices is recommended. It is likely that district policies were created in the late 1990s and that a modification will be necessary. These policy issues are discussed in chapter 11.

Reporting, Review, and Response Process

To address cyberbullying and cyberthreats effectively requires that students be willing to report such incidents to adults. The key factor necessary to encourage students to report incidents is the assurance that if they do report, effective steps will be taken to resolve the concerns. Students should be encouraged to report situations that are causing problems for themselves, as well as incidents involving other students—especially any cases where a student has posted a threat or suggestion of violence or suicide. Schools should establish a mechanism for students to file anonymous or confidential reports. Students risk retaliation if it becomes known that they have made such reports, which youth social norms define as tattling, and online retaliation can be extreme. However, the risks of retaliation can be significantly reduced with an anonymous or confidential reporting system. "Anonymous" means that the student can report without anyone finding out who the student is. In some situations, such disclosure will occur or will be necessary. School officials will need to assure students that their identity will be kept confidential.

The anonymous or confidential reporting system could have a deterrent effect on cyberbullying. Except for situations involving one-on-one harassment or stalking, other students will witness many instances of cyberbullying. An anonymous or confidential reporting system places bullies or prospective bullies in a situation where they will never know who might download the harmful material and provide it to a school administrator.

Another practice that should be considered is an online reporting system for cyberbullying and cyberthreats, as well as any other bullying and harassment concerns. The home page of the district and school Web sites could have a link to an online complaint reporting form. The page could include district policies and information on how to file a complaint. This system should have the capacity to allow students to file an electronic complaint and to forward any harmful material to an appropriate administrator.

Chapters 8 and 9 have presented the recommended review and response process. Schools will need to decide which staff members are responsible for the tasks involved in following this process. Again, the most important strategy to encourage student reporting is to respond effectively to those reports so that students recognize that their reports will lead to positive efforts to resolve the problems.

Professional Development

A triage approach to professional development is recommended—providing the professional development necessary to educators based on the prospective role they might play in addressing these concerns:

- Several key people at the district level should become highly knowledgeable about these issues—one person with technical expertise and one with bullying and suicide prevention expertise. These individuals can serve as key resources for school administrators in addressing specific incidents. In cases where small schools are served by an intermediary service district, the key staff may be employed at the intermediary level.

- All members of the district and safe schools planning and educational technology committees will need sufficient knowledge about these concerns to be able to implement effective prevention, review, and response activities.

- Teachers who will be providing student education should have a full understanding of the behavioral aspects of cyberbullying and cyberthreats. An understanding of the material provided in chapters 1 through 6 should be considered necessary.

- All other educational staff should be made aware of the concerns. Cyberbullying does not generally directly affect life in the classroom, as is the case with face-to-face bullying. However, educators need to be aware that signs of student distress or failure may be an indication of bullying or cyberbullying activities. Any educators who work with students when using the district's computers, including substitute teachers, need to be aware of the potential of cyberbullying occurring through the district's Internet system and be sensitive to the signs that a student has had a negative online experience.

Parent Outreach

Because the majority of student online activity is occurring at home, parents must be better educated about these concerns. Parents should be encouraged to make it clear to their children that engagement in cyberbullying is not acceptable and should encourage their children to report any instances of cyberbullying that are directed toward them or that they witness. Parents must be aware of concerns related to involvement with dangerous online groups and issues around cyberthreats—the importance of reporting any online material that appears to be threatening and of not posting material that could be perceived as a threat. The chief need is for parents to understand the importance of monitoring their children's online activities and know how to do so effectively.

It is notoriously difficult to provide parent education. Busy parents generally do not have time available to attend parent meetings. The parents who do attend parent meetings are frequently the ones who are least likely to actually need the guidance because they are already more actively engaged with their children. Material sent home may or may not be read. The time when parents are most likely to pay attention to these concerns is when they are seeking information necessary to respond to a particular situation.

The key to success will be in providing multiple communications, ranging from brief to more extensive. The following are possible options:

- Provide information about cyberbullying and cyberthreats in the context of a larger workshop for parents on the Internet and youth risk.

- Provide brief information about cyberbullying and cyberthreats in the context of some other meeting or gathering that parents are likely to attend. For example, a brief presentation on cyberbullying issues could be incorporated into meetings for parents of incoming students, included in a meeting addressing a range of healthy youth concerns, or even included as part of the program when the school choir or band performs.

- Send written information home. Appendix L includes a one-page informational document that can be sent home in a school newsletter.

- Provide more extensive written information in the front office, counselor's office, or health office and provide this material to parents whose children are involved in an actual incident. Appendix K, the *Parent Guide,* is a more extensive document that can be provided in this manner.

- Include brief cybersafety tips periodically in school newsletters. These tips may be related to local or national news articles.

- Provide the brief and comprehensive information documents (Appendixes J, K, and L) through the district and school Web sites in conjunction with an online reporting mechanism.

Community Outreach

A community outreach program should be designed to reach three communities:

- Law enforcement and mental health professionals

- Other community organizations

- Local news media

Law Enforcement and Mental Health Professionals

Generally, representatives from law enforcement and the mental health community serve on the district safe schools committee and may serve on other school committees. These individuals will have insight to offer in the context of planning and implementation. Additionally, the resolution of a specific incident may require involvement of law enforcement or referral to mental health services. These individuals need to have a good understanding of the district's review and response approach.

It will also be helpful for all mental health professionals in the community to have a better understanding of these concerns because they may be working with students and their families privately. The mental health representatives who serve on the district safe schools committee can assist in developing strategies to better educate this community. All mental health professionals in the community should be made aware of the district's plan of action and the resource material available through the district. This may be accomplished through news coverage, professional association meetings and newsletters, or direct mail.

Community Organizations

Community organizations that are involved in youth activities—including groups such as Boy's and Girl's Clubs, Boy Scouts, Girl Scouts, Campfire, and the like, as well as faith-based organizations—can provide an additional mechanism to educate parents and youth. Any organization that provides youth with access to the Internet outside school, such as the public library and after-school programs, should be included in the educational efforts. These organizations can be made aware of the district's plan and available resource material through news coverage or direct mail. The district may wish to invite representatives from these programs to parent or staff training workshops.

Local News Media

Press coverage of the district's efforts in addressing these concerns can be an additional conduit of information to both community members and parents. If a reporter contacts the district about a specific incident, the district can seek to ensure that information is included in the news report on how parents can prevent and respond to the concerns the incident raises. Make sure the district press contact knows which staff members will handle communication with any reporters in relation to any of these concerns.

Student Education

The basic information that needs to be communicated to students about cyberbullying and cyberthreats is not extensive. Appendix J, the *Student Guide to Cyberbullying and Cyberthreats,* can be reproduced and provided to students. This document includes essential information that can be conveyed quickly. It is recommended that the *Student Guide* be disseminated and discussed on an annual basis and made available in the front office, counselor's office, health office, library, and computer lab, as well as on the district's Web site.

A variety of instructional strategies can be used to enhance the educational effectiveness of this document:

- Present students with the results of the recent student needs assessment and use this data as the basis for engaging in a discussion about how to address local concerns. Ask the students to prepare a joint document presenting their advice on these issues to the school or district safe schools committee.

- Ask students to research news articles online that discuss cyberbullying or cyberthreats and discuss or write about the incidents reported. Ask students to put themselves into the story and outline the steps they would take if they witnessed or experienced incidents similar to those reported.

- Have students engage in a debate about one of the key social norms that supports online social aggression: "On the Internet, I have a free-speech right to post whatever I want, without regard for the possible harm it might cause to someone else."

- Ask students to interview their parents about family values that apply to online activities. Download some of the terms of use agreements from popular social networking sites. Provide copies of the district's Internet use policy. Have the students create an extensive chart outlining the standards expressed by their parents, the terms of use agreements, and the district's Internet use agreement. Identify the commonalities and any differences. Following this analysis, ask the students to create their own personal statement of standards for online behavior.

Performance Measurement and Evaluation

An important component of the comprehensive approach is the establishment of a process by which the district or school will establish performance measures and regularly gather and analyze data to evaluate activities and guide planning and implementation. Performance measurement is used for determining progress toward goals and evaluating the effectiveness of programs.

The template for a comprehensive plan of action provided in Appendix D includes suggested approaches to conduct performance measurements for various aspects of the program. Some of these performance measures involve an evaluation report following an event such as a workshop.

Because these concerns are so new, it will be very helpful for the district to consistently evaluate specific incidents. An incident report form is provided as Appendix C. School administrators can submit this report form to the district safe schools committee so that aggregated data can be maintained and patterns of concern can be identified. School administrators should also request feedback from all parents and students involved in any incident and summarize this feedback on the report made to the district. This analysis will provide insight into the effectiveness of professional development, parent education, and student education efforts, as well as the effectiveness of the school response.

The student needs assessment survey, provided as Appendix E, should be administered on a periodic basis to provide an overall assessment of progress toward objectives. The recommended data analysis is included in this appendix.

In conclusion, the most important step in a performance measurement model is use of the data for evaluation and program modification. Evaluation should lead to the continuation of program components that have been determined to be working effectively— and to the modification of program components that do not appear to be working properly. Because of the newness of these concerns, a strong focus on performance measurement and evaluation is essential.

CHAPTER 11

Management of Internet and Personal Digital Devices

This chapter provides an overview of key aspects of Internet and cell phone use management that can reduce the potential for cyberbullying and cyberthreats.

MISUSE OF INTERNET AND PERSONAL DIGITAL DEVICES

As noted in chapter 3, in a recent survey of young people between the ages of 12 and 17, one-third reported that they had been cyberbullied.[1] Of those who reported the cyberbullying, 30 percent reported that they were cyberbullied at school. One-sixth of the children between the ages of 6 and 11 reported that they had been cyberbullied, and 45 percent indicated that this occurred at school. The district needs assessment will provide local data about the degree of concern that students are cyberbullying each other at school.

It can be anticipated that the potential for misuse of the district's Internet system and personal digital devices used at school to engage in cyberbullying will continue to grow. Communication activities are becoming integrated into many Web sites—too many to block effectively without damaging the ability to use the Internet for educational purposes. Furthermore, many students have cell phones, and in coming years, it can be anticipated that students will be increasing their classroom use of other personal digital devices, including computers and PDAs.

As discussed in chapter 5, failure to take reasonable precautions to address such concerns could lead to liability. Reasonable precautions include addressing policies and practices for Internet use through the district Internet system, as well as for the use of cell phones and other personal digital devices by students on campus.

Four key factors should be addressed to reduce the potential for misuse of the district's Internet system: strong focus on educational use, enhanced supervision and monitoring, a clear and comprehensive Internet use policy that is communicated effectively and enforced appropriately, specific policies to address electronic communications, and appropriate management of the Internet filter.

Districts have significantly increased their use of the Internet in schools within the last decade. It is quite likely that the policies and practices to manage student Internet use were formulated when the Internet was first implemented. Those policies and practices must be revisited to address the challenges of the current environment.

Educational Use

When teachers are prepared to lead students on exciting learning adventures on the Internet, many of the concerns related to misuse of the Internet will disappear. Students who are engaged and excited about what they are discovering will focus their efforts on meeting the instructional requirements, not entertainment. The demand for the available computers for completing assignments will become so high that Internet recess use in open computer labs will simply not be considered acceptable.

What is "Internet recess?" The term refers to the use of the Internet for entertainment and low-quality surfing, gaming, or gabbing. Unfortunately, in some districts, or schools within districts, there is simply too much Internet recess—and the risks of bullying behavior during recess are high.

It is important to understand why computers and the Internet tend not to be used consistently for high-quality educational activities. Some of the factors that conflict with educational use are specific to the United States; others are more universal.

- When technologies, including the Internet, were coming into schools in the United States, the No Child Left Behind (NCLB) Act was being implemented at the same time. School administrators have focused significant efforts on the implementation of NCLB requirements, leaving insufficient time to focus on technology. What is more, NCLB requires testing, with potential for significant punishment of the school if certain performance standards are not met. This creates an environment that reduces the inclination to engage in the exploration and risk-taking necessary to support integration of new learning opportunities.

- In U.S. schools, funds to support the acquisition of new technology are provided through the E-rate program. This program provides funds to support telecommunications and Internet access for schools and libraries. While this program provides funds for networking and equipment, it does not provide funds for professional and curriculum development. As technology came into schools, concerns about student access to pornography were raised, and filtering software was strongly promoted as the solution. To this day, many educators think that it is perfectly safe to simply allow students to explore the Internet because the filtering software will protect them.

- Schools obtained Internet access before many families, especially lower income families, were able to do so. This led to the perspective that schools needed to provide public access to the Internet for students—that students ought to be able to engage in free-time use of the Internet, much as they would in a public library.

- In many districts, the Internet is perceived primarily as a technical service and not an essential component of instruction. In many districts, the staff who are responsible for providing professional development to teachers on computer and Internet use are affiliated with the technology services department, not the curriculum and instruction department. This arrangement reflects a lack of understanding about technology and instruction.

- Technology is also still frequently considered a separate area of curriculum. Schools generally have instructional objectives for specific technology skills. These objectives are important, but it is equally important to ensure that districts develop strategies to integrate effective use of technology to improve student learning in other subject areas, especially language arts, social sciences, and science.

- There has been a lack of accountability with respect to the professional preparation of teachers to use the Internet for high-quality instructional activities. Schools should periodically survey their teachers to determine how they are using technology and the Internet in their classrooms, their skill level in doing so, and their perceived need for professional development and curriculum resources.

Assessing Educational Use

There has also been a lack of accountability with respect to assessing Internet use in schools to determine the degree to which students are using it for educational rather than entertainment or other low-quality purposes. The following assessment is recommended.

During three typical school days, capture the URLs of 100 sites accessed at 10:00, 12:00, and 2:00. This will result in the capture of 900 URLs. Divide the list of URLs among the district's library media specialists and have them visit and categorize the sites according to a classification system along these lines:

- Search engines
- Instructional or reference sites
- News sites
- Sports sites
- E-commerce sites
- Music, gaming, and entertainment sites
- Community sites
- Other sites

An analysis of the degree to which students are accessing these various kinds of sites will provide a helpful basis for determining the degree to which the Internet is being used in schools for instructional purposes. An excessive amount of activity on sports, e-commerce, music, gaming, entertainment, and community sites equates to a significant amount of Internet recess. It is during such recess that harmful online activities are most likely to occur.

Enhancing Educational Use

To support high-quality educational use, the school needs to take at least the following steps:

- Establish and define expectations for students and staff related to the educational purpose of the district's Internet system.
- Provide sufficient professional and curriculum development to ensure that teachers are well prepared and supported in using the Internet effectively for high-quality purposes.
- Establish a controlled research resources and communications environment.

Educational Purpose. Students and teachers should understand that use of the Internet while in school must be for an *educational purpose.* This term includes use of the system for classroom activities, continuing education, professional or career development, and high-quality, educationally enriching personal research. One way to explain this standard is to indicate that the Internet should be used for activities that are related to a specific class assignment or personal research on subjects that are similar to the kinds of subjects covered in classes or nonfiction material found in the school library.

The restriction against entertainment activities should not result in a complete ban on all entertainment-oriented sites. It should be recognized that innovative teachers can make great educational use of sites with what would normally be considered noneducational content. Such use should be allowed—but only if pursuant to clear instructional objectives.

Students should understand that these limitations are quite similar to the restrictions they can expect to encounter when they join the workforce. In fact, it is very important for students to understand the differences between personal access and access through a limited-purpose system—and to learn to manage their online activities responsibly given the purpose of the Internet system.

Some schools may have after-school programs that wish to allow students to use the Internet system after school hours as a public access service. Schools should enter into an agreement with the organization providing after-school care for the appropriate supervision of student use of the computers during this time. It should be made clear that such use must be in accord with the district's disciplinary code and Internet use policy, with the exception that entertainment activities are allowed.

Professional and Curriculum Development. Effective professional and curriculum development is essential! Unfortunately, far too many teachers are not yet adequately prepared to use technology and the Internet in an effective educational manner. Two recent reports that demonstrate this are the Pew Internet and American Life report *The Digital Disconnect: The Widening Gap between Internet-Savvy Students and Their Schools* and the National School Board Association (NSBA) report *Are We There Yet?*[2]

The Pew report reached the following conclusion:

While students relate examples of both engaging and poor instructional uses of the Internet assigned by their teachers, students say that the not-so-engaging uses are the more typical of their assignments. Students repeatedly told us that the quality of their Internet-based assignments was poor and uninspiring. They want to be assigned more—and more engaging—Internet activities that are relevant to their lives. Indeed, many students assert that this would significantly improve their attitude toward school and learning.[3]

The NSBA survey also found significant lack of teacher preparation. It made the following recommendations to address this concern:

- Treat technology as an integral tool for instruction and administration—not as an add-on. Technology is not a frill—it is essential to effective instruction and school vitality.

- Use the Internet for core educational priorities that matter most to student achievement. School district leaders report strong interest in online opportunities that match federal, state and local pressures, including standards, assessments and test preparation. School decision makers should be informed by these priorities as they make choices. At the same time, schools should understand that they can harness the power of the Internet to create and support diverse learning communities.

- Invest significantly in professional development for school leaders and teachers. A broad theme emerging from survey results is that teachers need help incorporating the Internet into regular classroom instruction. For new and veteran teachers alike, the Internet is a new frontier—and one that many have little time or training to explore. Teachers need technology training to be able to use the Internet as an effective, interactive tool for teaching, learning, communicating. Teachers also need to be prepared to guide and assess students in different ways.

Teachers who are early adopters of technology tend to take great delight in the independent development of innovative lesson plans using the Internet. Unfortunately, these early adopters tend to also be the most actively involved in district or school technology coordination and, unfortunately, sometimes do not recognize that the vast majority of teachers do not have the time, skills, or inclination to develop their own Internet-based learning activities and curriculum.

Early-stage adopters are quite comfortable taking risks using new technologies. Moving beyond this group requires a shift from approaches that support early adopters to approaches that support more pragmatic second-stage adopters. Second-stage adopters tend to want to manage any risks that might be present when they and their students step onto the Internet. This is the best way to engage second-stage technology adopters:

- Provide easy access to risk-free, easily implemented Internet-related lesson plans and activities that are directly related to district curriculum objectives. This can be accomplished through a district, state, or regional Web site or through links from the district site to such resources.

- Establish subject- and grade-oriented mailing lists where teachers can be encouraged to discuss curriculum issues or share lesson plans and where second-stage adopters can rapidly receive support.

- Enlist the aid of first-stage adopters to serve as mentors and provide predeveloped Internet curriculum to the second-stage adopters.

Educational Research Resources and Controlled Communications. The initial access point for teachers and students should be a district instructional Web page that immediately directs students to high-quality educational resources that have been reviewed by a credible source. Commercial services are available that provide access to sites that have been reviewed by information professionals and determined to be appropriate for research in a school setting.

The online activities of elementary school students should be limited to previewed sites or a specific Web page for a lesson. Elementary teachers need to know how to create a Web page to support a specific lesson—and support should be provided to those who cannot do so on their own. On the rare occasions elementary students need to use the more open Internet, close supervision is essential.

Secondary schools should generally encourage student reliance on the Internet research resource, but allow specific exceptions. Exceptions may be specific classroom activities that require open access or open access upon request in the library, if the student has been unable to find necessary information in the research resource.

Far too many high-quality educational activities require online communications for a district to take the perspective that students should not be allowed to communicate electronically. The key is to establish a controlled communications environment where students know that teachers have full access to everything they write or post online. The communications environment should allow for e-mail, real-time online communications, and both blogging and "wikis" (joint development of a document or project). Companies are now providing products that offer a controlled social networking environment.

At the elementary level, a classroom communications account may be all that is necessary. At the secondary level, students will probably require individual accounts.

Supervision and Monitoring

As noted, when the Internet came into schools, filtering software was strongly promoted as the way to protect children online. This is unfortunate, as filtering software has, and will always have, significant problems. It will never be entirely effective in blocking the sites it is supposed to block.

Students can find ways to bypass a school Internet filter. Filtering technologies will never address all concerns related to student Internet use—especially concerns related to inappropriate communications. And the communication concerns are likely to increase as the entire Internet becomes more interactive.

Further, reliance on filtering has led to a false sense of security and the perception among educators that the filter will keep students safe on the Internet, so supervision is not all that important. A locked fence will provide no protection or deterrence if it is possible to climb over or under the fence when no one is looking—and an active teen will always find more ways to deal with fences, whether online or off, than an adult educator is likely to be able to comprehend. More discussion on effective management of the Internet filter appears later in this chapter.

There are clearly some benefits to seeking to block access to sites deemed unacceptable, but effective supervision and monitoring is the real key to deterrence. The higher the risk of getting caught, the lower the risk that students will engage in inappropriate activity.

What effective supervision and monitoring do is to remove the perception of invisibility. Supervision and monitoring are the way educators remain hands-on—knowing where students are, what they are doing, and who they are doing it with. When young people are in an environment where adults have remained hands-on, they are much less likely to engage in risky or inappropriate behavior.

Supervision refers to activities where school staff members are present and attentive to student Internet use as it occurs. Monitoring refers to the use of technical systems that allow for an after-the-fact analysis of student use or the technical review of student activities during use. As noted repeatedly, students should have no expectation that their online activities at school will be private.

Supervision

Clear expectations should be conveyed to staff: When students are using the Internet, staff members are expected to be present and fully attentive to student online activities. However, supervision requirements should be appropriate to the age and circumstances of the students. Teachers who are sponsoring student teachers must also make sure that the student teachers also understand how to engage in effective supervision.

To facilitate effective supervision requires consideration of the physical placement of computers. To the greatest degree possible, all computers that are used by students should be positioned so that the screen is clearly visible to others. This is more difficult when students have laptops.

Teachers must know that it is essential to move around the classroom and specifically watch for signs that students are quickly changing screens when they approach—a clear indication that what just disappeared from the screen may not have been appropriate. Teachers should know that if they perceive a student engaging in this kind of suspicious behavior or any other suspicious behavior, it is advisable to review the history file of the sites the student has accessed.

Teachers should also periodically (but randomly) ask students to show them their history file as they walk around the room. This will help the teacher know how well the students are following the lesson guidelines. It also will serve as an extremely powerful deterrent, known in behavior management terms as "variable negative reinforcement." The possibility that the teacher may ask to see their browser history and will know if they have been visiting inappropriate sites will keep most students in line. Frequent requests to see the history file at the beginning of the year will help to establish an appropriate pattern of use.

It is likely that the greatest on-campus problems will occur when students have the ability to conduct independent research in the school library or computer lab. The same "show me your history file" technique should be used by librarian or computer lab monitor. This will help to create the understanding that use of the computer in these environments still must meet the district policy requirements of an educational purpose.

Secondary schools may also consider the use of student lab monitors to provide additional supervisory capacity. Students who have been granted such authority tend to take their jobs very seriously. They consider misuse by other students to reflect badly on the entire student body. Student supervisors are also very likely to be in tune with behavioral clues that other students may demonstrate if involved in misuse.

When developing school guidelines for supervision, it is also necessary to address the significant concerns presented when substitute teachers are managing classrooms while students are using the Internet. Frequently, the presence of a substitute leads students to think they have an opportunity for Internet recess. This is especially true if the teacher has not left appropriate lesson plans or the substitute teacher does not have good computer skills.

Schools must develop specific policies and standards for teachers whose students can be anticipated to be using computers at any time when they are absent. All substitute teachers need to have a good understanding of the district Internet use policy and their requirements under that policy. It may be appropriate to have a special designation for those substitute teachers who have the training and understanding to manage student use of the Internet effectively.

Monitoring

Effective monitoring of Internet usage will help to identify instances of inappropriate or unsafe use that may have gone undetected despite appropriate supervision. The implementation of an effective monitoring system is an excellent measure to prevent problems. When students know that they are leaving little cyberfootprints that can easily be tracked by the system administrator, they are much less likely even to think of doing something that will result in detection and discipline. And this is a concept they should become accustomed to, as many employers are also monitoring employee use of the Internet.

To ensure effective monitoring, secondary students should be provided with their own unique student user IDs. Many schools follow a practice whereby students may receive this user ID only upon completion of an Internet Use Policy class. The use of a unique student user ID should not be necessary at the elementary level because the focus at this level of schooling is protection in safe Internet spaces.

Real-time monitoring can occur through the use of technologies that allow the lab supervisor to remotely view any of the computer screens in the computer lab or school. In addition, intelligent content analysis monitoring technologies now coming onto the market provide excellent monitoring capability. These technologies use linguistic analysis to filter all Internet traffic, not only Web sites but also e-mail and any real-time communication activities, and report cases of suspected violations of the Internet use policy. Administrators can then review logs and messages to determine whether there was an actual violation.

Technical monitoring systems will never be totally effective. But as long as students perceive that there is a strong likelihood that inappropriate activity will be detected, the technical monitoring system will be an effective deterrent. Clear notice will enhance the effect. A large sign in the computer lab—"All computer activity is monitored"—will be helpful.

There is, however, one downside to reliance on monitoring that must be addressed. Students must know not to rely on the monitoring system to bring cyberbullying to the attention of lab monitors or teachers. The fear is that students will think that the monitoring system will identify any cyberbullying—when it simply cannot be expected to do so. Students must understand the importance of reporting any specific instances of cyberbullying. So a second sign in the computer lab will also help. This sign should say: "If you are being cyberbullied or see that someone is being cyberbullied, report this to the office."

INTERNET USE POLICY

The district Internet use policy must be written clearly, communicated effectively, and enforced appropriately.

Appendix H contains a district Internet use policy template, and Appendix I contains an Internet use agreement that can be provided to students and parents for signature. The Internet use policy covers many aspects related to Internet use that are not closely related to cyberbullying concerns and are therefore not addressed in this chapter. An online book, *Safe and Responsible Use of the Internet: A Guide for Educators,* on the Center for Safe and Responsible Internet Use Web site at http://csriu.org, provides additional guidance on these issues.

In the United States, Internet use policies must meet the standards outlined in the Children's Internet Protection Act (CIPA). The following information addresses the requirements for an Internet Safety Plan under the framework set forth in CIPA. For readers outside the United States, compliance with CIPA is not an issue, but the points addressed here are universal to any school.

CIPA was enacted as part of the Consolidated Appropriations Act of 2001.[4] CIPA requires all schools receiving funding through the E-rate program and technology funding through Title III of the Elementary and Secondary Education Act to comply with certain requirements. Most school districts in the United States are in compliance with CIPA. Under CIPA, in addition to implementing the use of a "technology protection measure," the district must adopt an Internet safety plan that addresses the following elements:

- Access by minors to inappropriate matter on the Internet and World Wide Web.

- Safety and security of minors when using electronic mail, chat rooms, and other forms of direct electronic communications.

- Unauthorized online access by minors, including hacking and other unlawful activities.

- Unauthorized disclosure, use, and dissemination of personal information regarding minors.

- Measures designed to restrict minors' access to materials harmful to minors.[5]

Frequently, Internet use policies are written at a language level that is too complex for students, parents, and teachers. The average student in 6th grade should be able to read and understand the policy as it is stated in the Internet use agreement. Restrictions on student activities should be written with sufficient clarity to allow the students and staff to have a good idea of the boundaries between appropriate and inappropriate behavior.

The Internet use agreement may be simply one of a large number of forms that students have to bring back signed. (More on signatures later in this chapter.) In addition to obtaining a signature, the provisions of the policy should be reviewed with students at the beginning of each school year and at the beginning of class sessions in a computer lab. Key provisions of the policy can be posted in computer labs, library spaces, and classrooms with computers. The provisions can also be posted in a rotating manner on the logon screen.

The Internet use agreement should be viewed as the foundation for the instruction students and staff will receive regarding the safe and responsible use of the Internet. The Internet use agreement will provide the rules. It is exceptionally important that students and staff understand the reasons for the rules. If students and staff are unable to understand the rules in the context of the concerns and issues the rules are meant to address, the policy will have limited value as a tool to promote the safe and responsible use of the Internet. One of the recommended instructional strategies to address cyberbullying is a suggestion to compare provisions of the Internet use agreement, terms of use agreements for popular youth Web sites, and parent standards.

Many districts go through a process of having students and parents sign the Internet use agreement on an annual basis. Most districts do not require students and parents to confirm their willingness to abide by the district's other disciplinary rules. However, there are three reasons why it is advisable to obtain a parental signature on an Internet use agreement.

Limitation of liability. The best way to prevent problems related to parental overreaction to issues of concern related to Internet use, which could lead to litigation, is through the use of a warning of the possible dangers on the Internet, a disclaimer of liability, and the option for parents not to allow their child to use the Internet.

Permission for disclosure of student information on the Internet. Prior to disclosing student information on the Internet, the district must have parental permission. Since such permission is absolutely necessary, it makes sense to include the provisions requesting permission for such disclosure in a full Internet use agreement.

Copyright permission. Prior to posting student work on the Internet, it is recommended that the district receive parental permission to post such work.

These three objectives can be met by having a parent and student sign the document upon enrollment at a particular school. This would shift the document from an enclosure in the annual set of forms to the packet of papers signed upon enrollment, where it is likely to be read with more care.

Addressing Electronic Communication Concerns

The CIPA requirement most closely related to cyberbullying is the provision requiring districts to address the safety and security of minors when using electronic mail, chat rooms, and other forms of direct electronic communications. The Internet use agreement should contain at least the following provisions addressing student safety and inappropriate language in online communications:

- Elementary and middle school students should not disclose their full name or any other personal contact information for any purpose. High school students should not disclose personal contact information, except to educational institutions for educational purposes or companies or other entities for career development purposes—or with specific staff approval. Personal contact information includes any information that would allow someone to locate the student off-line.

- Students should not disclose names or personal contact information about other students under any circumstances.

- Students should not use obscene, profane, lewd, vulgar, rude, inflammatory, threatening, or disrespectful language; post any information that, if acted upon, could cause damage or a disruption of school activities; engage in personal attacks, including prejudicial or discriminatory attacks; harass or bully another person, or recklessly post false or defamatory information about a person or organization.

- Students should promptly disclose to their teacher or another school employee any message they receive from any other student that is in violation of the restrictions on inappropriate language. Students should not delete such messages until instructed to do so by a staff member.

The use of a filtering product should be considered as only one component of a comprehensive approach to address student Internet use. Such use must ensure that students are not being subjected to inappropriate viewpoint discrimination, that an effective process is in place to ensure that if the filter has blocked access to an acceptable site it can be rapidly overridden, and that the concerns of students bypassing the filter have been addressed.

Inappropriate Viewpoint Discrimination

Districts must ensure that their district filter is not itself blocking in a discriminatory manner. It is hypocritical for a district to indicate to students that they should not harass students based on perceived sexual orientation or religious beliefs when the district filter is configured to block access to information and support sites for lesbian, gay, bisexual, transsexual, or questioning (LGBTQ) students or for students who are interested in nontraditional religions, as "inappropriate content."

An analysis of the blocking categories and practices of filtering products reveals that most have categories that raise concerns about discrimination against students based on controversial minority status—LGBTQ students and students who follow nontraditional religious beliefs, such as Wicca and modern pagan groups. Other controversial sites may also be blocked, but these two minority-status concerns are most visibly evident based on a review of common blocking categories. Assuming that the school libraries have reference materials to other religions and other types of sexual health information, and the district allows access to such material online for personal research, blocking access to sites that contain information about LGBTQ and nontraditional religions is unconstitutional—based on the principles of freedom of speech and freedom of religion.

Some filtering companies create difficulties for districts seeking to respect students' rights in these controversial areas. Frequently, the filtering companies have established categories that are unclear or even misleading. The company might have mistakenly decided that sexual orientation issues should be characterized as "lifestyle" and nontraditional religions should be characterized as "cults and occult." The company may be including other material in these same categories that is inappropriate for teens. For example, the company may be blocking access to the

Gay Lesbian Straight Education Network site in the same category as sites devoted to multiple-partner relationships or "swinging."

Until such time as the filtering companies are forced to ensure that their products do not block access from public institutions based on unconstitutional bias, districts will have to be selective and creative in their implementation of these products.

For example, it is likely that the risk of student involvement in a true cult site is very low, and the dangers of leaving the category blocking access to nontraditional religions unblocked are minimal. It is advisable for districts to simply leave any category that blocks access to nontraditional religion sites unblocked.

The filtering categories that block access to sites about LGBTQ issues are more problematic. It is quite possible that sites that are unacceptable for teens are blocked in the same category as the sites that should be considered acceptable. However, it is likely that the district filter is also blocking access to other sites containing appropriate information related to sexual health. Further, students who are seeking appropriate sexual health information can accidentally get into inappropriate sites.

This provides the opportunity for a comprehensive resolution of all concerns. The district can direct the health staff, health educators, counselors, and librarians to create a district Student Health and Wellness Web page that provides links to sites deemed appropriate by these professionals for student access. The district technology department should then ensure that these selected sites are not blocked. This approach will address concerns related to the full range of appropriate health and wellness sites that may be inappropriately blocked, including sites addressing LGBTQ issues.

Need to Override the Filter

It is also essential for the district to implement its filtering system in a manner that allows selected staff to immediately override the filter. This is necessary for safety reasons. Safe schools personnel may, at any time, receive a report from a student about worrisome material that has been posted online. Consider the potential concerns if a student reports to a counselor that another student has posted material that suggests a chance of suicide and the counselor cannot investigate because of inability to override the filter and get to the site where this material is posted.

It is imperative that all safe schools personnel—including administrators, counselors or psychologists, school resource officers, librarians, and computer staff—have the authority and ability to immediately override the filter for safe schools purposes. Some filtering products make it easier than others to provide override capacity. The manner in which the filtering product has been implemented also has a bearing on this. Frequently, filtering products provide two levels of override capacity—temporary override and the ability to permanently unblock a site. The temporary override capacity should be sufficient to address safe schools concerns. Filtering systems generally track the overrides to allow for review. This should be sufficient protection for the district against misuse.

Students' Ability to Bypass the Filter

Students can bypass most Internet filters by using a variety of strategies. For more insight, simply direct any search engine to "bypass Internet filter." As with other restrictions, students tend not to bypass the filter to access pornography—the onscreen evidence means there is too great a possibility of detection of that activity. Instead, many students bypass the filter simply to get to Web sites that contain appropriate material for instructional projects—material that has been inappropriately blocked by a filter. This bypassing occurs in schools that do not have appropriate—and constitutionally required—processes to provide for the prompt override of a filter.

In the United States, librarians and computer staff must have the authority and ability to override for constitutional reasons. The American Library Association challenged the constitutionality of the CIPA due to concerns that filtering products overblock and prevent access to appropriate material. The Supreme Court upheld the constitutionality of CIPA based on the understanding that if the filter was inappropriately preventing access to a site, it could be promptly overridden.[6]

But some students are also bypassing the district's filter to participate in social networking, send messages, play games, and engage in other inappropriate online activities while at school. It is necessary to address this issue in three ways:

- Librarians and selected teachers must have the authority and ability to review any blocked sites and independently make a decision to provide access to students to sites that are deemed appropriate. Librarians and teachers are highly educated professionals who should be considered to have insight that is superior to that of the staff at filtering companies when it comes to making decisions about the appropriateness of material for students. These override decisions must be made promptly so that the filter is not interfering with student research or teacher instruction. It is also recommended that schools establish a mechanism for students to anonymously request that sites be unblocked.

- The district must review the functionality of the filter to determine whether and how easily students can bypass it without fear of detection. Adjustments must be made to prevent this from occurring.

- Intentionally bypassing the filter to get to sites that are blocked should be considered a violation of the district policy.

PERSONAL DIGITAL DEVICES

Technologies are increasingly becoming more portable and accessible. Today's cell phones can now be used to access social networking sites and engage in instant messaging. As prices are coming down, many students have (or soon will have) other personal digital devices with wireless connectivity, including laptop computers, PDAs (such as Blackberrys and Palms), digital cameras, and even wristwatch computers.

District policy and practices must take into account the fact that these technologies are extremely popular among teens, that parents want their children to have electronic access for safety and logistical reasons, and that some technologies can be very helpful educationally. Policy must also account for the fact that these technologies can be misused by students on campus to engage in cyberbullying, as well as in other misuse, including drug dealing and school cheating. Most district policies are currently directed at cell phones and will need to be expanded to address other personal digital devices.

Districts currently have implemented a range of options for the management of cell phones. The most stringent approach, which is unlikely to be acceptable to parents, is that no cell phones may be allowed on campus. Given the challenges for working parents of having to safely coordinate the logistics of a wide range of after-school activities for their children, allowing student access to cell phones while on campus will probably be necessary.

Most schools prohibit the use of cell phones in the classroom but allow students to use cell phones before and after school. Some also allow students to use cell phones during lunch. Some may allow cell phone use in the halls. But these are all policy restrictions. The reality in most schools is that students are using cell phones in most locations in the building other than the classroom—and may even be using cell phones in the classroom if the teacher is not supervising effectively.

But cell phone technology is merging into PDA technology, and there are many ways for students to use PDAs for educational activities. In fact, many schools are implementing PDA programs to support instruction. In the very near future, schools will be faced with more and more students carrying personal laptops and PDAs to take notes in class—but that will also allow rapid access to social networking sites or the ability to text message or IM other students. These personal wireless technologies can circumvent any restrictions the district may have installed on the district Internet system.

The only way to handle this situation is to allow the use of personal laptops and PDAs in class for educational purposes—under the same provisions that the district Internet system can be used. This means that just as teachers might ask to review the history file while a student is using a school computer, they should also be able to routinely review all evidence of activities by a student using a personal laptop or PDA in the classroom.

Many current district policies regarding cell phones address when cell phones can be used. Use at a time or place that is unacceptable can lead to retention of the cell phone by a school administrator and the requirement that the parent come to school to retrieve the device. But use at an inappropriate time is only one consideration. From the perspective of the need to address cyberbullying and cyberthreats, the manner of use is also important. Students should know that the disciplinary code also applies to any use of any digital device on campus—whether at a legitimate time or not. This specifically includes district policies against bullying and harassment, as well as school cheating and other offenses.

Ideally, the search and seizure standard for such devices should make it clear that if there is a reasonable suspicion that students have used a cell phone or another personal digital device in a manner contrary to school policies, the records of their activity contained on the device can be searched. As noted in chapter 7, the legal ramifications of this issue are unclear as of this writing. As more insight is developed around this issue, it will be shared via the Center for Safe and Responsible Internet Use Cyberbullying Web site at http://cyberbully.org.

Checklist for Policy: Cell Phone and Other Personal Digital Devices

Given the lack of legal clarity, resolving these issues may require shifting to a contractual agreement between the school and parents. For example, the district could set forth a policy that no student would be allowed to have a cell phone or another personal digital device on campus without a signed parental agreement. The agreement would:

- Cover all personal digital devices and all use of such devices on school property or under school sponsorship, including school transportation and school events occurring off campus.

- Make it clear that the school disciplinary code and Internet use policy restrictions on inappropriate language apply to all use of any cell phone or other personal digital device used on school property. This specifically includes the provisions on bullying and harassment, illegal activities, school cheating, and the school's search and seizure rights.

- Allow the use of personal laptops and PDAs in the classroom only for educational activities, not for personal communications or entertainment activities.

- Provide that teachers have the ability to review the history of all student activities using such personal laptops or PDAs in the classroom, pursuant to the school's general ability to monitor or search personal items of students without cause.

- Provide that if there is reasonable suspicion that the student has used the digital device in the school building or school-sponsored activity in a manner that violates the disciplinary code, the parent agrees that the school may review all records of activity on the device.

- Include a provision for an internal review process if a parent disagrees with a school official's determination that the situation raised a reasonable suspicion, as well as an agreement to submit the issue to binding arbitration following this internal review to keep any incident from resulting in a court proceeding.

It may be possible to implement these suggestions under an implied consent approach. Suggestions should be reviewed by the district's legal counsel prior to implementation. As noted previously, updated information around this issue will be available on the Center for Safe and Responsible Internet Use Cyberbullying Web site at http://cyberbully.org.

NOT A COMPLETE SOLUTION

Districts must realize that while policies and practices for managing student use of the Internet and personal digital devices are important, such policies and practices will never be fully effective in preventing or detecting all instances of cyberbullying and cyber-threats. Encouraging students to report such incidents must remain the highest priority. One fortunate aspect of technology use is that evidence of misuse is generally preserved electronically. Such preservation eliminates "he said/she said" arguments. The bottom line is that the more effective a school is in responding to reports—as perceived by the students—the more inclined students will be to report.

Appendixes

The following appendixes may be reproduced by schools and other organizations who have purchased this book for nonprofit, educational use only, with proper credit to this book as the source. These documents are also available for download on the Center for Safe and Responsible Internet Use Cyberbullying site at http://cyberbully.org, where they may be updated from time to time.

Appendix A: Cyberbullying or Cyberthreat Situation Review Process   195

Appendix A is a schematic document that can be used by a safe schools or school threat assessment committee or by an administrator, counselor, or psychologist to guide the review of a situation involving a report of cyberbullying or a cyberthreat, as discussed in chapter 8.

Appendix B: School Actions and Options   197

Appendix B is a schematic document outlining the various responses to cyberbullying or cyberthreats, as discussed in chapter 9.

Appendix C: Incident Report and Evaluation Form   199

Appendix C is an incident report form to be completed by school administrators after addressing specific incidents. This report form includes questions necessary for effective evaluation.

Appendix D: Comprehensive Plan to Address Cyberbullying and Cyberthreats   201

Appendix D is a template for a plan of action that addresses the issues discussed in chapters 10 and 11.

Appendix E: Student Needs Assessment Survey   209

Appendix E is a student needs assessment survey, like the one discussed in chapter 10. This document also provides analysis recommendations.

Appendix F: Staff Needs Assessment Questions   217

Appendix F provides questions that can be asked in the context of a staff needs assessment, as discussed in chapter 10.

Appendix G: Request for Waiver of Principles of Effectiveness   221

Appendix G is a document districts in the United States can use to request federal funds through the Safe and Drug Free Schools and Communities Act for use in connection with the program recommended here. As discussed in chapter 10, programs supported by these funds must meet certain standards for research validation. Because the concerns of cyberbullying and cyberthreats are too new for sufficient research to have taken place, a school district must request a waiver of the standards. The template in this appendix can be used to seek such a waiver.

Appendix H: District Internet Use Policy   227

Appendix H includes a model Internet use policy. As discussed in chapter 11, this is a complete policy that addresses issues in addition to cyberbullying and cyberthreats.

Appendix I: Student Internet Use Policy and Agreement   245

Appendix I is an Internet use agreement designed to be provided to students and parents. As discussed in chapter 11, this is a complete policy that addresses issues in addition to cyberbullying and cyberthreats.

Appendix J: Student Guide to Cyberbullying and Cyberthreats   255

Appendix J is a text version of this program's student curriculum.

Appendix K: Parent Guide to Cyberbullying and Cyberthreats   265

Appendix K is a text version of the program's parent guide. It can be used in four ways:

- Provided as a handout for parents at parent education presentations.

- Made available in the school office and counselor's office for any parent who is seeking additional information.

- Provided to parents who have contacted the school because of concerns that their child is a target of cyberbullying.

- Provided to parents of any child who is suspected of engaging in cyberbullying.

In this last case, an administrator may wish to highlight the portion of this document providing recommendations for how parents can intervene to stop their child's harmful activity—and the section that discusses their potential increased liability if they know their child is engaging in activities that are harming another and fail to proactively address the concerns.

Appendix L: CyberbullyNOT— Stopping Online Social Aggression   281

Appendix L is the text version of a document for parents that can be distributed in school or newsletters.

Cyberbullying or Cyberthreat Situation Review Process

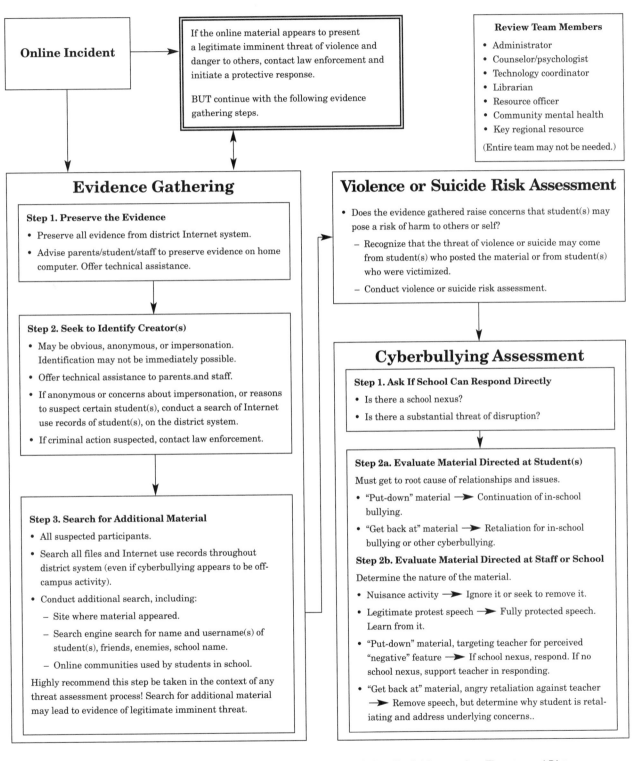

Online Incident

If the online material appears to present a legitimate imminent threat of violence and danger to others, contact law enforcement and initiate a protective response.

BUT continue with the following evidence gathering steps.

Review Team Members
- Administrator
- Counselor/psychologist
- Technology coordinator
- Librarian
- Resource officer
- Community mental health
- Key regional resource

(Entire team may not be needed.)

Evidence Gathering

Step 1. Preserve the Evidence
- Preserve all evidence from district Internet system.
- Advise parents/student/staff to preserve evidence on home computer. Offer technical assistance.

Step 2. Seek to Identify Creator(s)
- May be obvious, anonymous, or impersonation. Identification may not be immediately possible.
- Offer technical assistance to parents.and staff.
- If anonymous or concerns about impersonation, or reasons to suspect certain student(s), conduct a search of Internet use records of student(s), on the district system.
- If criminal action suspected, contact law enforcement.

Step 3. Search for Additional Material
- All suspected participants.
- Search all files and Internet use records throughout district system (even if cyberbullying appears to be off-campus activity).
- Conduct additional search, including:
  - Site where material appeared.
  - Search engine search for name and username(s) of student(s), friends, enemies, school name.
  - Online communities used by students in school.

Highly recommend this step be taken in the context of any threat assessment process! Search for additional material may lead to evidence of legitimate imminent threat.

Violence or Suicide Risk Assessment

- Does the evidence gathered raise concerns that student(s) may pose a risk of harm to others or self?
  - Recognize that the threat of violence or suicide may come from student(s) who posted the material or from student(s) who were victimized.
  - Conduct violence or suicide risk assessment.

Cyberbullying Assessment

Step 1. Ask If School Can Respond Directly
- Is there a school nexus?
- Is there a substantial threat of disruption?

Step 2a. Evaluate Material Directed at Student(s)

Must get to root cause of relationships and issues.
- "Put-down" material → Continuation of in-school bullying.
- "Get back at" material → Retaliation for in-school bullying or other cyberbullying.

Step 2b. Evaluate Material Directed at Staff or School

Determine the nature of the material.
- Nuisance activity → Ignore it or seek to remove it.
- Legitimate protest speech → Fully protected speech. Learn from it.
- "Put-down" material, targeting teacher for perceived "negative" feature → If school nexus, respond. If no school nexus, support teacher in responding.
- "Get back at" material, angry retaliation against teacher → Remove speech, but determine why student is retaliating and address underlying concerns..

APPENDIX B

School Actions and Options

Formal Disciplinary Action

Can impose formal disciplinary response if have established a school nexus and substantial and material disruption. BUT still need to address:

- Removal of materials and potential of retaliation by student or online "buddies."
- If "put-down" cyberbully, stop all in-school bullying. If "get back at" cyberbully, stop all in-school victimization.
- Support needs of target.

If cannot impose formal discipline, other action options still available.

Working With Parents

Child Who Is "Put-Down" Cyberbully

Assumptions

- Parents unaware, but actions are against family values.
- Initial response will be disbelief, followed by anger and humiliation.
- Parents naïve about strategies to manage Internet use.

Process

- Send downloaded material and Parent Guide to parents via certified mail.
- Request meeting following day.
- Seek parental commitment to:
  - Establish prohibitions.
  - Install and use monitoring software.
  - Limit student's access through other venues.

Increased potential for financial liability through civil litigation is a strong leverage.

Child Who Is Target, "Get Back At" Cyberbully, or Child Who Has Posted Distressing Material

- Parent could approach school, or school could find out from other source.
- Initial response of parent will be significant concern for safety and well-being of child.
- If contacting parent about reported concern, establish preliminary plan of action for support prior to meeting with parent.
- If working with parent of "get back at" cyberbully or student who has posted distressing material:
  - Ensure material is removed.
  - Install and use monitoring software.
  - Address underlying bullying or emotional concerns.
- If working with parent of target:
  - Explain limitations on formal response, but commit to assist in other ways.
  - Help parent file a complaint with the Web site or service provider.
  - Warn to watch for retaliation.

Working with Students

Working with Student Who Is Target

Addiction

- Address concerns of addiction to harmful online community.
  - Convince target to leave community.
  - Find way to get the cyberbullying to stop within the community.

Online Bully-Proofing

- Communications are preserved so student and counselor can evaluate and determine patterns of communication that may be precipitating bullying.
- Impact of harmful communication is invisible if target does not immediately respond.
- Delay in commincation can provide opportunity for target to calm down and respond with strength.

When to Ask for Help

Encourage students to tell an adult if:

- They are really upset and not sure what to do.
- The cyberbullying could be a crime.
- Any cyberbullying is or might be through the Internet or cell phone at school.
- They are being bullied by the same person at school.
- The cyberbully is anonymous.
- The cyberbully is bullying other students who may be more vulnerable.

Cyberbullying Response Options

- Target can tell cyberbully to stop.
- Target can ignore cyberbully.
- Target or advocate can:
  - File a complaint with Web site or service provider.
  - Contact cyberbully's parents.
  - Contact an attorney.
  - Contact the police.

APPENDIX C

Incident Report and Evaluation Form

Names of student(s) involved: Date:

Name(s) of district staff and any community professionals involved in resolution of incident:

1. Describe incident and attach all downloaded material:

2. Describe how the identities of the creator(s) of the material were identified:

3. Did the evidence gathered raise concerns that student(s) involved posed a risk of harm to others or themselves? If, "yes" how were these concerns addressed?

4. Was a determination made that the school could impose formal discipline? Describe the rationale for this decision:

5. Describe the underlying relationships between all parties:

6. Describe the actions taken to resolve the incident:

7. What insight or issues were raised by this incident that ought to be addressed in the context of the district's ongoing efforts to address these concerns?

8. *(To school administrator)* Following any incident, send a letter to all parents involved, stating the following:

   [School] is striving to respond in a highly effective manner to address concerns of cyberbullying and cyberthreats. Our objective is to resolve the incident so that our students can feel safe and secure at school and in their relationships with other students. Because you were recently involved in an incident, it would be very helpful to have your feedback on how effectively this incident was handled. The feedback you submit will be shared with the district safe schools committee. Your identity will be kept confidential.

   • In general, what are your overall feelings about the school's response to this incident?

   • How does your child feel about the response to the incident?

   • Are there any continuing problems that we should be aware of?

   • What aspects of the school's response were most helpful?

   • What aspects of the school's response were least helpful?

   • Are there any ways you think we could improve on our response?

9. *(To school administrator)* Summarize the responses of parents. Pose similar questions to students, preferably in written format.

From *Cyberbullying and Cyberthreats: Responding to the Challenge of Online Social Aggression, Threats, and Distress,* by N.E. Willard, © 2007, Champaign, IL: Research Press (800-519-2707; www.researchpress.com).

APPENDIX D

Comprehensive Plan to Address Cyberbullying and Cyberthreats

COMPREHENSIVE PLANNING

Objectives	Rationale	Action Steps	Responsibility	Timeline	Costs	Assessment
District and schools will achieve greater coordination between safe schools (SS) personnel and educational technology (ET) personnel to more effectively address concerns of cyberbullying and cyberthreats (CB/CT). (ET personnel include technology staff and library media specialists.)	SS personnel address youth risk issues but have limited experience with Internet use issues. ET personnel address Internet use issues, but have limited understanding of youth risk issues. To effectively address CB/CT concerns, requires both SS and ET expertise. Protective Factor Coordination of SS and ET staff will improve understanding and responsiveness.	District technology coordinator and library media specialist will become permanent members of district SS committee. ET personnel will be added to safe schools committees. (District may want to establish a work group of SS and ET committee members to create and implement comprehensive plan of action. SS committee would have ongoing management responsibility.)	District leadership School leadership SS/ET committees	SS committee membership changes implemented during _/_ school year and continued thereafter.	To be determined	Survey SS and ET personnel on an annual basis to assess effectiveness of current coordination arrangement.

From Cyberbullying and Cyberthreats: Responding to the Challenge of Online Social Aggression, Threats, and Distress, by N.E. Willard, © 2007, Champaign, IL: Research Press (800-519-2707; www.researchpress.com).

POLICY AND PRACTICES REVIEW

Objectives	Rationale	Action Steps	Responsibility	Timeline	Costs	Assessment
The district's Internet use policies and practices will reinforce the importance of use for educational purposes only, reduce the potential for misuse, and increase detection of misuse through effective supervision and monitoring. The district personal digital devices policy and practices reduce the potential for misuse and increase the detection of misuse. The district's Internet filter will be managed in a nondiscriminatory manner. Safe school and other staff will have prompt override capacity. All staff, students, and parents will have an excellent understanding of policy provisions.	District policies do not address current concerns. Policies must address appropriate uses and new technologies, be clearly linked with disciplinary code, establish monitoring and search and seizure standards, and address attempts to bypass school filter. Policies must be communicated effectively to staff, students, parents. Protective Factors • Students require a clear understanding of district policies. • Limiting Internet use to educational purposes will limit potential for misuse. • Increased potential for detection will reduce misuse. • Students will be more inclined to report concerns if they have a better understanding of the policies.	Survey staff about policy issues. Review Internet use records. Review existing policies and practices, revise language, approve new policies and practices. Develop strategies to communicate policies. Give staff authority and ability to override filter. Conduct needs assessment to reveal additional issues that should be addressed, possibly including: • Improving research resources. • Establishing controlled communications. • Offering more professional and curriculum development. • Acquiring different filtering product and/or monitoring technologies.	SS and ET committees (or work group) coordinate revision of policies and practices. Technology services director/ET committee coordinate other aspects of practices/management of Internet.	Implemented during __/__ school year and continued thereafter.	To be determined	• Survey school leadership on annual basis to determine effectiveness of new policies and practices. • SS and ET committees (or work group) review reports of policy violations to assess effectiveness of new policies. • Selected students and staff will be surveyed at the end of the school year to determine knowledge of policy provisions and effectiveness of practices.

Comprehensive Plan of Action (page 2 of 7)

REPORT, REVIEW, AND INTERVENTION PROCESS

Objectives	Rationale	Action Steps	Responsibility	Timeline	Costs	Assessment
District will establish and schools will implement a process to encourage student reports and allow for effective review and response to online risk concerns.	Adults are not generally present in online communities; therefore, student reporting of concerns is essential to resolving concerns before significant harm is incurred. Students are generally unwilling to talk with adults about Internet activities. They will not be willing to report online concerns unless they perceive that adults can and will effectively review and respond to address concerns. Protective Factor The key to encouraging student reporting of concerns to adults is an effective process to review and respond to such reports. (The recommended review and response process is set forth in Appendixes A and B.)	Schools will implement anonymous reporting mechanism. All members of SS committees will receive professional development in effective review and response process and options. District will establish online complaint-reporting process. Students will be informed about reporting, review, and response process.	District SS committee will establish guidelines for implementation at schools.	Implemented during __/__ school year and continued thereafter.	To be determined	The school review and response process will include required reporting to the district of any situations involving CB/CT. The reporting form will include an evaluation component. The district SS committee will review all reported situations on a regular basis to determine effectiveness of all aspects of intervention approach.

PROFESSIONAL DEVELOPMENT

Objectives	Rationale	Action Steps	Responsibility	Timeline	Costs	Assessment
All district staff will have sufficient knowledge of CB/CT, in light of position and job responsibilities, to ensure effective school response to online concerns.	The approach to providing professional development should be guided by position and job responsibilities. _Protective Factor_ Increased educator understanding will enhance effectiveness of the district's educational initiative and improve detection and intervention in specific instances.	Two key district staff members, one with technology expertise and one with safe schools expertise, obtain sufficient professional development to serve as resources for all district personnel. All school-level SS and ET personnel will receive sufficient professional development to enable them to fulfill roles necessary for review and response. Other district staff will be provided with general information about online youth risk concerns.	SS/ET committees (or work group)	Implemented during __/__ school year and continued thereafter.	To be determined	Staff evaluation of professional development programs following the completion of such programs. District SS evaluation of situation reports to determine necessary professional development improvements.

PARENT OUTREACH

Objectives	Rationale	Action Steps	Responsibility	Timeline	Costs	Assessment
Parents will gain sufficient understanding of the issues to enable them to provide guidance to their children on:	It is essential to enlist the assistance of parents to address these concerns because much of youth online activity occurs at home.	The district will post information for parents on the district Web site.	SS committee School leaders	Implemented during __/__ school year and continuing thereafter.	To be determined	Parent "leaders" (e.g., PTA leadership) requested to solicit input from other parents and report on the perceived effectiveness of the information dissemination.
• Appropriate standards for online communications.	Many parents are not providing sufficient guidance to their children or monitoring their online activities.	Schools will send brief information home to parents in a newsletter.				
• Effective strategies to prevent and respond to cyberbullying and other online risk situations.	Providing parent education is difficult; therefore, many different approaches are necessary.	Schools will offer a workshop on Internet safety and responsible use issues to parents.				Parents who attend a parent workshop will be requested to complete an evaluation after the workshop.
• Concerns about posting material that could be viewed as a threat and the importance of reporting any possible threats or situations involving cyberbullying to appropriate adults.	The community outreach program will provide an additional approach to parent outreach. Protective Factor Increasing parental involvement will reduce CB/CT concerns and improve responsiveness to specific incidents to reduce harm to students.	Schools will provide more in-depth information to parents at school. Safe schools personnel will provide in-depth information to any parents whose children have become involved in a risky online situation.				Parents of children who have become involved in risky online situations and who receive informational material will be requested to provide an evaluation regarding the helpfulness of the material.
• How to more effectively monitor their child's online activities and detect and respond to concerns.						

Comprehensive Plan of Action (page 5 of 7)

205

COMMUNITY OUTREACH

Objectives	Rationale	Action Steps	Responsibility	Timeline	Costs	Assessment
Key community partners, especially law enforcement (LE) and community mental health (CMH) organizations, will have a sufficient understanding of online youth risk concerns so that school officials can coordinate responses to specific situations when necessary. The district will seek to enlist the aid of other community organizations that serve youth and parents—including the public library, youth organizations, and faith-based organizations—in the dissemination of information about CB/CT. The district will work with local news media to assist in educating parents and the general public.	Resolution of specific situations may require collaboration with LE and/or CMH professionals. Providing informational materials and education to community organizations will reinforce parent and student education. Some community organizations also provide students with Internet access. Local press can provide an effective conduit for education. <u>Protective Factor</u> A community-wide approach will enhance the effectiveness of the district's educational initiative and intervention in specific instances.	The LE and CMH representatives on the SS committee will develop a plan of action to engage other relevant representatives of these communities. The district will (options): • Send informational materials to key community organizations. • Provide information to the local newspaper about the availability of informational materials. • Host a workshop for local community organizations. The district's press contact will know which knowledgeable staff members can serve as press contacts about these concerns. The district will seek to use press contacts as a vehicle to educate parents and other community members.	SS committee	Plan of action to be developed ___ (date).	To be determined	Following any situations involving LE and/or CMH, participants will be requested to submit evaluations. Organizations that request or who have been known to use informational materials will be asked to provide information on how those materials were/are being used and their perceived effectiveness.

Comprehensive Plan of Action (page 6 of 7)

206

STUDENT EDUCATION

Objectives	Rationale	Action Steps	Responsibility	Timeline	Costs	Assessment
Starting at the ___ grade level, students will receive instruction on CB/CT issues.	It is necessary to provide students with sufficient information about these concerns so that they understand the risks and know how to take steps to protect themselves independently. Influencing student attitudes about appropriate norms for online behavior and willingness to involve adults in situations are the foundation for effective prevention and response. Protective Factors Students will: • Develop and articulate personal responsible standards for online communications. • Implement effective strategies to prevent and respond to cyberbullying. • Not post material that could be viewed as a threat. • Report threats or situations involving cyberbullying to adults.	To initiate this new program, students in all grades will receive introductory instruction about these concerns. Thereafter, instruction will be incorporated into appropriate classes, as determined by each middle and high school. Instruction will use basic informational materials and relevant news stories about incidents.	School SS committees	Implemented during ___/___ school year and continuing thereafter.	To be determined	The instructional materials conclude with questions posed to students about these concerns. Student classroom discussions will serve as informal focus groups to assess student experiences, understandings, and attitudes. Teachers who provide instruction will report to SS committees about student reception of the instruction and comments made during discussions related to experiences, understandings, and attitudes. Students who are involved in incidents as bystanders, reporters, or participants will be requested to provide feedback to district on effectiveness of education and district response.

Comprehensive Plan of Action (page 7 of 7)

Student Needs Assessment Survey

The following survey is seeking information from students about cyberbullying and cyberthreats. The results of this survey will help your school respond to these concerns. Your responses to this survey are confidential. You may also choose not to complete this survey. (The term *parent* means anyone serving in a parenting role.)

Survey Questions

1. What grade are you in? ____

2. What is your gender? ___ M ___ F

3. Do you use the Internet at home? ___ Yes ___ No

4. Approximately how many hours are you online on a typical day during the week? ___

5. What are your favorite online activities? (Please check all that apply.)

   ___ Communicating with school friends.

   ___ Meeting new people in online social communities.

   ___ Surfing to look for stuff or learn new things.

   ___ Playing online games.

   ___ Shopping.

   ___ Homework.

   ___ Designing Web sites or profiles.

   ___ Other: _____.

6. Do you use a cell phone to communicate with other students while at school?

___ Yes ___ No

7. Have your parents talked with you about how you should treat others online?

___ Yes ___ No

8. How often do your parents look at what you are doing online?

___ Frequently ___ Occasionally ___ Never

9. Do you have a profile on a social networking site like MySpace or Xanga?

___ Yes ___ No

   a. If you have a profile, how often do your parents look at your profile?

   ___ Frequently ___ Occasionally ___ Never

10. How often do you discuss what you are doing online with your parents?

___ Frequently ___ Occasionally ___ Never

11. In the last six months, have you:

   a. Been in an online fight?

      ___ Yes, 1 to 4 times ___ Yes, 5 or more times ___ No

   b. Received online messages that made you very afraid for your safety?

      ___ Yes, 1 to 4 times ___ Yes, 5 or more times ___ No

   c. Received mean or nasty messages from someone?

      ___ Yes, 1 to 4 times ___ Yes, 5 or more times ___ No

   d. Sent mean or nasty messages to someone?

      ___ Yes, 1 to 4 times ___ Yes, 5 or more times ___ No

   e. Been put down online by someone who has sent or posted cruel gossip, rumors, or other harmful material?

      ___ Yes, 1 to 4 times ___ Yes, 5 or more times ___ No

f. Put down someone else online by sending or posting cruel gossip, rumors, or other harmful material?

___ Yes, 1 to 4 times ___ Yes, 5 or more times ___ No

g. Had someone pretend to be you and send or post material that damaged your reputation or friendships?

___ Yes, 1 to 4 times ___ Yes, 5 or more times ___ No

h. Pretend to be someone else to send or post material to damage that person's reputation or friendships?

___ Yes, 1 to 4 times ___ Yes, 5 or more times ___ No

i. Had someone share your personal secrets or images online without your permission?

___ Yes, 1 to 4 times ___ Yes, 5 or more times ___ No

j. Shared someone's personal secrets or images online without that person's permission?

___ Yes, 1 to 4 times ___ Yes, 5 or more times ___ No

k. Been excluded from an online group by people who are being mean to you?

___ Yes, 1 to 4 times ___ Yes, 5 or more times ___ No

l. Helped exclude someone else from your online group?

___ Yes, 1 to 4 times ___ Yes, 5 or more times ___ No

12. How frequently do you think other students at your school are cyberbullied?

___ Frequently ___ Occasionally ___ Never ___ Don't know

13. Have you seen, or do you know of, material posted online that denigrates or puts down a school staff member?

___ Yes ___ No

14. Have you seen, or do you know of, any students who posted material online that threatened or suggested violence?

___ Yes ___ No

15. Have you seen, or do you know of, any students who posted material online that threatened or suggested suicide?

___ Yes ___ No

16. Have you seen, or do you know of, any students who participate in online hate groups?

___ Yes ___ No ___

17. Have you seen, or do you know of, any students who participate in online gangs?

___ Yes ___ No ___

18. How often do you think cyberbullying occurs when students are using school computers?

___ Frequently ___ Occasionally ___ Never ___ Don't know

19. How often do you think cyberbullying occurs through cell phones or PDAs used at school?

___ Frequently ___ Occasionally ___ Never ___ Don't know

20. How often do students bypass the district's Internet filter to get to sites that have been blocked by the filter?

___ Frequently ___ Occasionally ___ Never ___ Don't know

21. If you saw that someone was being cyberbullied, how likely is it that you would do the following:

a. Join in by posting similar material.

___ Very likely ___ Somewhat likely ___ Somewhat unlikely ___ Very unlikely

b. Support the cyberbully.

___ Very likely ___ Somewhat likely ___ Somewhat unlikely ___ Very unlikely

c. Read the material, but not contribute.

___ Very likely ___ Somewhat likely ___ Somewhat unlikely ___ Very unlikely

d. Avoid or leave the online environment.

___ Very likely ___ Somewhat likely ___ Somewhat unlikely ___ Very unlikely

e. Complain to others, but not directly to the cyberbully.

___ Very likely ___ Somewhat likely ___ Somewhat unlikely ___ Very unlikely

f. Try to help the victim privately.

___ Very likely ___ Somewhat likely ___ Somewhat unlikely
___ Very unlikely

g. Tell the cyberbully to stop.

___ Very likely ___ Somewhat likely ___ Somewhat unlikely
___ Very unlikely

h. Support the victim publicly.

___ Very likely ___ Somewhat likely ___ Somewhat unlikely
___ Very unlikely

i. Report the cyberbullying to someone who can help.

___ Very likely ___ Somewhat likely ___ Somewhat unlikely
___ Very unlikely

22. What are some things you can do that could reduce the possibility that you might be cyberbullied? (Please list all actions you can think of.)

23. If you were being cyberbullied, what would you do? (Please list all actions you can think of.)

24. If you were being cyberbullied and you could not get it to stop by yourself, would you tell your parents?

___ Very likely ___ Somewhat likely ___ Somewhat unlikely
___ Very unlikely ___ Not sure

25. If you were being cyberbullied at school, would you tell a school staff member?

___ Very likely ___ Somewhat likely ___ Somewhat unlikely
___ Very unlikely ___ Not sure

26. If you saw or knew that another student was being cyberbullied, would you tell your parents or a school staff member?

___ Very likely ___ Somewhat likely ___ Somewhat unlikely
___ Very unlikely ___ Not sure

27. If you saw or knew that a student had posted material threatening or suggesting violence or suicide, would you tell your parents or a school staff member?

___ Very likely ___ Somewhat likely ___ Somewhat unlikely ___ Very unlikely ___ Not sure

28. If you saw or knew that a student was participating in a hate group or gang, would you tell a school staff member?

___ Very likely ___ Somewhat likely ___ Somewhat unlikely ___ Very unlikely ___ Not sure

29. What would your concerns about telling your parents be?

30. What would your concerns about telling a school staff member be?

Thank you for your help.

Student Survey: Data Analysis and Evaluation

Questions 1 through 6 will provide basic demographic data. Over time, the district will be also able to track the amount of Internet use and activities.

Questions 7 through 10 address the important issue of parental involvement. An increase in the percentage of students reporting greater parental involvement would indicate success of the parent education program.

Question 11 asks about personal involvement in cyberbullying, as a target or as a perpetrator. For those districts interested in a more sophisticated analysis, the data in this question can be compared to data in questions 1 through 10 to determine the relationship between age, gender, online activity, and parental involvement and reports of cyberbullying involvement.

Questions 12 through 17 provide an indication of the degree to which students believe that these harmful activities are occurring. The questions were phrased "Have you seen . . ." because it is likely that students will more freely report behavior they witness than they will report their own online activities, if those activities are considered inappropriate.

Ideally, the numbers of students reporting personal involvement or knowledge of these online harmful activities will decrease. However, districts are advised to be cautious in their reliance on this data to determine effectiveness for two reasons:

- There may be an increase in reports because increased awareness of concerns has led to increased sensitivity to the issue.

- All indications are that these concerns are increasing, along with the amount of teen online activity. As noted in chapter 3, in a survey that was originally administered in 2000 and then readministered in 2006, the rate of reported cyberbullying doubled.[*]

Given the lack of understanding about these concerns, a district that holds the incident rates stable or has only a modest increase may be addressing the concerns in a highly effective manner.

Questions 18 through 20 will provide specific insight into the effectiveness of the district's current policies and practices around Internet, cell phone, and PDA use.

Question 21 assesses bystander responses. Responses "a" and "b" can be considered harmful; responses "c" and "d" are neutral; and responses "e" through "i" are favorable responses. Over time, a decrease in students answering "very likely" or "somewhat likely" to responses "a" through "d" and an increase in these answers to responses "e" through "i" would indicate success in achieving the instructional objectives.

Questions 22 and 23 were specifically written open-ended to assess student knowledge of potentially effective ways to prevent and respond to cyberbullying incidents. The more potential responses a student can generate, the greater the personal power that student should feel in knowing how to prevent such incidents and respond to specific situations. An increase in the number of potentially effective ways to prevent and respond will indicate successful implementation of the student's education.

Questions 24 through 28 assess student comfort in reporting online concerns to adults. Questions 29 and 30 specifically solicit reasons for such reporting behavior. The answers to these questions can provide valuable insight into the development of educational and practical strategies to encourage reporting. Periodic assessment will allow the district to determine whether the educational program and the district's reporting, review, and response efforts have resulted in an increase in youth inclination to report online concerns to adults.

---

[*] Wolak, J., Mitchell, K., & Finkelhor, D. (2006). *Online victimization of youth: Five years later.*
www.unh.edu/ccrc/second_youth_Internetsafety-publications-html.

Staff Needs Assessment Questions

1. How significant are the following concerns:

    a. How significant is the concern of cyberbullying for your students?

    b. Is cyberbullying occurring when students are using school computers?

    c. Is cyberbullying occurring when students are using cell phones or other digital devices while at school?

    d. Are students posting material online that denigrates or puts down school staff members?

    e. Are students posting material online that appears to threaten violence?

    f. Are students posting material online that appears to threaten or suggest the possibility of an act of self-harm, such as suicide?

    g. Are students participating in online hate groups?

    h. Are students participating in online gang activity?

    i. Are students able to bypass the district's Internet filter to get to sites that have been blocked by the filter, including sites where they can communicate with other students or post information online?

2. How effective is the district's Internet use policy:

    a. Does the district's Internet use policy adequately address concerns of cyberbullying using the district Internet system?

    b. Is the Internet use policy clearly linked to the disciplinary code?

c. Are students aware that bypassing the filter is unacceptable?

d. Are students aware that the district's search and seizure standards apply to Internet use?

e. Is the policy readable?

f. Are issues related to appropriate Internet use addressed in other educational ways?

3. How effective is the district's cell phone and personal digital devices policy:

a. Does the district's cell phone policy adequately address concerns of cyberbullying by students using cell phones or other devices on campus?

b. Does the policy also cover personal digital devices that may be used by students in class?

c. Does the cell phone policy limit use of the cell phone during school hours?

d. Is the policy clearly linked to the disciplinary code?

e. Are students aware that the district's search and seizure standards apply to cell phones or other digital devices, including the ability to review messages if there is a reasonable suspicion of inappropriate activity?

f. Is the policy readable?

g. Are issues related to the appropriate use of cell phones and other digital devices addressed in other educational ways?

4. How effectively does the district's current Internet use management approach promote the effective educational use of the Internet?

a. Are teachers prepared to use Internet technologies for effective instructional activities?

b. Are teachers supervising student Internet use effectively?

c. Do current technical protection measures limit noneducational use?

d. Can current practices and technical protection measures detect instances of inappropriate use?

e. Can individual student use be tracked effectively?

f. Can teachers and librarians rapidly override the filter to access inappropriately blocked sites? (If they can't, this will be an argument used by students for why they have to bypass the filter.)

g. Is the district's filter blocking online material in a manner that is discriminatory and therefore could provide additional basis for cyberbullying or bullying?

5. How effective is district response to online concerns:

a. How inclined do students appear to be to report online concerns?

b. What factors might be encouraging or discouraging student reporting?

c. How well prepared are school leaders to respond to student reports of online concerns?

d. What factors might be reducing or enhancing the effectiveness of a school response (for example, legal, technical, parents)?

Request for Waiver of Principles of Effectiveness

BACKGROUND

All activities proposed for a Safe and Drug Free Schools and Communities Act (SDFSCA) plan must meet standards known as "principles of effectiveness."[1] These standards seek to ensure that state and local entities are held accountable for achieving measurable results. If a district is experiencing unique challenges and has ideas for new approaches that have not been fully tested through scientific research, the district may request a waiver of the SDFSCA requirement that the activity be based on scientifically based research.[2] The district must demonstrate that the proposed program or activity is innovative and has a substantial likelihood of success.

Addressing cyberbullying and related concerns is clearly a unique new challenge. The following kinds of information are considered necessary to support a waiver of the requirement that a program has been demonstrated to be effective through scientific research

- A needs assessment based on objective data that describes the problems or concerns currently faced.

- A description of the performance measure or measures the program or activity will address.

- The rationale for the program or activity, including how it is designed and why it is expected to be successful in accomplishing the improvements described in the performance measures.

---

[1]Section 4155(a)(1).
[2]Section 4115(a)(3).

- A discussion of the most significant risk and protective factors the program or activity is designed to target.

- A detailed description of the implementation plan, including a description of how the program or activity will be carried out, the personnel to be involved, the intended audience or target population, and the time frame for conducting the program or activity.

- A detailed description of all costs associated with carrying out the program or activity.

- An evaluation plan that addresses the methods used to assess progress toward attaining goals and objectives; the personnel who will conduct evaluation; the way the results of the evaluation will be used to refine, improve, and strengthen the district's comprehensive plan; and the way progress toward attaining objectives will be publicly reported.

- Evidence to support that the program has a "substantial likelihood of success," including a description of the prevention research and principles the program is based upon; a description of the results achieved from previous implementation of the activity or program in a setting similar to the one the district is proposing, together with a description of the rigor of evaluation conducted to determine such results; or, if the program has not yet been rigorously evaluated, a description of the plan and timeline for doing so.

The comprehensive plan set forth in Appendix D includes the components necessary to meet the requirements for a waiver of the principles of effectiveness. The following template can be used by districts as a guide for a district request for such a waiver in the event the district desires to use SDFSCA funds to support a response to cyberbullying and cyberthreats.

Request for Waiver Template

[Name] School District requests a waiver of the Safe and Drug Free Schools and Communities Act requirement that programs meet the Principles of Effectiveness standard. [Name] School District seeks to use SDFSCA funds to implement and evaluate a comprehensive program to address cyberbullying, cyberthreats, and other Internet use concerns. These new concerns have emerged in recent years as a result of significantly increased youth activity on the Internet and use of cell phones and other personal digital devices.

The approach that will be implemented by [Name] School District has not yet been subjected to rigorous, scientifically based research to determine its effectiveness because the concerns have just recently emerged, and there has been insufficient time to conduct research on effectiveness of strategies.

The comprehensive approach the district will implement has been developed by the Center for Safe and Responsible Internet Use and is fully outlined in the book *Cyberbullying and Cyberthreats: Responding to the Challenge of Online Social Aggression, Threats, and Distress*. This book describes the challenges and the prevention research and principles upon which the approach is based. A copy of the book can be provided upon request.

This approach incorporates key components of programs that have been determined to be successful in preventing face-to-face bullying—specifically, the Olweus Bullying Prevention Program, along with current practices in threat assessment, as recommended by the U.S. Secret Service, and with suicide prevention plans. The approach additionally incorporates components necessary to address the management of technology use in schools, issues related to the ways in which youth are using and misusing technologies, and legal restrictions on school-imposed discipline that result from free-speech protections for student off-campus speech.

Further, the approach implemented by the district will incorporate ongoing evaluation and analysis, which will provide insight into the effectiveness of the program and the opportunity to modify the program when necessary. The district will remain in communication with the Center for Safe and Responsible Internet Use to both provide and gain updated recommendations on effective strategies to address these concerns.

Needs Assessment

[Name] School District has conducted two types of needs assessment:

- *Student Survey.* This survey, administered to selected middle and high school students, assessed the following: general information, Internet use, parent or guardian involvement in Internet use, personal experiences and insight into other students' experiences with cyberbullying and other concerns, bystander behavior, and reporting behavior.

- *Staff Assessment.* The staff needs assessment assessed the degree to which safe schools and educational technology personnel perceive problems. This assessment solicited insight into perceptions about the adequacy of current school policies and implementation of those policies, Internet use management issues, and reporting and response concerns.

The results of the needs assessments are attached. These results indicate significant concerns related to student involvement in cyberbullying, as well as some concerns related to cyberthreats.

Comprehensive Plan of Action

The attached comprehensive plan of action has been developed by [specify—probably a work group consisting of members of the district safe schools committee and educational technology committee]. This plan of action has been reviewed and approved by [specify— probably the full district safety committee, including community members, the district educational technology committee, and the district leadership council].

The comprehensive plan of action includes the following:

- Objectives
- Rationale and protective factors
- Action steps

- Responsibilities
- Time line
- Costs
- Assessment and evaluation plan

Substantial Likelihood of Success

There is a substantial likelihood of success in the implementation of this program because it is grounded in research and principles that are known to be effective in reducing bullying behavior, as well as insight into the emerging concerns. Further, a comprehensive evaluation approach has been built into the plan of action, and the [Name] School District will be communicating regularly with others who are also implementing this program to exchange information about effective strategies.

District Internet Use Policy

A. BASIC PROVISIONS

1. The [Name] School District is providing Internet access to its employees, board members, and students. The district's Internet system has a limited educational purpose and has not been established as a public access service or a public forum. The district has the right to place restrictions on use to ensure that use of the system is in accord with its limited educational purpose.

2. Student use of the district's Internet system will be governed by this policy, related district and school regulations, and the student disciplinary code. Staff use will be governed by this policy, related district and school regulations, district employment policy, and the collective bargaining agreement. The due process rights of all users will be respected in the event there is a suspicion of inappropriate use of the district Internet system. Users have limited privacy expectations in the contents of their personal files and records of their online activity while on the district system.

3. Students' constitutional rights to freedom of speech and freedom to access information will be protected when they use the Internet in school. The district Internet system is a limited public forum. The district may restrict access to materials or may place restrictions on student speech for valid educational reasons. The district will not restrict student access to information or speech on the basis of viewpoint discrimination.

4. The district makes no warranties of any kind, either express or implied, that the functions or the services provided by or through the district Internet system will be error-free or without defect. The district will not be responsible for any damage users

may suffer, including but not limited to loss of data, interruptions of service, or exposure to inappropriate material or people. The district will not be responsible for the accuracy or quality of the information obtained through the system. The district will not be responsible for financial obligations arising through the unauthorized use of the system. Users or parents of users will indemnify and hold the district harmless from any losses sustained as the result of misuse of the system by that user. Use of the system by students will be limited to those students whose parents have signed a disclaimer of claims for damages against the district.

5. The district has developed and approved this policy in accord with the statutory requirements of the Children's Internet Protection Act. The policy was developed with input and feedback from staff, students, parents, and community members. The policy represents the district's good-faith efforts to promote the safe, ethical, responsible, and legal use of the Internet, support the effective use of the Internet for educational purposes, protect students against potential dangers in their use of the Internet, and ensure accountability.

B. DUE PROCESS

1. The [Name] School District will cooperate fully with local, state, or federal officials in any investigation involving or relating to any unlawful activities conducted through the district Internet system.

2. User access to the district Internet system will require the use of an account name and password to enable individual users to be identified. [Optional: You may wish to add "Elementary students may use the Internet through a classroom user account and password" here.]

3. In the event of an allegation that a student has violated this policy, the student will be provided with notice and an opportunity to be heard in the manner set forth in the student disciplinary code.

4. Employee violations of this policy will be handled in accord with district policy and the collective bargaining agreement.

5. Notice of student or staff violation of this policy shall be forwarded to the [name of committee] to facilitate evaluation of the policy and the implementation strategies.

C. EDUCATIONAL PURPOSE

1. The district's Internet system has a limited educational purpose.

   a. The term *educational purpose* includes use of the system for classroom activities, continuing education, professional or career development, and high-quality, educationally enriching personal research.

   b. Students may not use the system for personal commercial purposes, including offering or purchasing products or services. Staff may use the system for personal commercial purposes if such use is extremely limited.

   c. Users may not use the system for lobbying activities, as defined under [applicable statute prohibiting use of public funds for lobbying]. This provision shall not limit the use of the system by students or staff for the purposes of communicating with elected representatives or expressing views on political issues.

   d. Staff may use the district Internet system for communications related to collective bargaining and union organizational activities.

   e. A school may establish an after-school "open access" program or enter into an agreement with an authorized after-school activities provider to allow open access to the Internet for noneducational purposes. All student use during open access hours must be closely supervised. It shall be made clear to students that the district Internet use agreement will cover all use, with the exception that noneducational use of limited access material may occur.

2. The district will provide professional development opportunities for teachers to help them learn how to use the Internet effectively for instructional purposes, disseminate Internet-based lesson plans, and provide technical and instructional support to students.

   a. Substitute teachers must be specifically certified to instruct in classrooms where students are accessing the Internet.

Certification requirements will ensure that substitute teachers have a standard level of technical proficiency and understand Internet safety and responsible use issues, this policy, and the obligations related to supervision of students in their use of the Internet.

Unless they are under the direct supervision of their cooperating teacher, student teachers must be certified to instruct in classrooms where students are accessing the Internet.

3. Student use and activities will be structured in a manner that is appropriate to the age and skills of students, recognizing the importance of providing more secure environments for younger students and supporting safe and responsible independent use by older students.

4. The district will establish student research resources to facilitate and promote the effective use of the Internet for educational purposes and reduce the potential for student access to inappropriate material. The student research resources will provide access to materials that have been prescreened by educators and other professionals to ensure the appropriateness of the material for educational purposes.

5. Teachers will be encouraged and supported in the creation of classroom Web sites that will direct students to sites with information pertinent to current studies. All sites linked to through the classroom Web site should be prescreened by the teacher to ensure such sites are appropriate in light of the age of the students and relevance to the course objectives.

6. The district and teachers will seek to limit student exposure to commercial advertising and product promotion, especially advertising or promotion of youth-oriented products and services, in the development of the district or classroom Web sites or other assignments that make use of the Internet.

7. For students at the elementary school level, access to information on the Web will be generally be limited to access available through the student research resources or through classroom Web sites. Any student access to material outside such prescreened sites must be closely supervised by the teacher.

8. For students at the secondary school level, access to information on the Web should generally be through the student research resources or through classroom Web sites. Students may access other sites upon approval by their teacher.

9. If use of the online material constitutes fair use under copyright law, teachers may download information from the Web that is necessary for classroom instructional purposes and provide this information to students who do not have Internet access. This information may be provided either in hard-copy form or through a computer system without live access to the Internet.

10. District health personnel, health education teachers, and counselors shall establish a student health and well-being online resource that will provide access to high-quality sites that provide information and support for students facing a wide range of adolescent health issues. The selection of these sites will be based on known youth health and well-being concerns and shall not be limited based on viewpoint discrimination.

11. The district will establish or authorize the use of a controlled communications environment that will allow the students to communicate electronically for educational purposes. Such communications may include e-mail, chat, instant messaging, and blogging.

D. PROTECTIONS AGAINST ACCESS TO INAPPROPRIATE MATERIAL

1. Inappropriate material

    a. The [Name] School District has identified the following types of material as prohibited, restricted, and limited access material.

        i. *Prohibited material.* Prohibited material may not be accessed by the students or staff at any time for any purpose. This category includes material that is obscene, child pornography, and material that is considered harmful to minors as defined by the Children's Internet Protection Act. The district has designated the following types of materials as prohibited:

        Obscene materials.

        Child pornography.

        Material that appeals to a prurient or unhealthy interest in, or depicts or describes in a patently offensive way, violence, nudity, sex, death, or bodily functions.

        Material that has been designated as being for adults only.

Material that promotes or advocates illegal activities.

ii. *Restricted material.* Material that may arguably fall within the description provided for prohibited material but has clear educational relevance, such as material with literary, artistic, political, or scientific value, will be considered to be restricted. In addition, restricted material includes promotion or advocacy of the use of alcohol and tobacco, hate and other potentially dangerous groups, school cheating, weapons, and [list other issues of concern to the district]. Material that is restricted may not be accessed by elementary or middle school students at any time for any purpose. Restricted material may be accessed by high school students in the context of specific learning activities that have been approved by the building principal.

iii. *Limited access material.* Limited access material includes anything generally considered to be noneducational or for entertainment. Limited access material may be accessed in the context of specific learning activities that are directed by a teacher. Limited access material includes electronic commerce, games, jokes, recreation, entertainment, and investments. [*Author's note:* Some schools may wish to allow open access times when access to these noneducational sites would be allowed— for example, at an after school program. Any open access allowed must be closely supervised.]

b. Any user who inadvertently accesses material that is considered prohibited or restricted should immediately disclose the inadvertent access in a manner specified by their school. This will protect users against an allegation that they have intentionally violated the policy.

c. The determination of whether material is prohibited, restricted, or noneducational shall be based on the content of the material and the intended use of the material, not on the response of a technological protection measure. The fact that the technological protection measure has not protected against access to certain material shall not create the presumption that such material is appropriate for users to access. The fact that the technological protection measure has blocked access to certain material shall not create the presumption that the material is inappropriate for users to access.

2. Technological protection measures

   a. Technological protection measures include technologies that seek to block user access to certain sites (filtering software), block inappropriate material from being sent to district users, ensure the security of the district network, and monitor Internet use.

   b. The district has selected technological protection measures for use with the district Internet system and has specified the manner in which these measures will be configured. This selection and configuration is described in the attached document.

   c. District filtering software will always be configured to protect against access to material that is obscene, child pornography, and material that is harmful to minors, as defined by the Children's Online Privacy Protection Act. The district or individual schools may, from time to time, reconfigure the technological protection measures to best meet the educational needs of the district or schools and address the safety needs of the students.

   d. The district safety and responsible use committee will conduct an annual analysis of the effectiveness of the selected technological protection measures and make recommendations to the superintendent regarding selection and configuration.

3. Override, nondiscrimination, disabling, and bypass of filtering software

   a. All district administrators, library media specialists, computer lab coordinators, and safe schools personnel shall have the authority to temporarily override the filtering software to review a Web site that has been blocked and to make the professional decision to provide immediate student access to that site. Other school staff may be designated by a building principal to have override authority.

   b. Students' free-speech rights of access to information within an educational environment shall be fully protected. Care will be taken in the selection and configuration of the filtering software to ensure that viewpoint discrimination does not occur.

c. An anonymous process shall be established to allow students to request that a site be permanently unblocked. Decisions about unblocking should generally take no longer than two school days.

d. The determination of whether material is appropriate or inappropriate shall be based on the content of the material and the intended use of the material, not on the protective actions of the filtering software.

e. The filtering software may not be disabled at any time that students may be using the district Internet system if such disabling will cease to protect against access to materials that are prohibited under the Children's Internet Protection Act. The filtering software may be disabled for system administrative purposes when students are not using the system.

f. Students and staff may not use external proxy servers or other similar technologies to bypass or seek to bypass the filtering software.

E. SUPERVISION, MONITORING, SEARCH AND SEIZURE, AND RETENTION OF RECORDS

1. Student use of the district Internet system will be supervised by staff in a manner that is appropriate to the age of the students and circumstances of use. The building administrator or a designee in each school will develop and disseminate staff supervision requirements. Computers used by students in classrooms and labs will be positioned to facilitate effective staff supervision.

2. The district will monitor student and staff use of the Internet through a regular analysis of Internet usage. Individual schools may implement any additional monitoring systems, as desired.

3. Users have a limited privacy expectation in the contents of their personal files and records of their online activity while on the district system. Users will be fully and regularly informed about the district's supervision and monitoring activities and the limitations on their privacy that result from such supervision and monitoring.

4. Routine maintenance and monitoring of the system may lead to discovery that a user has violated or is violating district policy, regulations, or the law. An individual search will be conducted if there is reasonable suspicion that such violations have occurred. The nature of the investigation will be reasonable and in the context of the nature of the alleged violation. Individual search of a user's e-mail must be approved by a district administrator responsible for supervision of the student or staff member or by the superintendent or a designee. In the event an individualized search is conducted, a record will be established detailing the reason for the search, the extent of the search, and the results.

5. The superintendent or a designee will implement an Internet records retention system that is in accord with the state public records law [specify relevant legislation]. Internet records that are not subject to retention will be destroyed on a regular basis. Staff will be regularly informed that the contents of their personal files may be discoverable under state public records laws.

F. ELECTRONIC COMMUNICATION

1. Staff will be provided with individual e-mail accounts. Staff will use a signature file that identifies who they are and their position with the district. Staff use of these district e-mail accounts will be for professional purposes.

2. The district or schools will establish controlled electronic communications services, including e-mail, blogs, and real-time electronic communications, for students to use for educational purposes.

3. Teachers will supervise and regularly review all electronic communications of students.

4. Students may not establish or access Web-based e-mail accounts or commercial services through the district Internet system unless such accounts have been approved for use by the individual school.

G. UNLAWFUL, UNAUTHORIZED, AND INAPPROPRIATE ACTIVITIES

1. Unlawful activities

a. Users will not attempt to gain unauthorized access to the district Internet system or to any other computer system through the district system, or go beyond their authorized access. This includes attempting to log in through another person's account or access another person's files.

b. Users will not make deliberate attempts to disrupt the computer system performance or destroy data by spreading computer viruses or by any other means.

c. Users will not use the district Internet system to engage in any other unlawful act, including arranging for a drug sale or the purchase of alcohol, engaging in criminal gang activity, or threatening the safety of any person.

2. Inappropriate language

a. Restrictions against inappropriate language apply to all speech communicated through the district Internet system, including public messages, private messages, and material on Web pages or in blogs, or posted in any other manner.

b. Users will not use obscene, profane, lewd, vulgar, rude, inflammatory, threatening, or disrespectful language.

c. Users will not post information that, if acted upon, could cause damage or a danger of disruption to the district, a school, or any other organization or person.

d. Users will not engage in personal attacks, including prejudicial or discriminatory attacks.

e. Users will not harass or bully another person.

f. Users will not knowingly or recklessly post false or defamatory information about a person or organization.

g. Students will promptly disclose to their teacher or another school employee any message they receive from any other student that is in violation of the restrictions on inappropriate language. Students should not delete such messages until instructed to do so by a staff member.

3. Plagiarism and copyright infringement

a. Users will not plagiarize works that they find on the Internet.

b. Users will respect the rights of copyright owners in their use of materials found on, disseminated through, or posted to the Internet.

H. SYSTEM SECURITY AND RESOURCE LIMITS

1. System security

   a. Users are responsible for the use of their individual account and should take all reasonable precautions to prevent others from being able to use their account, including protecting the privacy of their password.

   b. Users will immediately notify the system administrator if they have identified a possible security problem. However, users will not go looking for security problems, because this may be construed as an unlawful attempt to gain access.

   c. Users will avoid the inadvertent spread of computer viruses by following the district virus protection procedures.

2. Resource limits

   a. Users will not download large files unless absolutely necessary. If necessary, users will download the file at a time when the system is not being heavily used and immediately remove the file from the system computer.

   b. Users will not misuse district, school, or personal distribution lists or discussion groups by sending irrelevant messages.

   c. Users will check their e-mail frequently, delete unwanted messages promptly, and stay within their e-mail quota.

   d. Users will subscribe only to approved high-quality discussion groups that are relevant to their education or professional and career development.

   e. Excessive use of the district Internet system may raise a reasonable suspicion that a user is using the system in violation of district policy.

I. PROTECTION OF STUDENT CONFIDENTIALITY AND PRIVACY

1. All contracts with third-party providers of data management services for the district will be reviewed to ensure compliance with federal and state student privacy and records retention laws.

2. Staff transmission of student confidential information via e-mail must be in compliance with all federal and state student privacy laws.

a. E-mail transmission will be used only when the circumstances justify the need for immediacy in the transmission of information.

b. The subject line of the e-mail should provide an indication that the e-mail contains confidential student information.

c. A hard copy of any e-mail containing student confidential information will be retained in accord with district student records retention requirements.

3. Teachers will ensure the protection of student personal information when establishing any relationship with a third-party site or system.

a. Teachers may require, encourage, or allow students to establish individual accounts on a third-party site or system only under the following circumstances:

    i. The establishment of the account is necessary to achieve an identified educational purpose.

    ii. There is no commercial advertising for youth interest products or services on the third-party system.

    iii. Student personal information and student use data will not be collected, analyzed, or used for commercial advertising or marketing purposes.

    iv. A minimum amount of information is collected for the purpose of establishing the account, and no personal contact information is provided.

    v. The third-party system has committed to maintain the privacy of any information provided.

    vi. The third-party system provides a process by which parents may access, review, and remove their child's account information.

b. Signed parental permission must be obtained prior to the establishment of the student account. Notice to the parent about proposed student accounts on third-party systems must include the following information:

    i. The name, URL, and privacy policy of the third-party system.

    ii. Description of the educational purpose for establishing the account.

iii. The period of time for which the account will be established.

iv. Information on how parents can access their child's records on the third-party site.

4. Collection, analysis, or sale of student use data for commercial purposes: The district may not enter into any agreement with a third-party supplier of Internet-related services if the third-party service provider intends to collect, analyze, or sell individual or anonymous student use data for the purpose of commercial advertising and marketing research activities. The collection and analysis of student use data strictly for the purpose of evaluation and improvement of the educational site is acceptable.

5. Privacy and communication safety standards: Students will abide by the following privacy and communication safety standards when using the district Internet system, including use of electronic communications and the Web.

a. In this context, "personal contact information" includes the student's name, together with other information that would allow an individual to locate the student, including parent's name, home address or location, work address or location, or phone number.

b. Elementary and middle school students will not disclose their full names or any other personal contact information for any purpose.

c. High school students will not disclose personal contact information except to educational institutions for educational purposes, companies or other entities for career development purposes, or with specific staff approval.

d. Students will not disclose names, personal contact information, or any other private or personal information about other students under any circumstances.

e. Students will not forward a message that was sent to them privately without permission of the person who sent them the message.

f. Students will promptly disclose to their teacher or other school employee any message they receive that is inappropriate or makes them feel uncomfortable. Students should not delete such messages until instructed to do so by a staff member.

6. The following provisions address the disclosure of student information, posting student-created material, and posting pictures of students on the district Web site or any school Web site. The district or schools may establish password-protected Web sites that will restrict access to staff, students, and their parents. Parents must approve any disclosure of student information and posting of student-created material.

   a. For students in elementary and middle school, the following standards apply to any material posted on a publicly accessible site:

      i. Students will use a username that will disguise their full name.

      ii. Group pictures without identification of individual students are permitted.

      iii. Student work may be posted with limited student identification.

      iv. All student-posted work will contain the student's copyright notice, using the student's username.

   b. For students in elementary and middle school using a password-protected site, parents may approve either the elementary or middle school standards for publicly accessible sites or the following standards:

      i. Students may be identified by their full name.

      ii. Group or individual pictures of students with student identification are permitted.

      iii. Student work may be posted with student name.

      iv. All student-posted work will contain the student's copyright notice, including the student's name.

   c. For students in high school on publicly accessible sites or password-protected sites, parents may approve either the elementary or middle school standards or the following standards:

      i. Students may be identified by their full name.

      ii. Group or individual pictures of students with student identification are permitted.

      iii. Student work may be posted with student name.

iv. All student-posted work will contain the student's copyright notice, including the student's name.

J. COPYRIGHT MANAGEMENT

1. The district will respect the copyright rights of students and staff.

   a. Students own the copyright to their creative works, including works created using district resources. The Internet agreement signed by parents will include a request for permission from parents to post student work on the Internet. All student work posted on the Internet will contain a copyright notice indicating the ownership of that work by the students.

   b. District staff own the copyright to works created outside the scope of their employment responsibilities and without the use of district resources. District staff may post such work on the district Web site to facilitate access by students or staff. Notice of such posting and claim of ownership must be provided to [state to whom it must be given]. By posting such work on the district's Web site, the staff member will grant an nonexclusive license or permission for any staff or student within the district to freely use such work.

   c. The district shall own the copyright on any works created by district staff within the scope of their employment responsibilities.

2. The district will promote respect for the copyright rights of others.

   a. The district will provide instruction to staff and students on their rights and responsibilities with respect to the copyright ownership rights of others.

   b. No material may be disseminated through the district Internet system or posted on the district Internet site unless that material is original, in the public domain, used in accord with the fair use provisions of the copyright law, or is disseminated or posted with permission of the copyright owner.

K. DISTRICT WEB SITE REGULATIONS

1. District Web site: The district will establish a district Web site. Material appropriate for placement on district Web site

includes district information, school information, teacher or class information, student projects, and student extracurricular organization information. Personal information unrelated to education will not be allowed on the district Web site.

a. The superintendent will designate a district Web publisher to be responsible for maintaining the official district Web site and monitoring all district Web activity. The Web publisher will develop style and content guidelines for official district and school Web materials and develop procedures for the placement and removal of such material.

b. All official material originating from the district and posted on the district Web site must be approved through a process established by the district Web publisher.

2. School Web pages: The building principal will designate a school Web publisher to be responsible for managing the school Web site and monitoring class, teacher, student, and extracurricular Web pages. All official material originating from the school will be consistent with the district style and content guidelines and approved through a process established by the school Web publisher. The school Web publisher will develop additional guidelines and placement processes for the school Web site.

3. Teacher or classroom Web pages and blogs: Teachers may establish Web pages and blogs for use with class activities or that provide a resource for other teachers. Teachers will be responsible for maintaining their class or educational resource sites and previewing any student work prior to posting.

4. Noninstructional staff Web pages and blogs: Noninstructional staff may develop Web pages and blogs that provide a resource for others. Staff will be responsible for maintaining their resource sites.

5. Student Web pages and blogs

a. Students may create a Web page and blog as part of a specific instructional activity. Material presented on a student class activity Web page and blog must meet the educational objectives of the instructional activity and be created and maintained under the direct supervision of a teacher.

b. It will not be considered a violation of a student's right to free speech to require removal of material that fails to meet established educational objectives or that is in violation of a provision of the Student Internet Use Policy or student disciplinary code. However, student material may not be removed on the basis of disagreement with the views expressed by the student.

   c. Student Web pages and blogs must include the following notice: "This is a student Web page. Opinions expressed on this page shall not be attributed to the district."

   d. Student Web pages and blogs will be removed at the end of the school year unless special arrangements are made.

6. Extracurricular organization Web pages and blogs

   a. With the approval of the building principal, extracurricular organizations may establish Web pages, including blogs. Material presented on the organization Web page or blog must relate specifically to organization activities.

   b. Organization Web pages must include the following notice: "This is a student extracurricular organization Web page and blog. Opinions expressed on this page shall not be attributed to the district."

7. Web Page and blog requirements

   a. All Web pages and blogs associated with the district are considered to be a limited public forum. All material posted on Web pages and blogs using the district domain will be developed in such a manner as to reflect well upon the district and its schools, staff, and students.

   b. All new district Web site and all school, class, and distance education materials will be fully compliant with disability information technology access standards. The district will develop a plan to revise all existing Web site material to achieve compliance with access standards.

   c. All Internet use policy provisions, including those addressing inappropriate language, privacy, and copyright, will govern material placed on the district Web site.

   d. Web pages and blogs shall not contain the identification information or pictures of the student or student work unless such provision has been approved by the student's parents or guardians, as has been provided in Section I (6).

e. Material placed on the Web site is expected to meet academic standards for proper spelling, grammar, and accuracy of information.

f. All Web pages and blogs should have a link at the bottom of the page that will help users find their way to the appropriate home page.

8. Web site concerns

a. The district Web site and each school Web page will have a "Web Site Concerns" link. This link will take the reader to a page that provides the following information:

i. [Name] School District seeks to ensure that all materials placed on the district or school Web sites are placed in accord with copyright law and do not infringe on the rights of or harm others in any way.

ii. We have provisions in our Internet Use Policy that address copyright, defamation, harassment, invasion of privacy, and other harmful speech.

iii. We will promptly respond to any issues of concern. If you have a concern about material placed on our Web site, please contact us. [Add link to e-mail address of an administrator who has the responsibility of promptly responding to any complaint.]

Student Internet Use Policy and Agreement

This document sets forth the rights and responsibilities for students under the district's Internet Safe and Responsible Use Policy.

A. EDUCATIONAL PURPOSE

1. The district Internet system has been established for a limited educational purpose. The term *educational purpose* includes classroom activities, continuing education, professional or career development, and high-quality, educationally enriching personal research.

2. The district Internet system has not been established as a public access service or a public forum. The district has the right to place reasonable restrictions on the material you access or post through the system. You are also expected to follow the rules set forth in this policy, the student disciplinary code, and the law in your use of the district Internet system. The student disciplinary code will govern any violations of this policy.

3. You may not use the district Internet system for commercial purposes. This means you may not offer, provide, or purchase products or services through the district Internet system.

B. ACCESS TO ONLINE MATERIALS

1. The material you access through the district's Internet system should be for class assignments or for personal research on subjects similar to what you might study in a class or in the school library. Use for entertainment purposes is not allowed.

2. You will not use the district Internet system to access the following: material that is obscene; child pornography; material that depicts, or describes in an offensive way, violence, nudity, sex, death, or bodily functions; material that has been designated as for adults only; material that promotes or advocates illegal activities; material that promotes the use of alcohol or tobacco, school cheating, or weapons; or material that advocates participation in hate groups or other potentially dangerous groups.

3. If you mistakenly access inappropriate information, you should immediately report this access in the manner specified by your school. This will protect you against a claim that you have intentionally violated this policy.

4. The district has installed filtering software to protect against access to inappropriate material.

   a. If you feel that the filtering software is blocking your access to an appropriate site, report this to a school librarian, computer lab coordinator, principal, or teacher. You may also submit an anonymous request to have the site unblocked.

   b. You will not seek to bypass the filtering software by using a proxy site or some other technology.

C. PRIVACY AND COMMUNICATION SAFETY REQUIREMENTS

1. "Personal contact information" includes your full name, together with other information that would allow an individual to locate you, including your family name, your home address or location, your work address or location, or your phone number.

2. If you are an elementary or middle school student, you will not disclose your full name or any other personal contact information online for any reason.

3. If you are a high school student, you may disclose personal contact information to educational institutions, companies or other entities for career development purposes, or with specific staff approval.

4. You will not disclose names, personal contact information, or any other private or personal information about other students. You will not forward a message that was sent to you privately without permission of the person who sent you the message.

5. You will promptly disclose to your teacher or other school staff any message you receive that is inappropriate or makes you feel uncomfortable. You should not delete such messages until instructed to do so by a staff member.

D. UNLAWFUL, UNAUTHORIZED, AND INAPPROPRIATE USES AND ACTIVITIES

1. Unlawful activities

   a. You will not attempt to gain unauthorized access to the district Internet system or to any other computer system through the district Internet system or go beyond your authorized access. This includes attempting to log in through another person's account or to access another person's files.

   b. You will not make deliberate attempts to disrupt the district Internet system or any other computer system or destroy data by spreading computer viruses or by any other means.

   c. You will not use the district Internet system to engage in any other unlawful act, including arranging for a drug sale or the purchase of alcohol, engaging in criminal gang activity, or threatening the safety of any person.

2. Inappropriate language

   a. Restrictions against inappropriate language apply to all speech communicated through the district Internet system, including public messages, private messages, and material posted on Web pages.

   b. You will not use obscene, profane, lewd, vulgar, rude, inflammatory, threatening, or disrespectful language.

   c. You will not post information that could cause damage or a danger of disruption to your school or any other organization or person.

   d. You will not engage in personal attacks, including prejudicial or discriminatory attacks.

   e. You will not harass or bully another person.

   f. You will not knowingly or recklessly post false or defamatory information about a person or organization.

g. You will promptly disclose to your teacher or another school employee any message you receive from any other student that is in violation of the restrictions on inappropriate language.

3. Plagiarism and copyright infringement

a. You will not plagiarize works that you find on the Internet. Plagiarism is taking the ideas or writings of others and presenting them as if they were yours.

b. You will respect the rights of copyright owners in your use of materials found on, disseminated through, or posted to the Internet. Copyright infringement occurs when you inappropriately reproduce a work that is protected by a copyright.

E. SYSTEM SECURITY AND RESOURCE LIMITS

1. System security

a. You are responsible for your individual account and should take all reasonable precautions to prevent others from being able to use your account. Under no conditions should you provide your password to another person.

b. You will immediately notify a teacher or the system administrator if you have identified a possible security problem. However, do not go looking for security problems, because this may be construed as an unlawful attempt to gain access.

c. You will avoid the inadvertent spread of computer viruses by following the district virus protection procedures.

2. Resource limits

a. You will use the system only for educational and career development activities and limited, high-quality personal research.

b. You will not download large files unless absolutely necessary. If necessary, you will download the file at a time when the system is not being heavily used and immediately remove the file from the system computer.

c. You will not misuse district, school, or personal distribution lists or discussion groups for sending irrelevant messages.

F. YOUR RIGHTS AND EXPECTATIONS

1. Free speech

   a. Your right to free speech and access to information applies to your use of the Internet. The district may restrict access to materials for valid educational reasons. The district will not restrict your access to information and ideas based on a disagreement with the views expressed. The district may restrict your speech for valid educational reasons. The district will not restrict your speech on the basis of disagreement with the opinions you are expressing.

2. Copyright

   a. You own the copyright to works that you create in school or for a class assignment. If the work is created by a group, each student will share joint ownership of the copyright. You and your parent or guardian must agree before your work will be posted on the district Web site. Your work should be posted with your copyright notice.

3. Privacy

   a. You should expect only limited privacy in the contents of your personal files on the district Internet system and records of your online activity. All student use of the Internet will be supervised and monitored. The district's monitoring of Internet usage can reveal all activities you engage in using the district Internet system.

   b. Routine maintenance and monitoring of the district Internet system may lead to discovery that you have violated this policy, the student disciplinary code, or the law. An individual search will be conducted if there is reasonable suspicion that you have violated this policy, the student disciplinary code, or the law. The investigation will be reasonable and related to the suspected violation.

   c. Your parents have the right to request to see the contents of your computer files at any time.

4. Due process

   a. The district will cooperate fully with local, state, or federal officials in any investigation related to any unlawful activities conducted through the district Internet system.

b. In the event there is a claim that you have violated this policy or student disciplinary code in your use of the district Internet system, you will be provided with notice and opportunity to be heard in the manner set forth in the student disciplinary code.

c. If the violation also involves a violation of other provisions of the student disciplinary code, it will be handled in a manner described in the code. Additional restrictions may be placed on your use of your Internet.

G. LIMITATION OF LIABILITY

The district will not guarantee that the functions or services provided through the district Internet service will be without error. The district will not be responsible for any damage you may suffer, including but not limited to loss of data, interruptions of service, or exposure to inappropriate material or people. The district will not be responsible for the accuracy or quality of the information obtained through the system. The district will not be responsible for financial obligations arising through the unauthorized use of the system. Your parents can be held financially responsible for any harm that may result from your intentional misuse of the system. You may use the system only if your parents have signed a disclaimer of claims for damages against the district.

Student Internet Account Agreement

Student Section

Student Name _____ Grade _____

School _____

I have read the district's Student Internet Use Policy. I agree to follow the rules contained in this policy. I understand that if I violate the rules, my account can be terminated and I may face other disciplinary measures.

Student Signature _____ Date _____

Parent or Guardian Section

I have read the district's Student Internet Use Policy.

I hereby release the district, its personnel, and any institutions with which it is affiliated from any and all claims and damages of any nature arising from my child's use of, or inability to use, the district system, including but not limited to claims that may arise from the unauthorized use of the system to purchase products or services or exposure to potentially harmful or inappropriate material or people. I understand that I can be held liable for damages caused by my child's intentional misuse of the system.

I will instruct my child regarding any restrictions against accessing material that are in addition to the restrictions set forth in the district policy. I will emphasize to my child the importance of following the rules for personal safety.

For Parents or Guardians of Elementary School Students

I hereby give ❏ do not give ❏ permission for my child to use the Internet. I understand that this permission includes permission for my child to access information through the Web, receive e-mail communications through a class account, and engage in other educationally relevant electronic communication activities.

I hereby give ❑ do not give ❑ permission for the school to post the following information and material on the Internet: Students will use a limited student identification (first name and last initial or other school-developed identifier). Group pictures without identification of individual students are permitted. Student work may be posted with the limited student identification. All student-posted work will contain the student's copyright notice using the limited student identification (for example, © 2007, jjwill, Student at Adams Elementary School).

For Parents or Guardians of Middle School Students

I hereby give ❑ do not give ❑ permission for my child to use the Internet. I understand that this permission includes permission for my child to access information through the Web, receive an individual e-mail account, and engage in other educationally related electronic communication activities.

I hereby give ❑ do not give ❑ permission for the school to post the following information and material on the Internet: Students will use a limited student identification (first name and last initial or other school-developed identifier). Group pictures without identification of individual students are permitted. Student work may be posted with the limited student identification. All student-posted work will contain the student's copyright notice using the limited student identification (for example, © 2007, jjwill, Student at Adams Middle School).

For Parents or Guardians of High School Students

I hereby give ❑ do not give ❑ permission for my child to use the Internet. I understand that this permission includes permission for my child to access information through the Web, receive an individual e-mail account, engage in other educationally related electronic communication activities, and provide personal information to others for education or career development reasons or as approved by school staff.

I hereby give permission for the school to post the following information and material on the Internet:

❑ Option 1: Students will use a limited student identification (first name and last initial or other school-developed identifier). Group pictures without identification of individual students are permitted. Student work may be posted with the limited student identification. All student-posted work will contain the student's copyright notice, using the limited student identification (for example, © 2007, jjwill, Student at Adams High School).

❏ Option 2: Students may be identified by their full names. Group or individual pictures of students with student identification are permitted. Student work may be posted with student name. All student-posted work will contain the student's copyright notice, including the student's name.

❏ Option 3: No information or material may be posted.

Parent Signature _____ Date _____

Parent Name _____

Home Address _____ Phone _____

****

Space Reserved for System Administrator

Assigned Username _____

Assigned Temporary Password _____

For students in elementary and middle school, the following standards apply to any material posted on a publicly accessible site: Students will use a username that will disguise their full name. Group pictures without identification of individual students are permitted. Student work may be posted with the limited student identification. All student-posted work will contain the student's copyright notice, including the student's username.

For students in elementary and middle school using a password-protected site, parents may approve either the elementary/middle school publicly accessible sites standards or the following standards: Students may be identified by their full name. Group or individual pictures of students with student identification are permitted. Student work may be posted with student name. All student-posted work will contain the student's copyright notice, including the student's name.

For students in high school on publicly accessible sites or password-protected sites, parents may approve either the elementary/middle school standards or the following standards: Students may be identified by their full name. Group or individual pictures of students with student identification are permitted. Student work may be posted with student name. All student-posted work will contain the student's copyright notice, including the student's name.

Student Guide to Cyberbullying and Cyberthreats

CYBERBULLYING

Cyberbullying is being mean to others by sending or posting harmful material or engaging in other forms of social aggression using the Internet or other digital technologies. Here are some examples of kinds of cyberbullying:

- Flaming—Online fights using electronic messages with angry and vulgar language.

  Joe and Alec's online fight got angrier and angrier. Insults were flying. Joe warned Alec to watch his back in school the next day.

- Harassment—Repeatedly sending nasty, mean, and insulting messages.

  Sara reported to the principal that Kayla was bullying another student. When Sara got home, she had 35 angry messages in her e-mail box. The anonymous cruel messages kept coming—some from strangers.

- Denigration—"Dissing" someone online. Sending or posting gossip or rumors about a person to damage his or her reputation or friendships.

  Some boys created a "We Hate Joe" Web site where they posted jokes, cartoons, gossip, and rumors, all dissing Joe.

- Impersonation—Pretending to be someone else and sending or posting material to get that person in trouble or danger or to damage that person's reputation or friendships.

Laura watched closely as Emma logged on to her account and discovered her password. Later, Laura logged on to Emma's account and sent a hurtful message to Emma's boyfriend, Adam.

- Outing—Sharing someone's secrets or embarrassing information or images online.

  Greg, an obese high school student, was changing in the locker room after gym class. Matt took a picture of him with his cell phone camera. Within seconds, the picture was flying around the phones at school.

- Trickery—Tricking someone into revealing secrets or embarrassing information, then sharing it online.

  Katie sent a message to Jessica pretending to be her friend and asking lots of questions. Jessica responded, sharing really personal information. Katie forwarded the message to lots of other people with her own comment, "Jessica is a loser."

- Exclusion—Intentionally and cruelly excluding someone from an online group.

  Millie tries hard to fit in with a group of girls at school. She recently got on the "outs" with a leader in this group. Now Millie has been blocked from the friendship links of all the girls.

- Cyberstalking—Repeated, intense harassment and denigration that includes threats or creates significant fear.

  When Annie broke up with Sam, he sent her many angry, threatening, pleading messages. He spread nasty rumors about her to her friends and posted a sexually suggestive picture she had given him in a sex-oriented discussion group, along with her e-mail address and cell phone number.

Preventing Cyberbullying

There are several important things that you can to do to avoid being a target of cyberbullying:

- *Protect yourself.* Never provide any information or images in electronic form that could be used against you.

- *Examine how you are communicating.* If you find that people are frequently attacking you, look closely at how you are communicating with them. You might be communicating in a way that is irritating others or hurting their feelings.

- *Find some new friends.* If you are trying to fit into a group of people who are treating you badly, it might be easier to simply find some nicer friends. Life's too short to waste time trying to be friends with mean people.

Don't Give Power to Bullies

Bullies want to achieve power and be seen by others as stronger and better. If you lose your cool or respond in another way that shows lack of strength, a bully can boast about it to others—and will probably keep bullying you. So the key to handling bullies is to stay calm and not make it fun to harass you. The Internet can actually help you if you are the target of bullying. If you are bullied online, you have several advantages:

- No one can see your initial reaction. If you do lose your cool, which is natural and normal, no one will ever know—as long as you keep your hands off the keyboard until you calm down.

- Internet communications are delayed. If you choose to respond, you can take the time to write a calm, strong, assertive response. You can even show your response to others to get feedback before you send it.

- You might not feel as strong and powerful as the person bullying you. But you can act like you are stronger and more powerful when you are online. Just pretend you are creating a character in an online game—a character who is stronger than you currently think you are.

A Very Important Rule

Never retaliate! A bully wants you to get upset. If you get mad and strike back in an attempt to hurt the bully as badly as you were hurt, it just won't work. No matter what you think of, all it does is give the bully a "win." It makes you look bad. You could also set yourself up for trouble. People who see your post may think you are the one who is causing the problem, not the bully. If someone shows your message to an adult, you could be the one who gets into trouble.

Don't Be a Cyberbully

People lose their temper from time to time. Many people have sent a message on the Internet that was angry—and wrong. This does not make you a bully. If you have sent an angry or hurtful message, apologize. If you have posted angry or hurtful material, remove it and apologize. Try to make things right.

Bullies don't just lose their temper and make a mistake. Bullies intentionally put other people down so that they can make themselves feel more important. Bullies try to defend their actions in a number of ways. They say or think things like these:

> *"I didn't do anything wrong." It wasn't my fault." "The stupid kid deserved it." "I was just playing around." "It was just a joke."*

If you are acting like a bully, the most important question you need to ask yourself is "Why?" What are you trying to gain by putting others down?

What you should understand about cyberbullying is that whenever you use electronic communications you are leaving traces—"cyber-footprints" that lead right back to you. Eventually, people will be able to figure out who you are and hold you accountable for the harm you have caused.

What You Should Do If You Are Cyberbullied

There are different ways to respond to cyberbullying. Decide what to do based on who is cyberbullying you and how bad the cyberbullying is. Try to figure out what you think might work best to get the cyberbullying to stop.

- Always save the evidence. Download the harmful material. Save any chats or instant messages. But don't keep looking at it—this will only make you feel worse.

- Decide if you need to involve an adult. Sometimes you can resolve these situations on your own. Tell an adult if:

  You are really upset and are not sure what to do.

  The cyberbully is also bullying you in real life.

  You have been threatened with harm.

  The cyberbullying is doing things that can really damage your reputation and friendships.

  The cyberbully is also bullying other students.

  You tried some of the other steps to get the cyberbully to stop, but it didn't work.

- Tell the cyberbully to stop. Send the cyberbully a private message stating something like this: "Stop sending me messages" or "Remove the material you posted." Depending on your relationship with this person, you might be able to work out a friendly truce. Make sure your message is nonemotional and strong. You could also tell the cyberbully that if the harm does not stop, you will take other steps to stop it.

- Ignore the cyberbully. Stop going to any group where you are being cyberbullied. Remove the cyberbully from your buddies list.

- Have your parents contact the cyberbully's parents. They might talk with the parents or send them a letter. If they send a letter, it will be helpful if they include the harmful material you have downloaded.

- File a complaint with the Web site or service. Most sites and services prohibit bullying behavior. You can generally find an e-mail contact on the home page. Explain what has happened and provide the links to the harmful material or attach any harmful messages. Request that the material be removed and perhaps also that the account of the cyberbully be terminated.

- Talk to your school. If the cyberbully goes to your school, and especially if the cyberbully is also bullying you at school, tell your principal or school counselor. Provide the material you have downloaded.

- Contact an attorney or the police. You will need your parents to help you with this. Sometimes cyberbullying is so bad your parents could sue the parents of the cyberbully for money. Or the cyberbullying could be a crime. Of course, it's better if things do not get to this point—but it's useful to know these options are there if things get really bad.

Be a Friend

Bullies love an audience. Many teens do not like to see others being bullied, but are not sure what to do. Here are some things you can do:

- Speak out against cyberbullying in your online communities.

- Help the target in private.

- Encourage the target to report the cyberbullying.

- File a complaint with the site yourself.

- Report the cyberbullying to the school the target attends. You can download this material and report anonymously.

- Tell your parents and ask their guidance.

CYBERTHREATS

Cyberthreats are either threats or "distressing material"—statements that make it sound like the writer is emotionally upset and may be considering harming someone else, harming himself or herself, or committing suicide.

> *Jeff wrote in his blog: "I'm a retarded [expletive] for ever believing that things would change. I'm starting to regret sticking around. It takes courage to turn the gun on your self, takes courage to face death."*

> *Celia met Andrew in a chat room. Andrew wrote: "bring a gun to school, ur on the front of every. . . . i cant imagine going through life without killing a few people. . . . people can be kissing my shotgun straight out of doom. . . . if i dont like the way u look at me, u die. . . . i choose who lives and who dies."*

> *Greg set up an anonymous IM account and sent a threatening message to his older sister suggesting that she would be killed the next day at school.*

Sometimes when teens post what appears to be a threat, they are just joking. Other times, the threat could be very real. Here are two very important things that you must understand about online threats:

- *Don't make threats online.* If you post a threat online, adults may not be able to tell whether the threat is real. There are criminal laws against making threats. If you make a cyberthreat, even if you are just joking, you could be suspended, expelled, or even arrested.

- *Report threats or distressing material.* If you see a threat or distressing material posted online, it could be very real. It is extremely important to report this to an adult. If the threat is real, someone could be seriously injured.

Just in case you are wondering—these are all true stories. Jeff killed nine people and then killed himself. Celia reported her online conversation to her father, who contacted the police. The police found that Andrew had many weapons, including an AK-47. He is now in prison. Greg's sister told her parents, her parents told the school, and the school went into "lockdown." Greg was identified easily—and arrested for making a threat.

REPORTING ONLINE CONCERNS

Many teens think that it is really not okay to talk with adults about what is happening online. They may think that adults will overreact—which, admittedly, in some cases they do. Or they may be afraid that other teens will retaliate.

The problem is that teens are being harmed by others or are posting material that raises real concerns about their safety or the safety of others. And responsible adults are not present in the online communities where this is occurring. So if teens who witness online concerns don't report, someone might be really hurt.

> *A group of girls at his school had been taunting Alan through IM, teasing him about his small size, daring him to do things he couldn't do. They dared him to commit suicide. He discussed this with them. The girls thought it was a big joke. One afternoon, Alan got his grandfather's shotgun, loaded it, and killed himself. He left this message, "The only way to get the respect you deserve is to die."*

> *Just in case you are wondering—this is a true story. How might this story have ended differently if one of the girls had told her parents or someone at school that Alan was being cyberbullied and was talking about killing himself?*

If you see something happening online that worries you, here is what you can do:

- Download all the materials. Provide written instructions for how to find these materials online or where the communications occurred.

- If there is a possibility of immediate harm, report your concern to the local police or to a school violence or suicide prevention hotline.

- To report other concerns, show the materials to the principal or school counselor or put the documents and instructions into an envelope, write "IMPORTANT" on the envelope, and put the envelope in your principal's or school counselor's office or mailbox.

- If the student does not go to your school, see if you can find out where the student does go to school by searching for the school Web site. Look for an e-mail address for the school principal or counselor. Send a "high priority" message explaining your concerns and telling this person where to find the material online.

THINKING IT THROUGH

1. What are your personal standards for how you intend to treat other people online?

2. What steps will you take to make it less likely that you will be cyberbullied?

3. What are four things you could do if you were being cyberbullied?

4. What should you not do if you are cyberbullied?

5. What can you do if you see someone else being cyberbullied?

6. Why is it not a good idea to post material that an adult might think is a threat?

7. Why is it a good idea to report any online material that appears to be a threat, even if it may just be a joke?

8. Review the terms of use agreement for a popular teen Web site. What kinds of communications and activities does this agreement prohibit?

9. What are your thoughts on the following statement: "On the Internet, I should have the free-speech right to post whatever I want, even if I might hurt someone else."

FOR THE TEACHER: INSTRUCTIONAL RECOMMENDATIONS

The following are additional instructional strategies:

- Present students with the results of a recent student needs assessment and use this data as the basis for engaging in a discussion about how to address local concerns. Ask the students to prepare a joint document presenting their advice on these issues to the school or district safe schools committee.

- Ask students to research news articles online that discuss cyberbullying, cyberthreats, or dangerous online communities, then have them discuss or write about the incidents reported. Ask students to put themselves into the story and outline the steps they would take if they witnessed or experienced any incidents similar to those that were reported. The goal of this exercise is to reinforce the recommendations for how students can productively address these concerns.

- Have students debate about one of the key social norms that supports online social aggression: "On the Internet, I have a free-speech right to post whatever I want, without regard for the possible harm it might cause to someone else."

- Ask the students to interview their parents, asking for their guidance on family values around online activities. Download some of the terms of use agreements from popular social networking sites. Provide copies of the district's Internet use policy. Have the students create a major chart outlining the standards expressed by their parents, the terms of use agreements, and the district's Internet use agreement. Identify the commonalities and any differences. Following this analysis, ask the students to create their own personal statement of standards.

APPENDIX K

Parent Guide to Cyberbullying and Cyberthreats

Young people have fully embraced the Internet as both an environment and a tool for socializing. Via the Internet and other technologies, they send e-mail, create their own Web sites, post intimate personal news in blogs (online interactive journals), send text messages and images via cell phone, contact each other through IMs (instant messages), chat in chat rooms, post to discussion boards, and seek out new friends in teen sites.

Unfortunately, there are increasing reports of teenagers (and sometimes younger children) using these technologies to post damaging text or images to bully their peers or engage in other aggressive behavior. There are also increasing reports of teens posting material that raises concerns that they are considering an act of violence toward others or themselves.

This guide provides parents with insight into these concerns and guidelines to prevent your child from being victimized by or engaging in online harmful behavior. It also provides guidance on things you can do in either case.

CYBERBULLYING

Cyberbullying is being cruel to others by sending or posting harmful material or engaging in other forms of social aggression using the Internet or other digital technologies. Cyberbullying can take different forms:

- Flaming—Online fights using electronic messages with angry and vulgar language.

Joe and Alec's online exchange got angrier and angrier. Insults were flying. Joe warned Alec to watch his back in school the next day.

- Harassment—Repeatedly sending nasty, mean, and insulting messages.

Sara reported to the principal that Kayla was bullying another student. When Sara got home, she had 35 angry messages in her e-mail box. The anonymous cruel messages kept coming—some from strangers.

- Denigration—"Dissing" someone online. Sending or posting gossip or rumors about a person to damage his or her reputation or friendships.

Some boys created a "We Hate Joe" Web site where they posted jokes, cartoons, gossip, and rumors, all dissing Joe.

- Impersonation—Pretending to be someone else and sending or posting material to get that person in trouble or danger or to damage that person's reputation or friendships.

Laura watched closely as Emma logged on to her account and discovered her password. Later, Laura logged on to Emma's account and sent a hurtful message to Emma's boyfriend, Adam.

- Outing—Sharing someone's secrets or embarrassing information or images online.

Greg, an obese high school student, was changing in the locker room after gym class. Matt took a picture of him with his cell phone camera. Within seconds, the picture was flying around the phones at school.

- Trickery—Talking someone into revealing secrets or embarrassing information, then sharing it online.

Katie sent a message to Jessica pretending to be her friend and asking lots of questions. Jessica responded, sharing really personal information. Katie forwarded the message to lots of other people with her own comment, "Jessica is a loser."

- Exclusion—Intentionally and cruelly excluding someone from an online group.

Millie tries hard to fit in with a group of girls at school. She recently got on the "outs" with a leader in this group. Now

Millie has been blocked from the friendship links of all of the girls.

- Cyberstalking—Repeated, intense harassment and denigration that includes threats or creates significant fear.

  When Annie broke up with Sam, he sent her many angry, threatening, pleading messages. He spread nasty rumors about her to her friends and posted a sexually suggestive picture she had given him in a sex-oriented discussion group, along with her e-mail address and cell phone number.

CYBERTHREATS

Cyberthreats are either threats or "distressing material"—general statements that make it sound like the writer is emotionally upset and may be considering harming someone else, harming himself or herself, or committing suicide.

> *Jeff wrote in his blog: "I'm a retarded [expletive] for ever believing that things would change. I'm starting to regret sticking around. It takes courage to turn the gun on your self, takes courage to face death." Jeff was also sharing his plans for an attack with a friend via e-mail.*

> *Celia met Andrew in a chat room. Andrew wrote: "bring a gun to school, ur on the front of every. . . . i cant imagine going through life without killing a few people. . . . people can be kissing my shotgun straight out of doom. . . . if i dont like the way u look at me, u die. . . . i choose who lives and who dies"*

> *Greg set up an anonymous IM account and sent a threatening message to his older sister suggesting that she would be killed the next day at school.*

Sometimes when teens post what appears to be a threat, they are just joking. Other times, the threat could be very real. There are two very important things that your child must understand about online threats:

- *Don't make threats online.* If you post a threat online, adults may not be able to tell whether the threat is real. There are criminal laws against making threats. If you make a cyberthreat, even if you are just joking, you could be suspended, expelled, or even arrested.

- *Report threats or distressing material.* If you see a threat or distressing material posted online, it could be very real. It is extremely important to report this to an adult. If the threat is real, someone could be seriously injured.

Just in case you are wondering—these are all true stories. Jeff killed nine people and then killed himself. Celia reported her online conversation to her father, who contacted the police. The police found that Andrew had many weapons, including an AK-47. He is now in prison. Greg's sister told her parents, her parents told the school, and the school went into "lockdown." Greg was identified easily—and arrested for making a threat.

HOW, WHO, AND WHY

- Cyberbullying or cyberthreat material—text or images—may be posted on personal Web sites or blogs or transmitted via e-mail, discussion groups, message boards, chat, IM, or cell phones.

- A cyberbully may be a person whom the target knows or an online stranger. Or the cyberbully may be anonymous, so it is not possible to tell. A cyberbully may solicit involvement of other people who do not know the target—cyberbullying by proxy.

Sue was really angry at Kelsey, who she thought stole her boyfriend. Sue convinced Marilyn to post anonymous comments on a discussion board slamming Kelsey. Marilyn was eager to win Sue's approval and fit into her group of friends, so she did as Sue requested.

- Cyberbullying and cyberthreats may be related to in-school bullying. Sometimes, the student who is victimized at school is also being bullied online. But other times, the person who is victimized at school becomes a cyberbully and retaliates online. Still other times, the student who is victimized will share his or her anger or depression online as distressing material.

Brad's blog is filled with racist profanity. Frequently, he targets black and Latino student leaders, as well as minority teachers, in his angry verbal assaults.

- Cyberbullying may involve relationships. If a relationship breaks up, one person may start to cyberbully the other person.

Other times, teens may get into online fights about relationships.

- Cyberbullying may be based on hate or bias—bullying others because of race, religion, physical appearance (including obesity), or sexual orientation.

- Teens may think that cyberbullying is entertaining—a game to hurt other people.

  Sitting around the computer with her friends, Judy asked, "Who can we mess with?" Judy started IM-ing with Brittany, asking her many personal questions. The next day, the girls were passing around Brittany's IM at school.

- Teens may have no one to talk with about how bad they are feeling and how horrible their life is, so they describe their feelings online. They might think that if they post this material online, they will meet someone who cares about them. Unfortunately, they may meet a dangerous stranger who will do them harm or other hurt teens, who only reinforce their bad feelings.

IMPACT OF CYBERBULLYING

It is widely known that face-to-face bullying can result in long-term psychological harm to targets. This harm includes low self-esteem, depression, anger, school failure, school avoidance, and, in some cases, school violence or suicide. It is possible that the harm caused by cyberbullying may be even greater than harm caused by traditional bullying because . . .

- Online communications can be extremely vicious.

- There is no escape for those who are being cyberbullied—victimization is ongoing, 24/7.

- Cyberbullying material can be distributed worldwide and is often irretrievable.

- Cyberbullies can be anonymous and can solicit the involvement of unknown "friends."

Teens may be reluctant to tell adults what is happening online or through their cell phones because they are emotionally traumatized, think it is their fault, fear greater retribution, or fear online activities or cell phone use will be restricted.

A group of girls at Alan's school had been taunting him through instant messaging, teasing him about his small size, daring him to do things he couldn't do, suggesting that the world would be a better place if he committed suicide. One day, he shot himself. His last online message was "Sometimes the only way to get the respect you deserve is to die."

BULLY, TARGET, AND BYSTANDER

If your child has been actively socializing online, it is probable that he or she has been involved in cyberbullying in one or more of the following roles:

- *Bullies:* "Put-downers" who harass and demean others, especially those they think are different or inferior, or "get-backers," who have been bullied by others and are using the Internet to retaliate or vent their anger.

- *Targets:* The targets of the cyberbully.

- *Harmful bystanders:* Those who encourage and support the bully or watch the bullying from the sidelines, but do nothing to intervene or help the target.

- *Helpful bystanders:* Those who seek to stop the bullying, protest against it, provide support to the target, or tell an adult. We need more of this kind of bystanders!

RELATED ONLINE RISKY BEHAVIOR

There are other concerns about youth online behavior that parents should be aware of. Teens who do not have strong real-world connections appear to be the ones most attracted to these risky behaviors.

- *Disclosing personal information:* Young people are disclosing personal contact information and massive amounts of sensitive personal information in public online sites or through personal communications. Teens seem to be unaware of the public and permanent nature of these disclosures and the ability of others to send the material they place in electronic form to anyone, anywhere.

- *Internet addiction:* Internet addiction is defined as an excessive amount of time spent using the Internet, resulting in lack of healthy engagement in other areas of life. The Internet offers a time-warped, 24/7 place where children and teens can get away from their real-world concerns.

- *Suicide and self-harm communities:* Depressed young people are interacting with sites and groups that provide information on suicide and self-harm methods (for example, cutting, anorexia, fainting) and encouragement for such activities.

- *Hate group recruitment and gangs:* Sites and groups that foster hatred against "others" are actively recruiting angry, disconnected youth. Some youth informally use the Internet to coordinate troublesome and dangerous activities.

- *Risky sexual behavior:* Young people are using Internet communities and matching services to make connections with others for sexual activities, ranging from online discussions about sex to "hook-ups." They may post or provide sexually suggestive or explicit pictures or videos.

- *Violent gaming:* Violent gaming frequently involves sexual or other bias-based aggression. Young people often engage in online simulation games, which reinforce the perception that all interactions online, including violent ones, are "just a game."

YOU CAN'T SEE ME—I CAN'T SEE YOU

Why is it that when people use the Internet or other technologies, they sometimes do things that they would never do in the real world? Here are some of the reasons:

- *You can't see me:* When people use the Internet, they perceive that they are invisible. The perception can be enhanced by creating anonymous accounts. People are not really invisible—online activities can be traced. But if you think you are invisible, this removes concerns about detection, disapproval, or punishment.

- *I can't see you:* When people use the Internet they do not receive tangible feedback about the consequences of their actions, including actions that have hurt someone. Lack of feedback interferes with empathy and leads to the misperception that no harm has resulted.

- *Everybody does it:* The perception of invisibility and lack of tangible feedback support risky or irresponsible online social norms, including these:

"Life online is just a game." Allows teens to ignore the harmful real-world consequences of online actions and creates the expectation that others will simply ignore or dismiss any online harm.

"Look at me—I'm a star." Supports excessive disclosure of intimate information and personal attacks on others, generally done for the purpose of attracting attention.

"It's not me. It's my online persona." Allows teens to deny responsibility for actions taken by one of their online identities.

"What happens online stays online." Supports the idea that one should not bring issues related to what has happened online into the outside world and should not disclose online activity to adults.

"On the Internet, I have the free-speech right to write or post anything I want regardless of the harm it might cause to another." Supports harmful speech and cruel behavior as a free-speech right.

STAY INVOLVED

Many parents think that if their children are home using a computer they are safe and not getting into trouble. Nothing could be further from the truth. Your child could be the target of cyberbullying or be causing harm to others from your own family room.

Some parents think they have protected their children because they have installed filtering software. Filtering software provides a false sense of security. Not only can youth still access material parents don't want them to access, filtering cannot prevent cyberbullying or address other concerns.

Make it your business to know what your child is doing online. Teenagers are likely to take the position that their online activities are their business. But parents have a moral, as well as legal, obligation to ensure that their children are engaged in safe and responsible behavior—including online behavior. Here are some ways to stay involved:

- Keep the computer in a public place in the house. Periodically check on what your child is doing. Discuss the kinds of Internet activities your child enjoys. Find out who your child's online friends are.

- Help your child distinguish between three kinds of personal information:

  Personal contact information: Name, address, phone number, and any other information that could allow someone to make contact in the real world. This information should be shared only in secure environments, when absolutely necessary, and with your permission.

  Intimate personal information: Private and personal information that should only be discussed with a relative, close friend, or professional. This information should never be shared in public online communities or through public communications such as chat or discussion groups. Disclosures in private communications with trustworthy friends or in professional online support environments may be appropriate.

  Personal interest information: Non-intimate information about interests and activities. This kind of information can generally be safely shared on public community sites or communication environments, including blogs, personal Web pages, chat, and discussion groups.

- Increase your child's online "stranger danger" awareness. Anyone your child meets online should be considered potentially dangerous until it is possible to determine from independent real-world sources who this person is and that this person has a background that provides assurances of safety.

- Be sure you know the online communities your child participates in and your child's usernames in these communities. Review your child's public postings, including your child's profiles, Web pages, and blogs. Discourage active involvement in the kinds of environments that promote excessive self-disclosure of intimate information and rude behavior. Your child may object and claim that these postings should be considered private. A child who makes this argument simply does not understand. The material posted on these sites is not private—anyone can read it. If your child is uncomfortable about your review of the material, then this is a good clue that the material should not be posted.

- Be up front with your child that you will periodically investigate the files on the computer, the browser history files and buddy lists, and your child's public online activities. Tell your child that you may review his or her private communication activities if you have reason to believe that you will find evidence of unsafe or irresponsible behavior.

- Watch out for secretive behavior. It's a danger sign if your child rapidly switches screens as you approach the computer or attempts to hide online behavior by emptying the history file.

- You can install keystroke monitoring software that will record all of your child's online activities. The use of such software raises trust concerns. The best way to use such software is as deterrence. Tell your child monitoring software has been installed but not yet activated and explain what actions on his or her part could lead to your investigation. These actions could include not being willing to talk about online activities, late night use, extensive use, decline in grades, evidence your child is seeking to cover his or her online tracks, report of inappropriate activity, appearing really upset after Internet use, and the like. If your child has engaged in unsafe or inappropriate behavior, the most appropriate consequence is the use of monitoring software and consistent review of all public and private online activity.

Important Note

If ever you find any evidence that your child is interacting with a sexual predator, do not confront your child. Your child could warn or run off with the predator. Call your local police and ask for a youth or computer crimes expert. If you suspect this kind of activity, consider installing or activating monitoring software but not telling your child.

PREVENT YOUR CHILD FROM BEING A CYBERBULLY

- Talk with your child about the value of treating others with kindness and your expectation that your child will act in accord with this value online.

- Make it clear that if your child engages in irresponsible online behavior, you will restrict Internet access, activate monitoring software, and review all online activity. Talk about the implications of cyberbullying that could lead to criminal arrest or civil litigation. Also, discuss the point that if your child misuses e-mail or a cell phone that is on a family account, the entire account may be terminated.

- Help your child develop self-awareness, empathy, and effective decision making by asking these questions:

Am I being kind and showing respect for others and myself?

How would I feel if someone did the same thing to me or to my best friend?

How do I feel inside?

What would a trusted adult, someone who is important in my life, think?

Is this action in violation of any agreements, rules, or laws?

How would I feel if others could see me?

Would it be okay if I did this in my home or at school?

How does this action reflect on me?

- Warn against online retaliation. Some teens who engage in cyberbullying are retaliating against teens who are bullying them face-to-face. Help your child understand that retaliating is not smart because when targets lose their cool, it allows the bullies to justify their behavior. Further, your child could be mistaken as the source of the problem. Ask the school counselor for resources to help you bully-proof your child and assistance to stop any bullying that is occurring at school.

IF YOUR CHILD IS CYBERBULLYING

If you become aware that your child is engaged in cyberbullying through your own investigation or through a report from the school or another parent, it is essential that you respond in a firm and responsible manner.

If you're like most parents, you will be motivated by a desire to stop your child from harming another. But you should also be aware that if you know your child is cyberbullying and fail to take action that stops your child from engaging in such harmful behavior—and that ensures the removal of material already posted—there is a significantly increased potential that you can be held financially liable for the harm caused by your child!

Useful actions to take are as follows:

- Establish very clear prohibitions about behaving in this manner.

- Warn against taking any action in retaliation or asking anyone else to engage in retaliation.

- Immediately install monitoring software, if you have not yet done so. Tell your child that all Internet activities will be monitored.

- Direct your child not to access the Internet anywhere but at school or at home, and advise that evidence of access from other locations will lead to further loss of privileges.

PREVENT YOUR CHILD FROM BECOMING A TARGET

It is important to bully-proof your child by building his or her self-confidence and resilience. Pay special attention if your child has traits that can lead to victimization, including obesity or the perception that your child is gay or lesbian. Your child may also be at risk if he or she is an alternative thinker, unwilling to play social games, and either wants desperately to be one of the "in crowd" or is inclined to reject association with them.

Ask your child whether he or she has been a target of cyberbullying or has witnessed it and what happened. Assure your child that you trust him or her to handle many of these kinds of situations, but that if a situation ever emerges that causes concerns, you are there to help. Make it clear that you will not respond by unilaterally restricting all Internet activities.

SIGNS OF VICTIMIZATION

If you are concerned that your child may be a target, try to engage your child in a conversation about bullying and cyberbullying and pay closer attention to what he or she is doing online. The following indicate that your child may be the target of cyberbullying:

- Signs of depression, sadness, anxiety, anger, or fear, especially if nothing apparent could be causing this upset or if your child seems especially upset after using the Internet or cell phone.

- Avoidance of friends, school, and activities, or a decline in grades, or both.

- Subtle comments that reflect emotional distress or disturbed online or in-person relationships.

If your child is highly depressed, appears to be suicidal, or has made a suicide attempt, it is critically important to find out what is happening to your child online. You may need the assistance of someone with greater technical expertise to help investigate.

ENCOURAGE YOUR CHILD TO BE A HELPFUL BYSTANDER

Cyberbullying is occurring in online environments where responsible adults are generally not present. Youth are also posting material that provides clues they are considering committing an act of violence against others or themselves in these online environments. Usually, the only people who know someone is being victimized or is depressed and considering violence or suicide are other teenagers. Increased teen intervention and reporting is essential!

Your child may ask you, "If I am just watching and am not part of the activity, then how could I be doing something wrong?" Good question. Here is an answer: "Bullies crave an audience. By paying attention to their bullying, you are encouraging their behavior. You are part of the problem. I want you to be part of the solution."

- Help your child gain a sense of responsibility for the well-being of others and the willingness to go out of the way to help another.

- Stress the importance of speaking out against bullies, or, if this is not safe, providing private help to the target or reporting such actions to you or another responsible adult.

- Make sure your child knows how important it is to report any direct threats or distressing material he or she may witness online to you, the school, a school violence or suicide hotline, or the police.

Review the two cyberthreat examples presented earlier:

Celia saved and reported the chat session. Andrew's intentions were found to be real, and he is now in prison. Many people knew Jeff was suicidal and planning an attack at his school. No one reported it. Jeff killed nine people and himself.

RESPONDING TO CYBERBULLYING

Help your child to . . .

- Develop personal guidelines for online involvement.

- Make a realistic evaluation of the quality of an online community and the benefits of remaining or leaving.

- Recognize the need to leave an online situation that has gotten out of control.

- Conduct a self-assessment of his or her behavior or communications that may be contributing to victimization.

- Learn how to respond to any harmful communications. Your child should know that if he or she is attacked online it is absolutely critical not to respond in anger. Anger shows weakness, which will encourage more bullying. Because Internet communications can be delayed, your child can take the time to calm down and prepare a response that is strong and assertive.

- Know when and how to gain assistance from an adult. Tell your child you expect that he or she can handle many incidents but that it is important to contact an adult if:

He or she is really upset and not sure what to do.

The cyberbullying could be a crime.

Any cyberbullying is (or might be) occurring through the district Internet system or via a cell phone at school.

He or she is being bullied by the same person at school.

The cyberbully is anonymous.

The cyberbully is bullying other teens who may be more vulnerable and too afraid to get help.

CYBERBULLYING RESPONSE OPTIONS

Save the Evidence

Save all e-mail and text messages, as well as records of chat or IM sessions. Download all Web pages. This should be done in all cases.

Identify the Cyberbully

Identification could require some detective work. Look for clues wherever the cyberbully is posting. Remember, a cyberbully may impersonate someone else or could be a proxy cyberbully. You may not need to know the identity of the cyberbully to take action.

- Ask your Internet service (ISP) provider to identify the source or contact a company that traces the identity of people online.

- If you can demonstrate that a student may be involved, have the district technology director search district Internet use records.

- If you intend to file a lawsuit, consider having an attorney help identify the cyberbully.

- If a crime has occurred, ask the police to identify the cyberbully.

Tell the Cyberbully to Stop

Your child can send the cyberbully a nonemotional, assertive message telling the cyberbully to stop.

Ignore the Cyberbully

Help your child block or filter all communications through his or her e-mail and IM contact list. Your child can also avoid going to the site or group where he or she has been attacked or change his or her e-mail address, account, username, or phone number.

File a Complaint

Cyberbullying is a violation of the terms of use of most Web sites, ISPs, and cell phone companies. File a complaint by providing the harmful messages or a link to the harmful material and ask that the account be terminated and any harmful material removed. Make sure you keep all communications. Here are the steps:

- If the cyberbully is using e-mail, contact the ISP of the cyberbully (you can determine the ISP from the e-mail address), contact the company at support@<ISP>, or look on the ISP's site for "Contact Us."

- If the material appears on a third-party Web site (with a URL such as www.webhostname.com/~kid'sname.html) go to the site's home page and file a complaint through "Contact Us."

- If the material is on a Web site with its own domain name (www.xyzkid.com), go to Whois (www.whois.net) to find the owner of the site and the host company. Go to the host company's Web site and file a complaint through "Contact Us."

- If the cyberbully is using a cell phone, trace the number and contact the company.

Contact Your School

Your school may not be able to discipline a student for totally off-campus actions because of free-speech protections. But if the cyberbully is using the district Internet system or is also bullying your child at school, or if your child's participation in school has been substantially disrupted, the school can intervene with formal discipline. Your school can also contact the parents of the cyberbully to get the cyberbullying to stop.

Contact the Cyberbully's Parents

The cyberbully's parents may be totally unaware that their child has engaged in this kind of activity, concerned about it when they find out, and both willing and able to get the cyberbullying to stop. Or they could become very defensive. Avoid meeting with them face-to-face. Instead, send the cyberbully's parents a certified letter that includes the downloaded material and requests that the cyberbullying stop and all harmful material be removed.

Contact an Attorney

Cyberbullying could meet the standards for defamation, invasion of privacy, or intentional infliction of emotional distress. An attorney can send a letter to the cyberbully's parents demanding that the cyberbullying stop. An attorney can also file a lawsuit against the cyberbully's parents for financial damages (money because your child has been harmed) and an injunction (requirement that the cyberbullying stop and material be removed).

Contact the Police

If the cyberbullying appears to be a crime, contact the police. Criminal cyberbullying involves threats of violence, coercion, obscene or harassing text messages, harassment or stalking, hate or bias crimes, creating or sending sexually explicit pictures, sexual exploitation, or taking a picture of someone in a private place.

CyberbullyNOT—Stopping Online Social Aggression

Cyberbullying is being mean to others by sending or posting harmful material using the Internet or a cell phone.

Types of Cyberbullying

- *Flaming:* Angry, rude arguments.

- *Harassment:* Repeatedly sending offensive messages.

- *Denigration:* "Dissing" someone online by spreading rumors or posting false information.

- *Outing and trickery:* Disseminating intimate private information or talking someone into disclosing private information, which is then disseminated.

- *Impersonation:* Pretending to be someone else and posting material to damage that person's reputation.

- *Exclusion:* Intentionally excluding someone from an online group.

- *Cyberstalking:* Creating fear by repeatedly sending offensive messages and engaging in other harmful online activities.

How, Who, and Why

- Cyberbullying may occur via personal Web sites, blogs, e-mail, discussion groups, message boards, chat, instant messaging, or voice, text, or image cell phones.

- A cyberbully may be a person whom the target knows or an online stranger. A cyberbully may be anonymous and may enlist the aid of others, including online "friends."

- Cyberbullying may be a continuation of, or in retaliation for, in-school bullying. It may be related to fights about relationships or be based on hate or bias. Some teens think cyberbullying is entertaining—a fun game.

Several factors may make teens unconcerned about the consequences of harmful online behavior:

- They think they are invisible or can take steps to become invisible, so they think they can't be punished.

- There is no tangible feedback about the harm they cause, so it seems like a game to them.

- Harmful online social norms support cyberbullying: "On the Internet, I have a free speech right to post whatever I want, regardless of the harm I cause."

The Harm

Cyberbullying can cause great emotional harm to the target. Online communications can be vicious, and cyberbullying can be happening 24/7. Damaging text and images can be widely disseminated and impossible to fully remove. Teens are reluctant to tell adults about problems online for fear of overreaction, restriction from online activities, and possible retaliation by the cyberbully. There are emerging reports of youth suicide and violence related to cyberbullying.

Responsible Management of Children's Internet Use

Parents have a moral and legal obligation to ensure that their children engage in safe and responsible behavior online! Useful steps to take:

- Keep the computer in a public place and supervise its use.

- Find out what public online sites and communities your child uses and periodically review what your child is posting. Emphasize that these sites and communities are public and that your child should never post personal contact information, intimate personal information, or provocative sexually oriented material. (Your child may argue that you are invading his or her privacy—but you can point out that what you're doing, anyone can do. These are *public* places!)

- Tell your child that you will investigate his or her private online communications if you have reason to believe that the child has engaged in unsafe or irresponsible behavior. You can install monitoring software to do this.

- Make joint Internet use management agreements with the parents of your child's friends—addressing the amount of time children can spend online, approved activities, and a mutual parental agreement to monitor and report.

Prevent Your Child from Being a Cyberbully

- Make it clear that all Internet use must be in accord with family values of kindness and respect for others and that any violation of this expectation will result in monitoring of all online activities, using Internet monitoring software.

- If your child is being bullied at school, work with the school to stop the bullying and make sure your child knows not to retaliate online.

Prevent Your Child from Becoming a Target of Cyberbullying

- Frequently discuss the concerns of public disclosure of intimate personal information and the value of modesty.

- Visit your child's favorite online communities and discuss the values demonstrated by others who participate there.

- Insist that the school intervene effectively to address any in-school bullying.

- Seek to bully-proof your child by reinforcing your child's unique individual strengths and fostering healthy friendships with teens you can trust to be kind.

Warning Signs That Your Child Might Be a Target

- Negative emotional reactions (sadness or anger) during or after Internet use.

- Withdrawal from friends and activities, school avoidance, decline of grades, and signs of depression and sadness.

- Indications that your child is being bullied at school or having any other difficulties with peers. Pay close attention if you see these indicators because these are the teens most often targeted by cyberbullies.

Action Steps and Options to Respond to Cyberbullying

- Save the evidence.

- Identify the cyberbully or bully group. Ask your Internet service provider for help.

- Clearly tell the cyberbully to stop.

- Ignore the cyberbully by leaving the online environment, blocking communications, or both.

- File a complaint with the Internet or cell phone company.

- Seek assistance from the school, if the cyberbully attends the same school. (But know that because of free-speech protections, if the cyberbullying is occurring totally off-campus, your school may be able to provide only informal assistance, not formal discipline.)

- Send the cyberbully's parents a letter that includes the evidence of cyberbullying. Demand that the actions stop and harmful material be removed.

- Contact an attorney to send a letter or file a lawsuit against the cyberbully's parents based on defamation, invasion of privacy, or intentional infliction of emotional distress.

- Call the police if the cyberbullying involves threats of violence, coercion, intimidation based on hate or bias, or any form of sexual exploitation.

Reporting Other Concerns

- If you have suspicions your child is involved with an online sexual predator, call the police. Do not talk to your child first—children in that situation often will warn the predator.

- If you see any online threats of school-related violence, call both the school and the police.

- If you see any material that raises concerns that a child is emotionally distressed and may be contemplating suicide, self-harm, or other violence, contact the counselor of the school the child attends.

Notes

CHAPTER 1

1. www.cbsnews.com/htdocs/pdf/colombine_affidavit.pdf.

2. www.detnews.com/2004/metro/0409/19/a01-277821.htm.

3. www.jeffweise.com/profiles.html. *Note:* This site provides access to material that reportedly reflects material that was presumably posted by Jeff Weise and was found and archived after the shooting. There is no source of the identity of the person(s) who have posted the material. Therefore, questions should be raised about the credibility of the site. However, news reports have referred to the same postings.

4. Rosario, R. (March 30, 2005). Investigators suspect wider attack planned. *Pioneer Press.* www.twincities.com/mld/ twincities/news/special_packages/red_lake/11262140.htm.

5. Bahrampour, T. (May 29, 2005). Message is clear in N.Va.: IM "threats" can bring teens trouble in an instant. *Washington Post.* www.washingtonpost.com/wp-dyn/content/article/2005/ 05/28/AR2005052800913.html.

6. Lystra, T. (April 13, 2006). Student charged for death threat. *Corvallis Gazette Times.*

CHAPTER 2

1. Technology does exist that can be used to verify age. This is a digital credential—a small piece of hardware that is coded with personal information that can be plugged into the USB port on the computer. But it is unrealistic to think that young people will independently use such a device to restrict their access to online communities, and online communities are highly unlikely to implement any technology that would require age verification.

2. Lenhart, A., & Madden, M. (2005). *Teen content creators and consumers*. Pew Internet and American Life Project. www.pewinternet.org/report_display.asp?r=166.

3. America Online Aim Fight. www.aimfight.com/.

4. Lenhart & Madden, *Teen content creators and consumers*.

CHAPTER 3

1. Most notably, Anne Collier, who publishes a weekly electronic newsletter on these issues; see http://netfamilynews.com.

2. Nansel, T. R., Overpeck, M., Pilla, R. S. et al. (2001). Bullying behaviors among U.S. youth: Prevalence and association with psychological adjustment. *Journal of the American Medical Association, 285*(16), 2094–2100.

3. Siegel, J., Dubrovsky, V., Kiesler, S., & McGuire, T. (1986). Group processes in computer mediated communication. *Organizational Behavior and Human Decision Processes, 37,* 157–187.

4. Kowalski, R., Limber, S. P., Scheck, A., Redfearn, M., Allen, J., Calloway, A., Farris, J., Finnegan, K., Keith, M., Kerr, S., Singer, L., Spearman, J., Tripp, L., & Vernon, L. (2005, August 18–21). *Electronic bullying among school-aged children and youth.* Paper presented at the annual meeting of the American Psychological Association, Washington, DC.

5. National Institute of Child Health and Human Development (NICHHD) study, cited in Nansel et al., *Bullying behaviors among U.S. youth.*

6. Bosworth, K., Espelage, D., & Simon, T. (1999). Factors associated with bullying behavior in middle school students. *Journal of Early Adolescence, 19,* 341–362.

7. American Association of University Women. (2001). *Hostile hallways: Bullying, teasing, and sexual harassment in school.* www.aauw.org/research/girls_education/hostile.cfm.

8. Macklem, G. (2003). *Bullying and teasing: Social power in children's groups.* New York: Kluwer Academic.

9. *Fight crime: Invest in kids.* (August 17, 2006). News release. www.fightcrime.org/releases.php?id=231.

10. Wolak, J., Mitchell, K., & Finkelhor, D. (2006). *Online victimization of youth: Five years later.* www.unh.edu/ccrc/second_youth_Internet_safety-publications.html.

11. Kowalski, Limber, S. et al. *Electronic bullying among school-aged children and youth.*

12. www.media-awareness.ca/english/research/YCWW/phaseII/

13. www.media-awareness.ca/english/research/YCWW/phaseII/key_findings.cfm.

14. Livingston, S., & Bober, M. (2004). *UK children go online: Surveying the experiences of young people and their parents.* http://personal.lse.ac.uk/bober/UKCGOfinalReport.pdf.

15. Lyznicki, J. M., McCaffree, M. A., & Robinowitz, C. B. (2004). Childhood bullying: Implications for physicians. *American Family Physician, 70,* 1723–1730.

16. Adams, L., & Russakoff, D. (June 12, 1999). Dissecting Columbine's cult of the athlete. *Washington Post,* p. A-1.

17. Newman, K. (2004). *Rampage: The social roots of school shootings.* Boulder, CO: Perseus Books.

18. Pellegrini, A. D., & Long, J. D. (2002). A longitudinal study of bullying, dominance, and victimization during the transition from primary school through secondary school. *British Journal of Developmental Psychology, 20*(2), 259–280.

19. Adler, P. A., & Adler P. (1998). *Peer power: Preadolescent culture and identity.* New Brunswick, NJ: Rutgers University Press.

20. Finlay, D. (October 15, 2005). Personal communication. Deborah Finlay is a school counselor in Virginia. A middle school student at her school committed suicide in the context of cyberbullying. She has become an authority on this issue and has provided very helpful from-the-trenches insight to this author.

21. Nansel et al., *Bullying behaviors among U.S. youth.*

22. Crick, N. R., & Grotpeter, J. K. (1995). Children's treatment by peers: Victims of relational and overt aggression. *Development and Psychopathology, 8,* 367–380.

23. Kaiser Family Foundation (2005). *Generation M: Media in the lives of 8–18-year-olds.* www.kff.org/entmedia/entmedia030905pkg.cfm.

24. Kowalski, Limber et al. *Electronic bullying among school-aged children and youth.*

25. Vossekuil, B., Fein, R., Reddy, M., Borum, R., & Modeleski, B. (2002). *The final report and findings of the Safe School Initiative: Implications for the prevention of school attacks in the United States.* U.S. Secret Service and U.S. Department of Education. www.secretservice.gov/ntac/ssi_final_report.pdf.

26. Reuters. (June 3, 2004). *Internet blamed for Japan school killing.* MSNBC. www.msnbc.msn.com/id/5110933/.

27. Nansel et al., *Bullying behaviors among U.S. youth.*

28. American Association of University Women, *Hostile hallways.*

29. Gay, Lesbian, Straight Educational Network. (2003). *National school climate.* www.glsen.org/cgi-bin/iowa/all/news/record/1413.html.

30. Harmon, A. (August 26, 2004). Internet gives teenage bullies weapons to wound from afar. *New York Times.* http://select.nytimes.com/gst/abstract.html?res=F10A17F9385A0C758EDDA10894DC404482.

31. Nansel et al., *Bullying behaviors among U.S. youth.*

32. Craig, W., & Pepler, D. (2000). Observations of bullying in the playground and in the classroom. *School Psychology International, 21*(1), 22–37; O'Connell, P., Pepler, D., and Craig, W., (1999). Peer involvement in bullying: Insights and challenges for intervention. *Journal of Adolescence, 22,* 437–452.

33. Pellegrini & Long, *A longitudinal study of bullying, dominance, and victimization.*

34. For example, see Slaby, R., Wilson-Brewer, R., & Dash, K. (1998). *Aggressors, victims, and bystanders: Thinking and acting to prevent violence.* https://secure.edc.org/publications/prodview.asp?15.

35. Stop Bullying Now. *Children who bully: SBN Tip 1–1.* U.S. Department of Health and Human Services, Health Resources and Services Administration. http://stopbullyingnow.hrsa.gov/ HHS_PSA/pdfs/SBN_Tip_1.pdf.

36. Lenhart, A. (2005). *Protecting teens online.* Pew Internet and American Life Project. www.pewInternet.org/PPF/r/152/ report_display.asp.

37. American Academy of Pediatrics et al. (2000). *Joint statement on the impact of entertainment violence on children.* Signed by American Academy of Pediatrics, American Academy of Child and Adolescent Psychiatry, American Psychological Association, American Medical Association, American Academy of Family Physicians, and American Psychiatric Association.

38. Media Awareness. (n.d.). *Marketing and consumerism: Special issues for tweens and teens.* www.media-awareness.ca/english/ parents/marketing/issues_teens_marketing.cfm.

39. Prichard, O. (December 11, 2005). A juggernaut called MySpace.com. *Philadelphia Inquirer.*

40. Nansel et al., *Bullying behaviors among U.S. youth.*

41. Rigby, K. (2001). Health consequences of bullying and its prevention in schools. In J. Juvonen & S. Graham, Eds., *Peer harassment in school: The plight of the vulnerable and victimized.* New York: Guilford Press.

42. Nansel et al., *Bullying behaviors among U.S. youth.*

43. Macklem, *Bullying and teasing.*

44. McEvoy, A. (2005, September). *Teachers who bully students: Patterns and policy implications.* Paper presented at the Hamilton Fish Institute's Persistently Safe Schools Conference. www.stopbullyingnow.com/ bullying%20by%teachers.htm.

45. Federal Bureau of Investigation. (2000). www.fbi.gov/ pressrel/pressrel00/school.htm, p. 7.

46. Ibid, p. 16.

47. www.mentalhealth.samhsa.gov/publications/allpubs/ walletcard/engwalletcard.asp.

48. Meadows, B., Bergal, J., Helling, S., Odell, J., Piligian, E., Howard, C., Lopez, M., Atlas, D., & Hochberg, L. (March 21, 2005). The Web: The bully's new playground. *People Magazine.*

CHAPTER 4

1. Wolak, J., Mitchell, K., & Finkelhor, D. (2003). Escaping or connecting? Characteristics of youth who form close online relationships. *Journal of Adolescence, 26*(1), 105–119. www.unh.edu/ccrc/Youth_Internet_info_page.html.

2. Young, K. S. (1998). *Caught in the Net.* New York: Wiley.

3. Whitlock, J. L., Powers, J. L., & Eckenrode, J. (2006). The virtual cutting edge: The Internet and adolescent self-injury. *Developmental Psychology, 42*(3), 407–417. www.apa.org/journals/releases/dev423407.pdf.

4. Franklin, R. A. (September 1, 2006). *The hate directory: Hate groups on the Internet.* www.bcpl.net/~rfrankli/hatedir.htm.

5. National Alliance of Gang Investigators Associations. (2005). *National gang threat assessment.* www.nagia.org/PDFs/2005_national_gang_threat_assessment.pdf.

6. CNN. (April 24, 2006). *Kansas students charged in alleged plot.* www.cnn.com/2006/LAW/04/24/kansas.plot/index.html; Johnson, K. (April 23, 2006). *Students had a hit list, mayor said. USA Today.* www.usatoday.com/news/nation/2006–04–23-school-plot_x.htm.

7. Finkelhor, D., Mitchell, K., & Wolak, J. (2000). Online victimization: A report on the nation's youth. National Center for Missing and Exploited Children. www.unh.edu/ccrc/Youth_Internet_info_page.html.

8. Denizet-Lewis, B. (May 30, 2004). Friends, friends with benefits and the benefits of the local mall. *New York Times Magazine.* www.nytimes.com/2004/05/30/magazine/30NONDATING.html?ex=1401249600&en=b8ab7c02ae2d206b&ei=5007&partner=USERLAND.

9. Associated Press. (October 12, 2005). Sexual predators lose an outlet. *Wired.* www.wired.com/news/politics/0,1283,69188,00.html. It is very disturbing that it took legal action to get Yahoo to close these chat rooms down.

10. Wolak, J., Finkelhor, D., & Mitchell, K. (2004). Internet-initiated sex crimes against minors: Implications for prevention based on findings from a national study. *Journal of Adolescent Health, 35,* 424.e11–424.e20. http://download.journals.elsevierhealth.com/ pdfs/journals/1054–139X/PIIS1054139X04001715.pdf.

11. Anderson, C., & Dill, K. E. (2000). Video games and aggressive thoughts, feelings, and behavior in the laboratory and in life. *Journal of Personality and Social Psychology, 78*(4).

CHAPTER 5

1. Damon, W. (1988). *The moral child.* New York: Free Press.

2. Kagen, J., & Lamb, S. (Eds.). (1987). *The emergence of morality in young children.* Chicago: University of Chicago Press.

3. American Academy of Pediatrics. (n.d.). *Understanding the impact of media on children and teens.* www.aap.org/family/mediaimpact.htm.

4. American Academy of Pediatrics et al. (2000). *Joint statement on the impact of entertainment violence on children.*

5. Hoffman, M. L. (1991). Empathy, social cognition and moral action. In W. M. Kurtines & J. L. Gewirtz, *Handbook of moral behavior and development,* Vol. 1 (pp. 275–301). Hillsdale, NJ: Erlbaum.

6. Erickson, E. (1963 [1950]). *Childhood and society* (2nd ed.). New York: Norton.

7. Erickson, Ibid.; Hoffman, 1991.

8. Damon, *The moral child;* Kagen & Lamb, *The emergence of morality in young children.*

9. Baumrind, D. (1989). Rearing competent children. In W. Damon (Ed.), *Child development today and tomorrow.* San Francisco: Jossey-Bass.

10. Nisan, M. (1991). The Moral Balance Model: Theory and research extending our understanding of moral choice and deviation. In W. M. Kurtines & J. L. Gewirtz, *Handbook of moral behavior and development,* Vol. 3 (pp. 213–250). Hillsdale, NJ: Erlbaum.

11. Bandura, A. (1991). Social cognition theory of moral thought and action. In Kurtines & Gewirtz, *Handbook of moral behavior and development,* Vol. 1 (pp. 45–104).

12. Joinson, A. N. (1998). Causes and implications of disinhibited behavior on the Internet. In J. Gackenbach (Ed.), *Psychology and the Internet: Intrapersonal, interpersonal and transpersonal implications* (pp. 43–60). New York: Academic Press.

13. Joinson, *Causes and implications of disinhibited behavior on the Internet;* Siegel, J., Dubrovsky, V., Kiesler, S., & McGuire, T. (1986). Group processes in computer mediated communication. *Organizational Behavior and Human Decision Processes, 37,* 157–187.

14. Hoffman, 1991.

15. Joinson, *Causes and implications of disinhibited behavior on the Internet.*

16. Turkle, S. (1995). *Life on the screen: Identity in the age of the Internet.* New York: Simon & Schuster.

17. Erickson, *Childhood and society.*

18. www.eff.org.

19. www.washingtonpost.com/wp-dyn/content/article/2005/05/28/AR2005052800913.html.

CHAPTER 6

1. www.myspace.com/misc/terms.html?z=1&Mytoken=20050418130053.

2. Restatement (Second) of Torts §316 (1965).

CHAPTER 7

1. *Katz v. United States,* 389 U.S. 347 (1967). The two-part test was first enunciated in Justice Harlan's concurring opinion and subsequently applied in other Fourth Amendment cases—for example, *Smith v. Maryland,* 442 U.S. 735, 740–41 (1979).

2. Ibid. at 350–52, 360.

3. Ibid. at 361 (Harlan, J., concurring).

4. 206 F.3d 392 (4th Cir. 2000).

5. 469 U.S. 325 (1985).

6. Ibid. at 341.

7. Ibid. at 342 (citations omitted).

8. Ibid. at 342.

9. Ibid. at 342 (citations omitted).

10. Check out the Circumventor system on the Peacefire Web site at www.peacefire.com. Circumventor was developed with funding by the U.S. government program that operates Voice of America to provide an inexpensive, easy-to-implement way for people in third-world countries with restrictive information access policies to get around filters. It is interesting that students in the United States are also using this technology.

11. 425 F. Supp. 2d 622 (E.D. Pa. March 30, 2006).

12. 393 U.S. 503 (1969).

13. 478 U.S. 675 (1986).

14. 484 U.S. 260 (1988).

15. Ibid. at 504.

16. Ibid. at 509.

17. Ibid. at 683.

18. Ibid. at 688.

19. Ibid. at 270.

20. 607 F.2d 1043 (2nd Cir. 1979).

21. Ibid. at 1044.

22. Ibid. at 1050.

23. Ibid. at 1052. n. 17.

24. 134 F.3d 821, 828 (7th Cir. 1998).

25 *Watts v. United States,* 394 U.S. 705 (1969).

26. *Rogers v. United States,* 422 U.S. 35 (1975).

27. 136 F. Supp. 2d 446 (W.D. Pa. 2001).

28. Ibid. at 455.

29. 757 A.2d 412 (Pa. Commw. 2000).

30. Ibid. at 421.

31. *Davis v. Monroe County Board of Education,* 526 U.S. 629 (1999).

32. 240 F.3d 200 (3rd Cir. 2001).

33. Ibid. at 14.

34. Ibid. at 15.

35. Ibid. at 27.

36. 47 U.S.C. 254 (I)(1)(A)(ii).

CHAPTER 8

1. National Center for the Analysis of Violent Crime of the Federal Bureau of Investigation. (2000). *The school shooter: A threat assessment perspective.* www.fbi.gov/publications/ school/school2.pdf.

2. United States Secret Service Safe Schools Initiative. (2002). *Threat assessment in schools: A guide to managing threatening situations and to creating safe school climates.* www.secretservice.gov/ntac_ssi.shtml.

3. www.sprc.org/.

4. For example, the Oregon Plan for Youth Suicide Prevention is online at www.oregon.gov/DHS/ph/ipe/ysp/2000plan/ index.shtml.

5. *Emmett v. Kent School District* No. 415 92 F. Supp. 2d 1088 (W.D. Wash. 2000).

6. Bahrampour, T. (May 29, 2005). Message is clear in N.Va.: IM "threats" can bring teens trouble in an instant. *Washington Post.* www.washingtonpost.com/wp-dyn/ content/article/2005/05/28/AR2005052800913_pf.html.

7. Robertson, T. (January 30, 2006). *Dozens knew school shooter's plans.* Minnesota Public Radio. http://news.minnesota. publicradio.org/features/2006/01/30_robertsont_redlake/.

CHAPTER 10

1. Title IV-A of the No Child Left Behind Act.

2. Section 4115 (a)(1).

3. The Center for the Study and Prevention of Violence at the University of Colorado has established a national violence prevention initiative to identify violence prevention programs that are effective. The project, called Blueprints for Violence Prevention, reviews programs in accord with a strict scientific standard of program effectiveness.

4. Section 4115 (a)(3).

5. Limber, S. P. (2004). Implementation of the Olweus Bullying Prevention Program: Lessons learned from the field. In D. Espelage & S. Swearer (Eds.), *Bullying in American schools: A social-ecological perspective on prevention and intervention* (pp. 351–363). Mahwah, NJ: Erlbaum.

6. Thornburgh, D., & Lin, H. S. (2002). *Youth, pornography, and the Internet.* National Academy of Science. www.nap.edu/books/0309082749/html/.

CHAPTER 11

1. *Fight crime: Invest in kids.* (August 17, 2006). News release. www.fightcrime.org/releases.php?id=231.

2. Levin, D., & Arafeh, S. *The digital disconnect: The widening gap between Internet-savvy students and their schools.* Pew Internet and American Life. Report released August 14, 2002. www.pewInternet.org/reportsww/toc.asp?Report=67; Grunwald Associates. (2002). *Are we there yet?* NSBA Foundation. www.nsbf.org/thereyet/index.htm.

3. Levin & Arafeh, *The digital disconnect.*

4. 42 U.S.C. 254. The best resource for a copy of the law is a version excerpted from the Appropriations Act that has been placed on the American Library Association Web site, http://aaa.ala.org/cipa/Law.PDF.

5. 47 U.S.C. 254(1)(1)(A).

6. *United States v. American Library Association*, 539 US 194 (2003).

Glossary

Blogs (short for "Web logs"): Interactive personal and often collective online diaries or journals, often found at social-networking sites. Teens share a significant amount of personal information in blogs. Others can submit comments. *Vblogs* are video journals; *Moblogs* are blogs that allow posting via cell phone.

Chat: Group communications (usually in text format, but increasingly in audio and video formats) that are happening in real time and have the capability to establish private (one-to-one) conversations.

Discussion groups or boards: Group communications around a topic posted for others to access in their own time (known as "asynchronous communications" because of the delay between sending and receiving), as on a physical bulletin board. Students often establish school-related discussion groups or boards.

E-mail: Electronic communication sent to individuals or to a discussion list over the Internet.

Instant messaging (IM): Private real-time communications with anyone on a contact or buddy list. IM includes chat. Depending on the IM service, teens can have up to 450 "friends" on their buddy list.

Online gaming: Taking part in interactive games that are played online in various formats: player versus player (one-to-one), player versus game software, and multiplayer (for example, MMORPGs, or massively multiplayer online role-playing games).

Personal Web sites: Sites where people post all forms of content: writings, drawings, photos, music, or video.

Profiles: Posted sets of personal information (likes and dislikes, interests, and so on). Students should be discouraged from including information that makes them personally identifiable. Established on community sites (social networking, blogging, and the like) or communication services (instant messaging, chat rooms, bulletin boards, and so on) during registration. Can generally be searched by other users.

Social-networking communities (sometimes mistakenly called "blogging sites"): Web sites that offer various combinations of features such as profiles, personal Web sites, blogs, discussion groups and bulletin boards, chat, gaming, music, video, e-mail, and messaging. Examples include www.myspace.com; http://xanga.com; http://facebook.com; and www.livejournal.com. *Important insight:* Terms of use for these communities generally prohibit harmful speech, but site owners do not review postings. Concerns must be reported to the site. Many sites have age limits, but youth know they can easily lie about their age during registration.

Text messaging: Messages sent via cell phones. Many cell phones can also transmit images.

Username: A fictitious name or "handle" that users establish during registration to identify themselves on that site (also known as a screen name). The usernames that a teen selects can provide insight into the image or persona the teen seeks to establish in the particular community.

Index

1

About the Author

NANCY E. WILLARD received a bachelor's degree of science in elementary and early childhood education from the University of Utah in 1975; a master's degree of science in special education from the University of Oregon, 1977; and a doctor's degree of jurisprudence from Willamette University College of Law in 1983. Before focusing her professional attention on issues of youth risk online, she taught at-risk children with emotional and behavior difficulties, practiced law in areas of computer law and copyright, and provided consulting services to schools on the implementation of educational technology.

Nancy is director of the Center for Safe and Responsible Internet Use. This center provides information for educators and other professionals on issues relating to youth risk online. She frequently lectures and conducts workshops for educators on policies and practices related to Internet use in schools and has written numerous articles on this subject. At present, she is expanding her use of Internet technologies to provide virtual workshops and classes.

Author of a book for parents titled *Cyber-Safe Kids, Cyber-Savvy Teens: Helping Young People Use the Internet Safely and Responsibly* (Jossey-Bass, 2007), Nancy lives in Eugene, Oregon, with her three children—Jordan, Allegra, and Bakul—plus various and assorted four-legged creatures.

You can contact Nancy through her Web sites: http://csriu.org and http://cyberbully.org.